The Communicator's Commentary

**1, 2 Thessalonians,
1, 2 Timothy,
Titus**

THE COMMUNICATOR'S COMMENTARY SERIES

Lloyd J. Ogilvie

General Editor

The Communicator's Commentary

1, 2 Thessalonians, 1, 2 Timothy, Titus

Gary W. Demarest

WORD BOOKS, PUBLISHER • WACO, TEXAS

Library of Congress Cataloging in Publication Data
Main entry under title:

The Communicator's commentary

  Includes bibliographical references.
  Contents: v. 9. 1, 2 Thessalonians, 1, 2 Timothy, Titus/
Gary W. Demarest
    1. Bible. N.T.—Commentaries—Collected works.
I. Ogilvie, Lloyd John. II. Demarest, Gary W.
BS2341.2.C65   225.7'7   81–71764
ISBN 0–8499–0162–6 (v. 9) (regular edition)   AACR2
ISBN 0–8499–3809–0 (v. 9) (deluxe edition)

Printed in the United States of America

9801239   AGF   987654

Contents

Editor's Preface

God has called all of His people to be communicators. Everyone who is in Christ is called into ministry. As ministers of "the manifold grace of God," all of us—clergy and laity—are commissioned with the challenge to communicate our faith to individuals and groups, classes and congregations.

The Bible, God's Word, is the objective basis of the truth of His love and power that we seek to communicate. In response to the urgent, expressed needs of pastors, teachers, Bible study leaders, church school teachers, small group enablers, and individual Christians, the Communicator's Commentary is offered as a penetrating search of the Scriptures of the New Testament to enable vital personal and practical communication of the abundant life.

Many current commentaries and Bible study guides provide only some aspects of a communicator's needs. Some offer in-depth scholarship but no application to daily life. Others are so popular in approach that biblical roots are left unexplained. Few offer impelling illustrations that open windows for the reader to see the exciting application for today's struggles. And most of all, seldom have the expositors given the valuable outlines of passages so needed to help the preacher or teacher in his or her busy life to prepare for communicating the Word to congregations or classes.

This Communicator's Commentary series brings all of these elements together. The authors are scholar-preachers and teachers outstanding in their ability to make the Scriptures come alive for individuals and groups. They are noted for bringing together excellence in biblical scholarship, knowledge of the original Greek and Hebrew, sensitivity to people's needs, vivid illustrative material from biblical, classical, and contemporary sources, and lucid communication by the use of clear outlines of thought. Each has been selected to contribute to this series because of his Spirit-empowered ability to help people live in the skins of biblical characters and provide a "you-are-there" intensity to the drama of events of the Bible which have so much to say about our relationships and responsibilities today.

The design for the Communicator's Commentary gives the reader an overall outline of each book of the New Testament. Following the introduction, which reveals the author's approach and salient background on the book, each chapter of the commentary provides the Scripture to be exposited. The New King James Bible has been chosen for the Communicator's Commentary because it combines with integrity the beauty of language, underlying Greek textual basis, and thought-flow of the 1611 King James Version, while replacing obsolete verb forms and other archaisms with their everyday contemporary counterparts for greater readability. Reverence for God is preserved in the capitalization of all pronouns referring to the Father, Son, or Holy Spirit. Readers who are more comfortable with another translation can readily find the parallel passage by means of the chapter and verse reference at the end of each passage being exposited. The paragraphs of exposition combine fresh insights to the Scripture, application, rich illustrative material, and innovative ways of utilizing the vibrant truth for his or her own life and for the challenge of communicating it with vigor and vitality.

It has been gratifying to me as Editor of this series to receive enthusiastic progress reports from each contributor. As they worked, all were gripped with new truths from the Scripture—God-given insights into passages, previously not written in the literature of biblical explanation. A prime objective of this series is for each user to find the same awareness: that God speaks with newness through the Scriptures when we approach them with a ready mind and a willingness to communicate what He has given; that God delights to give communicators of His Word "I-never-saw-that-in-that-verse-before" intellectual insights so that our listeners and readers can have "I-never-realized-all-that-was-in-that-verse" spiritual experiences.

The thrust of the commentary series unequivocally affirms that God speaks through the Scriptures today to engender faith, enable adventuresome living of the abundant life, and establish the basis of obedient discipleship. The Bible, the unique Word of God, is unlimited in its resource for Christians in communicating our hope to others. It is our weapon in the battle for truth, the guide for ministry, and the irresistible force for introducing others to God. In the New Testament we meet the divine Lord and Savior whom we seek to communicate to others. What He said and did as God with us has been faithfully recorded under the inspiration of the Spirit of God. The cosmic implications of the Gospels are lived out in Acts and spelled out in the Epistles. They have stood the test of time because the eternal Communicator, God Himself, communicates through them to those who would be communicators of grace. His essential nature is exposed, the plan of salvation is explained, and the Gospel for all of life, now and for eternity, is proclaimed.

A biblically rooted communication of the Gospel holds in unity and oneness what divergent movements have wrought asunder. This commentary series courageously presents personal faith, caring for individuals, and social responsibility as essential, inseparable dimensions of biblical Christianity. It seeks to present the quadrilateral Gospel in its fullness which calls us to unreserved commitment to Christ, unrestricted self-esteem in His grace, unqualified love for others in personal evangelism, and undying efforts to work for justice and righteousness in a sick and suffering world.

A growing renaissance in the church today is being led by clergy and laity who are biblically rooted, Christ-centered, and Holy Spirit-empowered. They have dared to listen to people's most urgent questions and deepest needs and then to God as He speaks through the Bible. Biblical preaching is the secret of growing churches. Bible study classes and small groups are equipping the laity for ministry in the world. Dynamic Christians are finding that daily study of God's Word allows the Spirit to do in them what He wishes to communicate through them to others. These days are the most exciting time since Pentecost. The Communicator's Commentary is offered to be a primary resource of new life for this renaissance.

In this volume on 1, 2 Thessalonians, 1, 2 Timothy, and Titus, by Dr. Gary Demarest we have a magnificent example of the quality of exposition of Scripture I've described. Dr. Demarest is a distinguished pastor, teacher, and missionary statesman. As pastor of the La Canada Presbyterian Church for the past nineteen years, he has given dynamic leadership as preacher, Bible teacher, and innovative initiator of new forms of parish renewal. In addition to the demanding tasks as leader of a large and growing suburban parish, Dr. Demarest has become an admired mentor of leaders both as a teacher of preaching at Fuller Seminary and as a speaker at church leadership conferences throughout the world. In recent years this ministry has taken him to East Africa where each year he leads pastor's conferences in Uganda, Kenya, and Tanzania.

The remarkable thing about this volume is the way Dr. Demarest plumbs the depths of the meaning of Paul's first and last epistles and then illustrates that meaning in the context of the most crucial issues facing us today. His obvious scholarship coupled with fresh metaphors from our time make this an example of exposition that really communicates.

Dr. Demarest writes in a very impelling way about what he has discovered through the years as a person, church leader, and world-wide spokesman for the faith. His interpretation of Paul's message in these strategic epistles is done in a way that grapples with the deeper meaning of each word and phrase. The original Greek is explained vividly, but never bogs down in obscurities. The author helps us understand the flow of Paul's thought, the issues to which the Apostle is responding, and utilizes the essential message for our times in a way that is gripping and moving.

This volume could well be a manual of the basics of the Gospel and church renewal. The important thing is that what the author writes, he has lived intensely. The rich resources of his own authentic faith are expressed with compelling witness. At the same time we are exposed to methods of preparation that have made him a preacher and speaker of excellence. He is primarily an expositor of the Scriptures. The well of wisdom and prophetic verve his congregation and audiences have come to expect is the result of the in-depth study of the Word we see displayed on the pages of this commentary. Added to that, he is an avid student of contemporary life, and he creatively interprets the implications of Scripture for the personal and social problems we all confront today. We have the opportunity to observe how this leading craftsman of communication lives in a passage, how he allows the Spirit to speak to him, what he seeks to communicate, and how he is engendered with boldness and authority in the declaration of that truth.

The author's intensely busy schedule has always included time for responsible scholarship. He is up to date on current theological trends, but never caught up in any of them. He speaks to issues, but makes none of them his central thrust. Here we have a parish pastor who is alive to what's going on in our world, but always addresses the concerns with a biblical plumbline.

In addition to preaching each Sunday, Dr. Demarest teaches a weekly Bible class in his church which attracts people from all over Los Angeles. The methods of exposition utilized in this commentary are the reason for the popularity of the class. There is a longing today for exposition which is personal and applicable to life. There are great preachers who are not also excellent Bible teachers. The author of this volume is both. That makes this commentary especially useful for preachers, teachers, and small group leaders. You will find the outlines of each passage particularly helpful. They will spark your own creativity in the crucial task of organizing your own material on the passage for your presentation.

Dr. Demarest accepted the assignment to do this particular volume after many of the other authors of the series had selected favorite books of the New Testament for their expositions. He admits that the epistles of Paul had not been the frequent focus of his preaching and teaching. I am thankful that it worked out that way. The result is a freshness and the excitement of a shared adventure. So often we are led back to more familiar passages for our preaching and teaching. It is challenging to approach portions of Scripture we would not immediately turn to as a more secure and tested basis of our expositions. The author shows us how to deal with difficult passages as well as those that yield more readily to explanation. The new insight he has brought to the exposition of Paul's earliest writing and those just before his death is an example of the unmined treasure awaiting us all in some of the neglected verses of the Bible.

A personal word. Gary Demarest is one of my most cherished friends. I have known him as a fellow pastor over the years and during the past eleven years as a covenant brother in a small group of pastors in our area who meet consistently. In the meetings he has been a great source of strength and encouragement to me. It is an honor to have this sensitive and empathetical interpreter of the Scriptures contribute this crucial volume in the Communicator's Commentary series.

Lloyd John Ogilvie

Author's Preface

If the letters of Paul that came to be included in the New Testament had been arranged chronologically, 1 and 2 Thessalonians would be first and the letters to Timothy and Titus would be last. In this volume we are thus dealing with the earliest and the latest of Paul's letters that have been preserved in the New Testament.

As you study these short but powerful letters, my prayer is that your journey through them will be as rewarding as mine has been in writing this commentary. I have not turned to these letters as often as I have other parts of the New Testament, nor have I preached or taught from them a great deal. However, having now taught through these letters with my weekly Bible classes, and having written this commentary, these remarkable letters are high on my list, and I shall live more with them in the future. I have been surprised by God!

If you study these five letters together, you'll discover some significant differences in attitudes and concerns. These differences have led some to conclude that Paul was not the author of all of them. I find this conclusion unwarranted. I see these differences as representative of the rapid and dramatic changes that took place in the early church during the last twenty years of Paul's life, or roughly in the period between A.D. 48 and A.D. 64.

Though they are the earliest and latest of Paul's letters, they share a common thrust that is vital and essential for Christians today. In each of them, Paul is addressing practical problems about daily Christian living. These problems have a direct bearing on the life of the church.

Three great themes breathe through all five letters: church government and organization; sound doctrine; quality in Christian living.

Taken as a whole, these letters establish for all time that church organization is not an end in itself but is important as a means of maintaining the doctrinal tradition with integrity. And doctrine must not become an end in itself but is essential to produce an authentic quality of life in and among the believers.

In our time, battles are raging around the issues of church government, doctrinal traditions, and Christian lifestyle. Serious study of these letters can give us new directions and dynamics for the present by putting us in touch with the past. We call the Bible the Word of God because of this continuing miracle in which the words written long ago to our specific and difficult situations become, by the Holy Spirit, God's Word to us today!

Introduction to 1 Thessalonians

In Paul's time, Thessalonica was the capital city of Macedonia, the northern part of Greece. The modern city of Salonika makes Thessalonica one of the New Testament towns with a continuous history to the present. It was noted for its hot springs and was called Therma until about 315 B.C., when it was renamed Thessalonica after the half sister of Alexander the Great who was also the wife of Cassander. It was a thriving city because of its location on the Via Egnatia, the major Roman highway connecting Rome with Constantinople.

Because of its location, it had to have a special place in the strategy of Paul. Here was the city that was the bridge between East and West. Once the Gospel was planted here, it had a base to reach to Rome in the West and all of Asia in the East. Thus, the coming of the Gospel to Thessalonica was a crucial event in Paul's missionary strategy to take the Gospel into the whole world. The story of the planting of the church in Thessalonica is recorded by Luke in Acts 17:1–9.

The church there was predominantly Gentile, and its beginnings were not without trouble. Indeed, the activists in the local synagogue did everything they could to destroy it. So much so that Paul and Silas were forced to leave, perhaps after only a few weeks there.

The Occasion of the Epistle

After their unceremonious departure from Thessalonica (Acts 17:10), Paul and Silas were given a warm reception in the next town south, Berea. But the same hotheads from Thessalonica caught up with them and forced yet another hasty departure (Acts 17:13). The next stop was Athens, where a greater climate of tolerance made life and ministry more tenable for Paul (Acts 17:15, 32–34).

While Paul was in Athens, he sent for Timothy and Silas, who had remained in Berea. A number of anxieties must have been pressing upon him. Were a few short weeks in Thessalonica enough to establish a beachhead for the Gospel? How were those converts doing? Should he return and try again? Only by sending Timothy back to Thessalonica from Athens could he get the information he needed (1 Thess. 3:1–5).

By the time Timothy returned from Thessalonica, Paul had moved to Corinth (Acts 18:1, 5). The report now received by Paul was good news and bad news. The good news was that the church in Thessalonica was standing strong and held Paul in high esteem and love. The bad news was that the church was experiencing some doctrinal divisions and some strong temptations from the surrounding culture. There were some real problems around the expectation of Christ's return. Some had quit their jobs in the belief that His Second Coming would be most any day. Others were upset and discouraged because their loved ones had died and had missed the imminently expected great event. And then there was the constant difficulty of adapting to an entirely different lifestyle than the one in which they had been raised, especially in the area of sexuality.

These were some of the things, good and bad, that prompted Paul to write his first letter to one of the young churches. And we can be grateful that this became a pattern for him, for his letters comprise about one-fourth of our New Testament.

An Outline of 1 Thessalonians

VIII. Life in the Church: 5:12–28
   A. Respect for Leaders in the Church: 5:12–13
   B. Discipline in the Church: 5:14–15
   C. Standing Orders for the Church: 5:16–18
   D. Life in the Spirit: 5:19–22
   E. And in Conclusion: 5:23–28

CHAPTER ONE

Grace and Peace

1 Thessalonians 1:1–2

There is a dangerous tendency to be in such a hurry to get into the heart of Paul's letter that we miss the meaning intended by him in the opening greeting:

> 1 Paul, Silvanus, and Timothy,
>
> To the church of the Thessalonians in God the Father and the Lord Jesus Christ:
>
> Grace to you and peace from God our Father and the Lord Jesus Christ.
> 2 We give thanks to God always for you all, making mention of you in our prayers,
>
> *1 Thess. 1:1–2*

The greetings in both 1 and 2 Thessalonians are unique among the thirteen letters of the New Testament bearing Paul's name. In all of the other eleven, he appends a title such as apostle, servant, or prisoner; but in these letters he refers to himself simply as Paul. This very likely indicates that Paul's apostolic authority was unquestioned among the Thessalonians, at least at this early date. It may also give us a clue that we are about to read a very personal letter. This simple greeting, different from all his other letters, certainly suggests that he feels a special intimacy with his brothers and sisters in Thessalonica.

The inclusion of Silvanus and Timothy, indicating that they somehow collaborated with Paul in writing the letter, is also worth pondering. Paul places them on an equal level with himself. For anyone who might think of Paul as a prima donna or a Christian celebrity, this greeting stands as a corrective. Nowhere is Paul's egalitarian attitude towards the ministry of others more clearly stated than in 1 Corinthians 1:10–17. A clear understanding of the nature of the Body of Christ in which every believer has a crucial place and in which the Holy Spirit distributes the gifts for ministry as He wills, is a rebuke to our cultic mania for Christian celebrities.

How refreshing that Paul, for whom we would want to develop some kind of "preacher of the century" award, begins this letter by placing himself on the very same footing with Silvanus and Timothy. There is a principle of relationships evident here, stated by Paul in Philippians 2:3, "Let nothing be done through selfish ambition or conceit, but in lowliness of mind let each esteem others better than himself." Growing, vital, deep relationships must be grounded in a sense of equality. If I ever allow myself to think that I am better than you, the possibility of a genuine relationship is gone.

And it is the Gospel that places us all in equality under God. The impeccable logic of Paul in Romans 1–3 settles this issue for all time. Good and bad, weak and strong, bright and dull—we all come to Christ at the very same level. So it was with Paul, Silvanus, and Timothy, and so it must be with us.

There is one more meaning to be found in this trilogy of men. They model the transcendence of the early church over the ethnic, social, and cultural divisions of its time. Paul we know well as a deeply religious Jew with the highest credentials (2 Cor. 11:22, Phil. 3:3–7) and as a Roman citizen by birth (Acts 22:28). Silvanus is the same man who is called Silas in Acts (Acts 15:22). A special companion and associate with Paul, he was also a Jew and a Roman citizen. Timothy was regarded by Paul as his "true son in the faith" (1 Tim. 1:2). We shall see the intimacy of Paul and Timothy in Paul's letters to him.

In these three friends who shared so much of life and ministry together, we have a living expression of the reality that in Christ "there is neither Jew nor Greek, there is neither slave nor free, there is neither male nor female; for you are all one in Christ" (Gal. 3:28). I can't escape the fact that the suburban congregation that I serve does not express this reality very well. We have not found ways to break free from the ethnic, social, and economic divisions around which our neighborhood has formed. Liberation from these social and cultural divisions and prejudices must become a higher priority on our church agendas.

Paul's simple way of addressing the church is also unique to these letters to the Thessalonians: *"To the church of the Thessalonians in God the Father and the Lord Jesus Christ . . ."*

The word "church" has suffered greatly from inflation in recent years. In most metropolitan Yellow Pages one can find listings for Buddhist churches, Unification ("Moonie") churches, Scientology churches, and many others with which we in traditional biblical Christianity have little or nothing in common.

While many of us like to think of "The Church" as strictly a body of believers in Christ, we must be aware that the word Paul uses here for church, *ekklēsia,* originally meant "a gathering of citizens called out by a herald from their homes into some public place." In Paul's time, any assembly of people called together to meet in a public place was an *ekklēsia.* Thus, "church" was a secular term appropriated by Paul, with an interesting background in both Greek and Hebrew thought.

In the classical tradition of ancient Greece, the *ekklēsia* was the assembly of all the citizens of a city who gathered to perform their civic rites. Such an assembly would not be unlike a gathering of all registered voters in one of our cities. The *ekklēsia* was called together by the state authorities for the purpose of electing magistrates, establishing laws and policies, making decisions regarding war and peace, raising and allocating funds, and even trying and judging citizens. It was a true democracy.

In the earliest Greek translation of the Old Testament, the Septuagint, *ekklēsia* is used to denote an assembly or congregation of the people of Israel. Examples of its usage are in Leviticus 10:17, Numbers 1:16, Deuteronomy 18:16, Judges 20:2, and 1 Kings 8:14. It occurs more than seventy times throughout the Old Testament. The clear sense behind *qahal* (the Hebrew word for congregation or assembly, translated by the Greek *ekklēsia*) is that the assembly or congregation gathers because God has called it together.

Thus, it is often pointed out that the word does not mean a group of people who have been "picked out" from others, but a gathering of people who have been called to come together to meet with God. God is the convenor of the gathering, and the invitation is to all who will come.

Here Paul uses the word *ekklēsia* with specific qualifiers both as to the location and to the characteristics of the assembly to which he writes. In this case he addresses the people gathered in Thessalonica. They are *"in God the Father and the Lord Jesus Christ."* Here is one of the simplest statements we have about the true nature of the Christian church. It is a company of believers in a particular place who affirm that they are children of God their Father and who acknowledge Jesus Christ as Lord.

The roots of Christian theology are here. We tend to take the idea of the fatherhood of God for granted. But nowhere else in the world's religions is the disclosure of God as a loving, caring Father as clear and focused as it is in Jesus Himself. We cannot ignore contemporary concerns about sexist language in the Bible and in the church. But we are in danger of losing an essential truth about God that comes to us in Jesus if we refer only to God as our parent. Masculine/feminine and fatherhood/motherhood characteristics are applied to God in the Bible from Genesis on. However, while the comfort of God is expressed as that of a mother for her children (Isa. 66:13), the portrayal of God as Father, especially by Jesus, is central in all of Scripture.

But this does not make a case for biblical masculine superiority. Quite the contrary! The Genesis narrative makes it clear that the man and the woman are both created in the image of God. "Then God said, 'Let Us make man in Our image, according to Our likeness; let them have dominion over . . . the earth.' So God created man in His own image; in the image of God He created him; male and female He created them. Then God blessed them, and God said to them, 'Be fruitful and multiply . . . have dominion . . . over every living thing that moves on the earth' " (Gen. 1:26–28). Conflict and the power struggle entered after the Fall. In God's design, both were given dominion together as a joint authority. Even the design for marriage was to create of the two "one flesh" (Gen. 2:24).

The contention that calling God "Father" is a sexist appendage of an outmoded male chauvinism is simply unwarranted. Let us not distort the fatherhood of God into a sexist aberration, but let us be faithful to the biblical disclosure of God as our Father. To know God as Father is to know His love, His care, His guidance, His protection, His constant self-giving, His watchfulness—and, yes, even His discipline, which is always exercised in our best interests.

Another root of Christian theology is found in Paul's phrase "The

Lord Jesus Christ." Each word of this title is crucial to our relationship with God. Jesus is His name. We worship and follow a real person who was born, who lived, died, and rose from the dead. We can visit Nazareth, Capernaum, Jericho, and Jerusalem. We can walk along the shore of Lake Galilee where He walked.

Christ is not His second name—it is a title out of the Old Testament. The term *Christos* is the Greek word for the Hebrew *Mashiach,* the promised "anointed one" to be sent by God for the redemption of Israel. It was the conclusion of Jesus' disciples that He was indeed the promised Messiah, the Christ promised by God. If we were to be precise in our language, we would call him Jesus *the* Christ. Such usage of "the Christ" is common in the Gospels, as in Peter's confession, "You are the Christ, the Son of the living God" (Matt. 16:16; see also Matt. 2:4, 22:42, 24:23; Mark 13:21; Luke 23:39, 24:26; John 7:31, 20:31). According to Luke, Paul regularly used the article in his preaching (Acts 9:22, 17:3, 18:5, 18:28). Yet, Paul does not use "the Christ" in his letters. Our usage has clearly been shaped by Paul's letters, but we must always remember that Christ is His title, not His name.

As Christ is Jesus' title designated by God, so Lord is the title which we may choose to give Him. To call Him Lord is to give Him absolute authority in one's life. The Greek word is *kurios,* which has a twofold emphasis—the authority of the one being called lord and choice of the one who is calling. Another word that we translate Lord is *despotēs.* It differs from *kurios* in that it denotes absolute ownership and uncontrolled power irrespective of the subject's feelings. *Kurios* indicated a relationship of total authority that was chosen by the subject.

To call Jesus Lord is a matter of choice. In Solmon's painting of Christ knocking at the door of the heart, there is no latch or knob on the outside of the door. It can only be opened from the inside. Christ never forces His way in. He only becomes Lord by our personal, free choice (Rev. 3:20).

When the church is a Christian church it is an assembly of people *"in God the Father and the Lord Jesus Christ"* (v. 1). It is to this community of faith that Paul sends *"grace"* and *"peace."* Here are two more words basic to our Christian vocabulary. Paul does a fascinating thing here. As we would say "hi" or "hello" today, the person in Paul's day would greet a friend with *"ch(k)airein"* or *"chaireh."* Instead of this common greeting, Paul uses *"charis"* which resembled the common greeting in sound but had an entirely different sense. Paul's greeting means "grace," a word used by him twice as often as all the other New Testament writers combined. Grace has been called Paul's code word.

The formal meaning of *charis* is "that which affords joy, pleasure, delight, sweetness, charm, loveliness." We refer to gracious speech, gracious manners, and graceful bearing. It is not used in the Gospels except in Luke 4:22, "gracious words," and in John 1:14, 16, and 17. When Paul reached for a word to express the rich meaning of God's redemptive love and action in Jesus, he chose the word *grace*. The source of all joy, loveliness, and genuine pleasure in life is the grace of God in Jesus Christ. Grace refers to the kindness of God in which He seeks us and brings us to Christ for our salvation. Grace contains the idea of receiving that from God which we can in no way earn or deserve. If you want one word that most nearly sums up all of the blessings and mercy of God given to us in Christ, that word is *grace*.

But it's not natural or easy to live by the grace of God. All of us have an inherent tendency to want to relate with God and with others on our own merit and achievement. Thus, the long, painful history of spiritual legalism—living by rules and regulations—achieving status by our goodness. In each of his letters, Paul strikes strong blows for grace alone. To the Romans, Paul argues that we are justified by grace alone through faith in Jesus Christ. To the Colossians he establishes emphatically that we are saved by Christ alone, not by regulations and ritual. To the Galatians, he claims freedom from all religious bondage in the name of Christ alone.

I couldn't number the people I've met across the years who have scorn and antagonism for Christ and the church because of their exposure in childhood and adolescence to grace-less Christianity. It is a dangerous thing to present Christ in terms of demands for moral perfection. It is a betrayal of the Gospel to offer salvation to people only on the basis of their goodness or religiosity. Salvation comes to those who cast themselves upon God's grace. Jesus' parable of the Pharisee and the tax collector (Luke 18:9–14) should have settled this for all time.

To receive the grace of God by faith results in *"peace,"* the second word of the greeting. Here, Paul chooses the Greek word *eirēnē*, which was used in the Greek translation of the Old Testament for the Hebrew word *shalom*. The Hebrews had come to use this word as a greeting which expressed the desire for safety, blessing, and well-being to a departing friend. In Israel today, *"Shalom"* is still the universal greeting of love and care.

The peace Paul refers to in his greeting is both external and internal. Grace is the basis of living in peace with one another. Two people sharing the grace of God have no option but to live in peace with each other. The style of Christian relationships is one of seeking and initiating peace with those around us. "Blessed are the peacemakers," said Jesus, "For they shall be called sons [and daughters] of God" (Matt. 5:9). The peace that comes with God's grace is not only external, but is also internal. In this sense, peace must be seen not merely as the absence of inner turmoil and conflict. Rather, peace is the inner calm in the midst of the storm. Paul sees peace as the active work of God in our lives which "surpasses all understanding" and which "will guard your hearts and minds through Christ Jesus" (Phil. 4:7).

In one form or another, this greeting of grace and peace occurs in each of Paul's letters. Grace points to God, who, in Jesus, is the source of all love and good in our lives. Peace points to the quality of life that grows out of grace. Both are the essence of the Christian lifestyle.

Paul completes his greeting by expressing his gratitude for them and assuring them that they are regularly in the prayers of Paul, Silas, and Timothy. Prayer is the binding force of the worldwide Body of Christ. I'm grateful for many people around the world with whom I have covenanted to share in mutual prayer. I have some clergy colleagues who pray for me every Saturday night, as I pray for them, and it's a source of great strength and meaning for us all. The development of a regular network of prayer relationships should be a high priority for every Christian.

Before going on, we need to observe that the remainder of this chapter, vv. 2–10, is one long and irregular sentence. Our translation breaks it up into five lengthy sentences, but we shall take the liberty of following the content rather than the punctuation. This, by the way, is typical of Paul's writing style, which has led many to believe that he most commonly dictated his letters, making the product a little less regular than had it been a written composition.

CHAPTER TWO

The Three Greatest Things in the World

1 Thessalonians 1:3

This is the first time that Paul uses what was to become one of his favorite trilogies—faith, love, and hope. These three are found together in Romans 5:1–5 where Paul shows how they sustain us in times of trouble. In Galatians 5:5–6 and in Colossians 1:3–5, faith is tied to hope and to love in special ways. In Ephesians 4:1–6, faith, love, and hope are set forth as the basis for a mature Christian life. The best known use of the trilogy by Paul is in 1 Corinthians 13:13 in the midst of his lengthy discussion of spiritual gifts: "And now abide faith, hope, love, these three; but the greatest of these is love."

> 3 remembering without ceasing your work of faith,
> labor of love, and patience of hope in our Lord Jesus
> Christ in the sight of our God and Father,
>
> *1 Thess. 1:3*

One of our favorite family activities through the years has been backpacking and camping. We've returned often to a small chain of lakes in the high Sierras tucked away in the midst of towering snowcapped peaks. There are no maintained trails. Over the years, we have placed trail markers along the way. We call them "ducks," each one made by stacking three rounded rocks of descending size on top of each other. What fun it is to begin the climb to our special place and find the trail markers guiding us along the way. Sometimes, right at the point where we're not sure of our bearing, we do not commit to a new direction until we have located another duck. How reassuring each one is at every crucial point!

I've long since come to think of faith, love, and hope as the indis-

26

pensable trail markers of my Christian journey. Sometimes the way is quite clear and the route is obvious. But often, I find myself uncertain and confused. And that's when I need most to pause until I've located faith, love, and hope. I'm finding that when I take my bearings on them, I can't stray too far from God's good way.

The Work of Faith

Paul points to the first trail marker by giving thanks for their *"work of faith."* For those who generally think of faith primarily as an intellectual exercise, this is a dramatic phrase. It's not often that we refer to faith as work. And the Greek word that Paul uses here, *ergou,* really has the sense of vocation as over against the sense of toil and labor.

Here is faith as vocation, faith as lifestyle. One Greek dictionary defines this phrase as "the course of conduct which springs from faith." A number of years ago Elton Trueblood entitled one of his books *Your Other Vocation.* His thesis is that your primary vocation is being a Christian. How you make your living is your *other* vocation. When someone asks me my vocation, I'm inclined to say that I'm a Presbyterian pastor. Instead, my instinctive response should be that I'm a follower of Jesus. I've seen many congregations transformed when the men and women of the church began to grasp that their real vocation is Christian discipleship, and their other vocation is how they make their living.

There's always the danger, though, that we make following Jesus mostly a matter of doing church work. Dick Halverson, now chaplain of the U.S. Senate, calls us to make a clear distinction between "church work" and "the work of the church." Church work, too often, becomes a matter of seemingly endless committee meetings preoccupied with maintaining the movement of wheels within wheels without producing genuinely meaningful ministry to people in need. Procter and Gamble developed a management principle that our church began using a few years ago. It's called the "elimination" approach. In essence, we analyzed every program and activity in our congregation by asking what would happen to the work of Christ in our town and world if we eliminated a particular program or committee. Some things that "we had always done" gave way to programs based upon specific needs of people.

This is not to say that only those things that are designated as

27

"religious" activities merit a place in a congregation's program, but it does demand that everything we do have some specific relationship to our faith in Christ and to serving the needs of people.

The same principle must also be at work in our personal lives as well as in our families. Faith seen as vocation becomes the basis for genuine stewardship of all that we are and have. Faith as vocation means that Jesus Himself becomes ultimately decisive in all areas of my life because I have freely chosen to call Him Lord. What would happen if we applied "the work of faith"—faith as primary vocation—to the areas of life that affect us most deeply—family life, work, and money?

Family life. Most everyone seems to agree that our troubles in family life are producing serious social and cultural consequences. And this isn't just an issue for the married. Each of us, married and single alike, participates in one or more forms of family life. I choose to define family not only in the more specific sense of parents and children, but also in the broader sense of being the family of God in Jesus Christ. Thus, faith as vocation involves us in family relationships and responsibilities at more than one level.

My mother, who has been widowed for a number of years, now lives in a Presbyterian retirement home. She's also an active member of our congregation. She really participates in three families. She is an active part of our personal family, sharing in the give-and-take of an energetic group of two headstrong parents and four independent teens-to-twenties daughters. Sometimes there's joy, sometimes sorrow, sometimes anger and conflict, but faith as vocation means that she's a part of it. As a member of the congregation, she has taken responsibilities to that family, as it has to her. And now as part of the Windsor Manor family, she participates in another set of relationships.

I'm convinced that we need to think of family life as all-inclusive. Even if we're not engrossed with parent-child relationships, we are still responsible to different families. No one is an island, especially in the Christian community.

Faith as vocation means that I not only accept the potential joys, rewards, and securities of family relationships, but that I accept my responsibility for the potential problems, conflicts, and struggles as well. To do this well, I have to approach all "family" relationships with realistic expectations.

It's clear to me that many of our relationships become problems because of unfair or unrealistic expections. The classic example occurs between parents and their young adult children. It's natural for parents to develop expectations as to education, lifestyle, career, and especially marriage partner. When the young adult deviates from or just plain rejects these expectations, the parents have to make some difficult choices. They choose either to accept the adult child's behavior or to press for change. Pressure to change can be applied in different ways. They can withdraw love and affection. They can withdraw or withhold emotional or financial support. They can try to coerce or manipulate. They can threaten and scold. But all efforts to change others primarily to realize our expectations for them are doomed to failure. Parents may get their desired results, but they have probably created a time-bomb that is waiting to explode.

I recall a tragic example, all too typical in pastoral counseling experience. The husband-to-be didn't even come close to mother's expectations for her daughter. All of the strategies possible were used by the mother to keep the daughter from the marriage. The final strategy was mother's refusal to attend the wedding. It wasn't long before mother was proven right. The marriage, indeed, turned out to be a disaster. But when the mother emotionally and physically invited her daughter back home, all efforts for reconciliation were rejected. The daughter said to me, "Mother has always tried to run my life to meet her expectations. I broke out and made a bad mistake. No way am I going to buy back into her need to control me." Whether this relationship will ever be restored is still questionable. And it will never be restored if mother can't control her expectations for daughter.

Faith as vocation is a corrective to faith as fantasy. Had mother learned to trust God rather than her expectations, she would have allowed her daughter freedom to make her mistakes. And she would still have her daughter in a strong relationship.

Faith as vocation focuses upon the work to be done in sustaining and building relationships. Such faith gives us the strength to transcend the pains and hurts in them. Keeping a tight rein on our expectations of others is the work of faith. And often it's hard work.

Faith as vocation is also crucial to another area of frequent tension in all family relationships. In many countries today, the whole family sleeps in one room, as they did in log cabins on the American frontier. We regard this with horror because of our quest for "space." One of the most frequent complaints I hear in the pastoral counseling room is that of not having enough "space" to oneself in the marriage and family. While all of us need some space, psychologist Dr. Bruno Bettelheim said, "If you need all that separateness, fine. I won't pass judgment. Just don't get married and have children."

The point is that being a marriage partner or participating in any family requires the sacrificing of a great deal of one's space. In other words, you have to give up something to have relationships. And the strength to give up space as needed is indeed the work of faith. I find, again and again, that my times of solitude with God give me the strength to sacrifice my space for the best interests of others around me.

Work. Faith as vocation helps put our "other vocation" into proper perspective. There's a great deal of emphasis these days upon stress in our work. Current stress research indicates that stress can be good or bad. Stress is essential to life—the only stressless condition is death. Hard and demanding work does not in itself produce crippling stress. Destructive stress comes at the point where our work does not have meaning for us, or when we allow our work to control everything else.

The term "workaholic" has become a common word in our vocabulary. It describes the person whose life has become addicted to a particular job or vocation. It's ironic to me that clergy are notorious workaholics. I say ironic because if any folks should have clear priorities that reflect their relationship with God, it ought to be those who preach and teach the Gospel.

The obvious cure for workaholism is a proper sense of vocation. To be committed to the vocation of faith is to put one's work into proper perspective. My primary vocation is to live a life that is pleasing to God and is alive and growing in personal relationships. Only as my work serves those higher ends can it merit my continuing involvement.

This means that life must consist of more than work. The late, great Vince Lombardi is regarded by all people in football as one of the greatest coaches of all time. He is reported to have opened his training camps for the Green Bay Packers with a rousing speech that concluded: "Remember at all times God, your family, and the Green Bay Packers—and always in that order!" It's a wise person who develops that perspective.

Faith as vocation keeps the relationships with God and with others as high priority. We simply will not sacrifice either for the sake of a better job, more money, or personal prestige. And even if the job is being the pastor of a thriving congregation, it has to be kept subordinate to the higher priorities of God and relationships.

But how do we change deeply entrenched, destructive work and stress patterns? With great difficulty. But change is what Christ always offers. In the Bible, change always begins with repentance, and this means that you choose to change. And what creates the desire for change? The awareness that there is something more fulfilling and rewarding.

A man I'll call Tom came into my study a few months ago. He described himself in all of the classic symptoms of workaholism—constant fatigue, a high level of irritability, feelings of distance from wife and children, more trips to the doctor and more medications, growing anger with people at work, more money but less happiness, and now some threats from his wife about the future of their marriage. Tom made it clear that he was convinced his relationship to work was at the center of his problems because most of his time and energy were consumed there. A successful entrepreneur, he was now controlled by the business he had started.

After a few conversations together, Tom saw that his problem was not how to control his business, but how to control himself. And with God's help he came to know Jesus Christ as Savior and Lord. As Christ became his vocational center, his business life came into a different perspective. In fact, he sold one business, cut down another, and rearranged his whole life with regard to Christ, the church, and his wife and children. Tom will freely tell you that he doesn't make nearly as much money as he once did and that his lifestyle has been greatly simplified. But if you could see the love and the warmth in that family that I see, you'd agree that his vocation of faith has made life very worthwhile.

Archbishop William Temple once said that for many of us life is like a department store in which someone went in during the night and mixed up all the price tags. Too many of us are paying very high prices for things of little lasting value. Only when we get a genuine sense of faith as our vocation can we hope to get the right price tags on the right values.

Money. Price tags and values have to do with money. We all learn early in life that money is one of the necessities of life. It is the way in which we exchange our skills and work for goods and services. If we didn't have money, we would need some other medium of exchange. There is no reason to regard money in itself as evil. Money becomes good or bad depending on its use. In the Bible, the question is always focused on the use of money.

How we use money is an expression of our sense of vocation. To become preoccupied with the accumulation of money reveals a false sense of the meaning of life. Jesus made this clear in the parable of the rich fool (Luke 12:15–21). Once the man was convinced that the abundance of life consisted in accumulating more and more wealth, he was doomed to missing the basic meaning of his life.

Faith as vocation is the basis for the management of money. We call it stewardship. A steward is one who is trusted to manage what belongs to someone else. The work of faith requires that I regard money as belonging to God and not to me. Money is to be managed for the service of God and others.

We will explore this theme in greater depth and breadth in our comments on 1 Timothy 6:3–21 (chapter 5, pp. 217–29).

The Labor of Love

From the "work of faith," Paul now introduces the second trail marker, the "labor of love." As we wrongly tend to think of faith as an intellectual matter, so we are inclined to regard love primarily as a matter of feeling. Here, Paul uses the Greek word *kopou,* meaning work as toil and hard labor—the kind of labor that produces fatigue and even exhaustion.

This becomes clear when we understand the full meaning of the word Paul uses for love, *agapē.* Paul intentionally uses *agapē,* for it defines a quality of love and life that is more a matter of acting than feeling.

This distinction is important. There are different kinds of love. The love celebrated by poets and put to music by lyricists is, for the most part, a matter of feelings. This kind of love, at its core, is deeply emotional. It is highly selective, and sometimes mysterious and virtually uncontrollable. Some people just naturally elicit strong feelings within us, while most people come and go without stirring any of our emotions.

The love of which Paul speaks here may or may not be related to emotional responses. It is intentional. It is what one chooses to do. This kind of love is increasingly difficult to get in touch with because we place so much emphasis upon our feelings. I'm grateful to live in a time when we are called upon to be in touch with our feelings. It is a well-established fact that being rightly related to our feelings is crucial to health and wholeness. But our heightened awareness of our feelings can become a barrier to this labor of love.

I've often faced this barrier in the counseling room. Anne had come to see me because she was struggling with guilt over her feelings for her aged mother. "She's so impossible. No matter what I do, I can't please her! I hate her! I hate her!" She sobbed uncontrollably, clenching her fists, knuckles white. In the course of three conversations, we reviewed many years of Anne's life with her mother.

It became clear that Anne had never experienced many warm and loving feelings for her mother—it just hadn't been that kind of a relationship. But it was also evident that across the years, Anne had been very kind and loving in her actions toward her mother. Again and again, she had tried to do what she felt would be in mother's best interests.

I recall saying to Anne, "You've really been describing *agapē* love." This is the love that acts whether or not it feels like acting. It acts in the best interests of the other person. Anne discovered that she really didn't hate her mother after all. Hate could not have done all the good things Anne had done. It was a joy to see the relief that came when she could make the distinction between her feelings and her actions. It was a relaxed and healed woman who exclaimed, "I really *don't* hate my mother. I'm just tired of getting nothing in return for my efforts!"

That's the labor of love! Love as action is hard work. To act in the other's best interests when I feel like striking out in anger is exhausting labor.

Now I can understand what Jesus demanded when He said, "Love your enemies, bless those who curse you, do good to those who hate you, and pray for those who spitefully use you and persecute you, that you may be sons of your Father who is in heaven" (Matt. 5:44–45).

I've never been able to generate very good or loving feelings for those who treat me as an enemy or who reject and hurt me. If Jesus commanded me to feel love toward them, I'd have to plead the impossibility of that. But when I understand His command as a call to behavior that acts in the best interest of the other, I am capable of obedience.

There's room in all of this for tough love. The labor of love may require confrontation that is unpleasant. It may require some painful honesty. It may require holding another responsible and accountable. It's here that I am no longer comfortable with the definition of *agapē* as unconditional love. The word unconditional is fine, but the word love is still not defined. *Agapē* love must always be defined in terms of actions and not just feelings. And the action must always be what one thinks is in the best interests of the other person. I plead for this definition of *agapē:* "acting in the best interests of the other person."

The more you do this kind of loving, the more you'll understand why Paul calls it the *"labor of love."* A very irate husband said to me, "I'm sick and tired of giving, giving, giving, and getting nothing in return." "Good," I said, "now you've begun the labor of love."

This kind of loving is never easy. It's always demanding and often exhausting. It's not possible for people turned in on themselves. But it's the most healing, redeeming, powerful force in all the world. For its classic definition, no one has been able to improve on Paul's: "Love suffers long and is kind; love does not envy; love does not parade itself, is not puffed up; does not behave rudely, does not seek its own, is not provoked, thinks no evil; does not rejoice in iniquity, but rejoices in the truth; bears all things, believes all things, hopes all things, endures all things" (1 Cor. 13:4–7).

The Patience of Hope

Paul now plants our third trail marker: the *"patience of hope."* The opposite of hope is despair, and there is good reason to believe that despair is at the root of many types of physical and mental illness. Hope is a powerful source of healing, but hope is hard to come by.

I'm one who keeps pretty well informed about current events. I have to confess that I depend more and more upon the printed media than upon television. I refuse to accept the format of the local TV news. It starts with the most dramatic murders, rapes, and crimes and then moves to any spectacular fires or accidents. I've found that I can get the weather and sports events coverage by tuning in at the fourteen minute mark of the newscast. Any in-depth coverage of what I consider to be significant news comes mainly in the printed media along with a few television specials.

A steady diet of television news is a pathway to despair. How does one find hope in the midst of all the bad news with which we are constantly bombarded? Many search for hope in some form of escapism. I have some friends who just avoid the news. They insist that they feel better by not knowing about all of the bad things going on in the world. Frankly, they remind me a bit of the story of the Hindu philosopher, who, because of his view of reverence for life, would not walk down the road without a sweeper in front of him lest he kill a living creature. He was a vegetarian for the same reason. One day, a friend gave him a microscope so that he could see the living organisms in the food he ate, challenging the consistency of his behavior. According to the story, he simply threw the microscope away. Yes, you can choose to be uninformed about the world around you, and you may even feel better; but hope is not based on escaping from reality through ignorance—and, by the way, have you ever pondered the word *ignore-ance?*

Others pursue hope through the escape route of diversion and pleasure. This has become one of the hallmarks of our relative affluence. I've watched the pattern from the perspective of a pastor in an affluent suburb for the past nineteen years. With financial success comes the freedom to purchase the second home, the motor home, the club memberships, and to pursue "the good life" with vigor and vim. I'm not arguing against vacations and quality family time, but I am convinced that this passionate pursuit of leisure and escape does not produce genuine hope.

Still others pursue hope through financial security. Some of my friends who are investment counselors, without divulging any confidential matters, have long since convinced me not to be timid about stating the needs for money for Christian causes throughout the world. In a community like ours, the accumulation of capital, euphemistically called "the estate plan," has become a way of life and even an obsession for many. But financial security does not produce genuine hope. How simply Jesus put it: "Do not lay up for yourselves treasures on earth, where moth and rust destroy and where thieves break in and steal; but lay up for yourselves treasures in heaven, where neither moth nor rust destroy and where thieves do not break in and steal. For where your treasure is, there your heart will be also" (Matt. 6:19–21).

The Hope in Jesus

Substitute "hope" for "heart" in that last sentence, and you have a good definition of hope. Hope is where your heart is! That's why none of the escape routes—ignorance, pleasure, diversion, financial security—produce genuine and enduring hope. Hope must be rooted in reality, lived out in service to others, and secure from "moths, rust, and robbers."

How, then, does one find hope in the midst of the realities that surround us? The New Testament sets forth a claim that is either stupendous or preposterous: Hope is found in Jesus Himself and Jesus alone! As Paul reminded the Corinthians, this claim "is foolishness to those who are perishing, but to us who are being saved it is the power of God" (1 Cor. 1:18).

This hope in Jesus is rooted in reality. In the Christian life we are not dealing merely with ideas, theories, theology, or doctrine. We are dealing with a person—Jesus Himself!

This hope in Jesus is lived out in service to others. Jesus majored in service to others. "I am among you as the One who serves" (Luke 22:27). "If I then, your Lord and Teacher, have washed your feet, you also ought to wash one another's feet" (John 13:14). To follow Jesus is to seek to serve others.

This hope in Jesus is secure from "moths, rust, and robbers." Genuine hope transcends all human boundaries, including death. That's why Paul stakes everything on the resurrection of Jesus from the dead: "And if Christ is not risen, then our preaching is vain and your faith is also vain. . . . But now Christ is risen from the dead" (1 Cor. 15:14, 20). His resurrection is the guarantee of God that death is not the end of our lives. And that means that this life is but an infinitesimal part of the whole. Genuine hope embraces the whole of life, not just this part.

This hope in Jesus gives us, then, a proper perspective for all of life. Hope must be geared both to this life of our years on earth, and to eternal life. All too often we lose our balance. The portrait of the "otherworldly" Christian is all too well known: he's so heavenly minded, he's of no earthly good! On the other hand, those who place all of their hope in this life, seeking either their own security and comfort or a just and perfect social order, become candidates for despair or false hope.

Hupomonē

Paul's use of "patience" with hope in verse 3 has profound significance especially because of the word he uses. The Greek word *hupomonē* has no single word equivalent in the English language. It occurs in the New Testament thirty times as a noun and about fifteen times as a verb. It is most often translated as patience, longsuffering, or endurance. *Hupomonē* is one of the great words of the New Testament. (For a much longer discussion of *hupomonē,* see pp. 262–64.) It suggests much more than patience. It portrays a way of taking on problems and suffering by which one not only endures, but out of the problem, actually creates opportunities.

It is thus the quality of *hupomonē* which sustains the power of hope. One whose hope is grounded in Jesus Himself, in this world and the next, finds the strength and perspective to bring *hupomonē* to each task and problem. Every difficulty and crisis is seen as an opportunity for serving God and others.

Hope and *hupomonē* are as inseparable as the chicken and the egg. Hope in Jesus is the source of *hupomonē,* and *hupomonē* sustains and nurtures genuine hope.

Here, then, at the beginning of Paul's very first letter are the basic trail markers of the Christian life: faith, love, and hope.

CHAPTER THREE

Jesus Christ Can Change Your Life

1 Thessalonians 1:4–10

"You can't teach an old dog new tricks." We may yawn at the old cliché, but most of us really believe that, don't we? We really don't see a lot of changes in people around us. Most folks are quite predictable, and their responses are pretty much the same. A husband probably knows exactly what his wife will say if he comes home from work two hours later than usual without having called. A wife probably has little difficulty anticipating her husband's response to a stopped-up toilet when he's on his way to a golf game. Some psychologists insist that our responses are quite predictable from the age of four or five on.

Can a person really experience significant change? That was the question Nicodemus asked Jesus (John 3), and it's an important question for all of us. The Christian faith is grounded upon the claim that people can be changed. While such change may not be as dramatic as that experienced by Paul (Acts 9), the central message of Jesus Christ is the possibility of radical transformation of the human personality by His love and grace.

As Paul continues his lengthy sentence of thanksgiving for the Christians at Thessalonica, he sets forth the great reality of the power of Christ to work deep and genuine change in human lives.

YOUR ELECTION BY GOD

4 knowing, beloved brethren, your election by God.

1 Thess. 1:4

38

The basis of Christian conversion is God's election. With the word "election" comes the word "predestination," and with them both, all kinds of anxieties and difficulties arise. The very thought of election or predestination places human freedom and responsibility in jeopardy. Thus in many of our discussions about Christian conversion, the "election" theme is mostly ignored or watered down.

But you can't escape this theme in Paul. Nowhere does he express it with greater brevity than here. And nowhere does he state it with more care than in Romans 8:29–30: "For whom He foreknew, He also predestined to be conformed to the image of His Son, that He might be the firstborn among many brethren. Moreover whom He predestined, these He also called; whom He called, these He also justified; and whom He justified, these He also glorified."

Does this mean that God has already determined who is to be saved and who is to be lost? If so, what's the use of appealing to people to respond to Christ, since they really have no choice in the matter?

Before we paint ourselves into a corner, let's begin by examining the question of human freedom and determinism. Among psychologists, philosophers, and theologians alike, there is no clear and simple answer to this question. Some behavioralistic schools of psychology go to the extreme of resolving the question by denying human freedom. Here it is declared that after the age of early childhood all of our patterns are established, and everything we do the rest of our lives is predetermined. This approach, based on psychological and behavioral theory, is akin to that of some Christian thinkers who interpret God's election to mean that from before our birth, some are elected to salvation and some are elected to damnation. This view is referred to as double-predestinarianism, meaning that predestination is the act of God in which people are consigned either to heaven or to hell.

The same question of freedom and determinism is answered by others to the other extreme. Some schools of philosophical thought reject completely the psychological emphasis upon conditioned human behavior. Here the emphasis is upon the freedom of the human spirit, the insistence that there is nothing that can interfere with free choice to responsible or irresponsible behavior. This is akin to some theological views which reject the idea of a sovereign God who is indeed in control of history. This view sees God, not only giving us complete freedom, but also insists that without that freedom one cannot be held responsible.

How can we resolve this age-old tension? I don't think we can. This presents a distressing dilemma for those who believe that there is one clear answer for every question. I've long since come to the conclusion that there are some mysteries in the universe beyond our understanding, not the least of which is God Himself. Theology has the task of helping us understand what we can, but it also has the responsibility of affirming unapologetically what we cannot comprehend.

One of the most profound statements of the fact that our knowledge of God is limited is found in the Old Testament. No one had ever been closer to God than Moses. The Book of Exodus is the story of that closeness. At a point of deep intimacy, Moses pleads boldly with God. "Show me Your glory" (Exod. 33:18). Moses is literally asking God to reveal Himself completely. And God replied: "I will make all My goodness pass before you, and I will proclaim the name of the Lord before you. I will be gracious to whom I will be gracious, and I will have compassion on whom I will have compassion. . . . You cannot see My face; for no man shall see Me, and live. . . . Here is a place by Me, and you shall stand on the rock. So shall it be, while My glory passes by, that I will put you in the cleft of the rock, and will cover you with My hand while I pass by. Then I will take away My hand, and you shall see My back; but My face shall not be seen" (Exod. 33:19–23).

What could be more clear? God does not make Himself fully known. There is more to His glory than we are allowed to see. "But," you say, "that's in the Old Testament. In Jesus, God has made Himself fully known." I think not, for Paul did not say that. To the Corinthians, he affirmed the limits of our knowledge of God: "For we know in part and we prophesy in part. But when that which is perfect has come, then that which is in part will be done away. . . . For now we see in a mirror, dimly, but then face to face. Now I know in part, but then I shall know just as I also am known" (1 Cor. 13:9–10, 12).

We do best, I'm convinced, to recognize at the outset that there are some things about God and His doings that we simply cannot and will not comprehend. I choose to regard this whole question of God's election as one of them.

But having said this, I'm just as convinced that we must keep both poles of the question in active tension. We must affirm that God is God. He does what He wills, showing mercy on whom He shows mercy. Paul did not hesitate to liken God to the potter and clay (Rom. 9:20–24). Yet we must also affirm human freedom. The invitation to the *ekklēsia* is trumpeted to all. Christ died for all people without distinction. Indeed, whoever will may come.

I find it helpful to distinguish between the past and the future as I wrestle with the question of divine election. When I look to the past, I find it quite evident that God indeed has chosen me and has been at work in my life. I have lived through enough tragedies and sorrows, both my own and others, to believe that God is active in bringing about His good purposes in our lives. But when I look ahead, I'm very much aware that there are choices and decisions to be made in which I have freedom and for which I am responsible.

This seems to be Paul's perspective here, for in verses 5–10 he makes clear some of the reasons why he was certain of the Thessalonians' election. It was the way in which they had responded to the Gospel that demonstrated the reality of their election.

The Gospel Is More than Words

> 5 For our gospel did not come to you in word only,
> but also in power, in the Holy Spirit, and in much
> assurance, as you know what kind of men we were
> among you for your sake.
>
> *1 Thess. 1:5*

The opening word *"for"* indicates a continuity of thought in this long, continuing sentence. The first evidence of their election was what happened in the events by which that first *ekklēsia* was found in Thessalonica. It was Paul's deep conviction that what had happened there through Silas and him could best be understood as the choice and work of God.

There's a never-ending mystery in this preaching and teaching of the Gospel. How does the human word become the divine word?— or perhaps it's better to ponder how the divine word becomes the human word. The Gospel must come in words. Though actions may speak louder than words, there is no communication of the Gospel until words have been spoken. For the Gospel is a story—the Good

News of Jesus Himself. But if the Gospel becomes merely a matter of words, it degenerates into a travesty.

Years ago, in the days of lower-grade technology, I can recall being in the movie theater when the screen went dark while the sound continued. As high school kids we would scream, clap, holler, and stomp until someone in the projection booth got the picture going again. It was frustrating to have just the sound and not the picture. How sad that many people never respond to the Gospel because they're only hearing the words without the picture. As Paul said elsewhere: "Though I speak with the tongues of men and of angels, but have not love, I have become as sounding brass or a clanging cymbal" (1 Cor. 13:1).

"Power." The first distinctive feature of the preaching event in Thessalonica was power. Wherever Paul went, he was ready to stake his life on the power of the Gospel Word. To the Romans he wrote: "I am not ashamed of the gospel of Christ, for it is the power of God to salvation for everyone who believes" (Rom. 1:16). To the Corinthians: "And my speech and my preaching were not with persuasive words of human wisdom, but in demonstration of the Spirit and of power, that your faith should not be in the wisdom of men but in the power of God" (1 Cor. 2:4–5).

Each of us who preaches and teaches the Gospel needs to be acutely aware of the power of this Word. The Word of God faithfully proclaimed is the most powerful force in the world. Somehow, God takes our teaching and preaching of His Word and uses it to change lives, to heal relationships, to build up and tear down just and unjust social structures, to do His work in the world.

"The Holy Spirit." The Word going forth in power is the Word going forth in the Holy Spirit. The Holy Spirit, God present and active, is the source of all power. The last recorded words of Jesus made this connection: "But you shall receive power when the Holy Spirit has come upon you; and you shall be witnesses to Me" (Acts 1:8).

The most vivid picture of the Holy Spirit has to be the "tongues, as of fire" sitting upon each of them (Acts 2:3). The fiery tongue is a symbol of the Word with power. Fire purges and cleanses; it consumes and changes. The Word proclaimed in the power of the Holy Spirit is a Word of fire.

There's always a danger that we reduce the Holy Spirit to some kind of a religious experience for our own sense of spiritual growth or well-being. Here we are reminded that the Holy Spirit is mission-oriented. God comes in His Spirit to empower the words used to proclaim the Gospel. The purpose of the power of the Spirit is to make us witnesses, not to entertain us or make us feel good. To be in Christ is to be in the Spirit, and to be in the Spirit is to be in God's power.

"In much assurance." The Word going forth in power and in the Holy Spirit also goes forth *"in much assurance."* This is a phrase that has to do with conviction—a settled and passionate conviction of the truth and power of the Gospel. Wherever Paul and his companions went, they proclaimed with absolute conviction the power of Jesus Himself to change human lives and to redeem the world. We find no uncertain sounds coming from Paul's heralding of the Word of Christ.

Does this mean that Paul had no lingering and unanswered questions about some aspects of the Gospel? Do we have to possess all of the answers before we can have this kind of assurance? No! There's an important distinction between questioning and doubting. Questioning is a matter of honesty. It is a willingness to be open to those parts of our understanding that are limited. Doubting, however, is a refusal to act in faith and obedience.

When Jesus came down from the mountain with Peter, James, and John after the transfiguration, He was met by the disciples who had been unable to bring healing to the son of a distressed father. When Jesus called the father to faith, the father confessed his confused mixture of faith and questioning. He cried out with tears, "Lord, I believe; help my unbelief!" (Mark 9:24). Jesus honored the man's honest anguish and healed the boy.

This story has always been precious to me, for it speaks to my condition. My intellectual journey with Jesus has always been a mixture of affirmations and questions. But I have chosen to distinguish between questioning and doubting. Questions there are, and there always will be. Doubt, to me, would be to choose to live by the unanswered questions rather than by faith in God. Doubting focuses on finding reasons not to trust in God. Questioning sees the same reasons but chooses to follow Jesus.

Having unanswered questions does not mean that we cannot proclaim the Word of the Gospel "with much assurance." We can have deep and settled convictions about the truth of the Gospel without needing to have all the answers.

Quality of life. The last distinctive feature of Christian witness to the Word is the quality of life of the proclaimers themselves: *"You know what kind of men we were among you for your sake."* Some scholars feel that this phrase could be just as well translated in the passive sense: "the kind of men God enabled us to be."

There's no question that the quality of our lives is an integral part of what we preach and teach. And we have that quality only by the grace of God. This is not to say that we do not have the right to proclaim the Gospel until or unless we have arrived at some special level of spiritual perfection. I was taught in seminary that we could not preach above the level of our own experience and that a congregation could not rise above the spiritual level of its pastor. I no longer accept that. While I take seriously my own responsibility to live an exemplary life, I've long since become aware that I must preach beyond my experience, because I preach Jesus, not me. And Jesus is always beyond where I am. I also am grateful for those men and women in the congregation I serve who model for me qualities of life in Christ to which I still aspire.

THE STRANGE UNION OF SUFFERING AND JOY

> 6 And you became followers of us and of the Lord,
> having received the word in much affliction, with joy
> of the Holy Spirit,
>
> *1 Thess. 1:6*

Paul continues to expand this long sentence, in which we are now but at midpoint! He apparently intends to add another reason for his certainty of their election: they had chosen to become followers of the apostles and Jesus. Our response is the confirmation of God's election.

What made their response so convincing was the fact that their reception of the Gospel resulted in a blend of suffering and joy. Had the Gospel just been a source of blessing and gain, their response might well have been attributed to selfish motives. But when they took on affliction voluntarily, a different set of dynamics became operative.

This raises a disturbing question to all of us involved in the communication of the Gospel in our day. There's no question that this is the era of the "me" generation. Our culture abounds in strategies for self-fulfillment. Whether through exercising, dieting, meditating, golfing, asserting, soaring, or spelunking, we have generated mass markets for delivering advice and techniques on how to find personal happiness and meaning.

Of greatest concern to me is not the obvious profit motives of the purveyors, but the underlying assumption that "the good life" consists of the absence or elimination of hardship, pain, and suffering. The assumption of the Gospel is just the opposite. The Gospel begins by facing the fact that life is difficult. All human experience is tied somehow to the Fall (Gen. 3). The story of Adam and Eve is *our* story. It is the story of rebellion against God and our stubborn insistence on doing things our way instead of His way. Disobedience to God is the root of human suffering and affliction. Suffering is unavoidable in this fallen world. The way to a life of meaning is to learn to handle suffering creatively and redemptively. Jesus is the model for life at its abundant best.

Yet the ease with which so many of our church leaders, clergy, and laity alike have bought the assumptions of our culture about "the good life" is alarmingly evident. In churches and in the media, the Gospel of Jesus is all too frequently marketed just like any other cure for hardship and suffering. "Trust in God and all will be well." "My career was at an all-time low, but I came to Jesus, and now I'm rich and famous." "Since Christ came into my life, every day is filled with happiness."

Is the Gospel primarily a way to emotional well-being and material success? All too often, it seems to be promoted that way. Whatever happened to the Jesus who said, "If anyone desires to come after Me, let him deny himself, and take up his cross daily, and follow Me" (Luke 9:23)? Whatever became of the Jesus who said, "Do not worry about your life, what you will eat; nor about the body, what you will put on. . . . But seek the kingdom of God, and all these things shall be added to you. . . . Sell what you have and give alms" (Luke 12:22, 31, 33)?

To rediscover the call of Christ as a call to sacrifice and suffering must become the highest priority for American Christians. We must be freed from our captivity to the cultural assumptions of "the good life." The chains of our bondage to the crass materialism and the flagrant self-centeredness of our generation must be broken.

The great discovery awaiting us is this strange union of suffering and joy. Paul states that *"the joy of the Holy Spirit"* came to them in their reception of the Word *"in much affliction."* For Paul and for them, obedience to God was always costly and frequently resulted in suffering (2 Cor. 11:22–33; Acts 17:1–10). But again and again they witness to the joy that comes in the suffering. Paul here uses the words for joy and suffering in the same sentence.

Perhaps one of the most completely concealed truths of our time is that suffering and joy go together. Life without problems and suffering is a fantasy and is not worth pursuing. If we live as followers of Jesus in the midst of a fallen world, a world at war with God and itself, we will suffer. But suffering will not break us or lessen our confidence in God. On the contrary, suffering for what we know in Jesus will only draw us closer to God. And in this suffering, the Beatitudes will come alive (Matt. 5:3–12).

THE INFLUENCE OF CHANGED LIVES

7 so that you became examples to all in Macedonia and Achaia who believe.

8 For from you the word of the Lord has sounded forth, not only in Macedonia and Achaia, but also in every place your faith toward God has gone out, so that we do not need to say anything.

9 For they themselves declare concerning us what manner of entry we had to you, and how you turned to God from idols to serve the living and true God,

10 and to wait for His Son from heaven, whom He raised from the dead, even Jesus who delivers us from the wrath to come.

1 Thess. 1:7–10

We now complete Paul's marathon sentence of verses 2–10. He celebrates the widespread influence of the witness of these Christians in Thessalonica.

Those of us who regularly preach the Gospel know very well that the measure of the sermon is determined as much by the congregation as it is by the preacher. Strong congregations make strong preachers. The Thessalonians, by the quality of their response to the Gospel, extended Paul's preaching throughout Greece. Through Macedonia in the north and Achaia in the south, their example and their faith became a source of strength for others.

Paul cites five ways in which their influence spread. In studying these verses it is important to ask ourselves, "Can any or all of these things be said of our group or congregation?" If not, why not?

Examples. The reputation of the Thessalonian Christians was outstanding. Paul pays them high tribute in calling them "examples" to believers everywhere. In fact, Paul never referred to any other church in this way.

The word translated "examples" is *tupos,* from which we derive our English word *type.* It originally meant the imprint made by a stroke or blow, as the mark of a hammer on the wood when you missed the nail. Then it came to mean the impression left by a seal, such as we place on a document by a notary public. Finally, it came to mean a pattern, such as I often see on the dining room table when a new dress is being made by one of our daughters.

What a compliment! What greater prayer is there for pastor and people than that our congregation might become an authentic pattern in which others may find shape and direction?

Trumpeters of the Word. From there the Word of the Lord had sounded forth. The word used here is the same that would be used to describe the sound of a trumpet or the booming of thunder.

In other words, the Word went out from Thessalonica with no uncertain sound. Would that we could discover that way of proclaiming the Gospel in our day. Too often our proclamation is an uncertain reaction to the agenda of the world around us. The "noise of solemn assemblies" too often bears little relationship to a clear trumpet sound or a sharp clap of thunder calling people to heed the Kingdom of God.

Even Paul could not add anything to their witness. Would he be able to say that of the word that is going out from us in our church?

Turning from idols. A great deal of their influence had to do with what they had rejected. They had *"turned to God from idols."* To us the word "idol" suggests ancient and pagan superstition—people worshiping statues or wood carvings. That, indeed, has been part of the history of idol worship. The ancient world abounded in deities to the point where it was impossible to determine whether the gods derived their existence from the people or the people from their gods.

But with all of our high technology, the religious situation hasn't changed all that much, not if we define religion in terms of what holds the trust and allegiance of men and women. We, too, are surrounded by a plurality of deities of our own making.

Wealth and its accumulation holds a far higher place in our loyalties than any ceramic idol in a primitive tribal village. Doesn't the arms race between Russia and America reveal a worship of military might far greater than any obeisance to wooden or stone gods of war in ancient cultures? And then there is sex. The fertility rites in ancient Greece were but a prelude to our preoccupation with sexual pleasure.

To turn to the living and true God is to reject all of the idols that have their grip on a given generation. And what does our community see in us? Has anyone asked us lately why we are so different from the world around us?

Turning to and serving God. To have rejected and turned away from the idols is one thing. But it's not only what you turn *from* that is important. Of greater importance is what you turn *to,* and what you do after you've turned.

The Christians in Thessalonica had turned from the idols of their day and become *servants* of God. The word used here is the same word used for a slave. We live in an age that prefers to think of God as a partner rather than as a slave owner. We may grant Him chairmanship of the board, but to give Him absolute, unqualified authority in our lives meets resistance. But the God of the Bible is the God who made Himself known on Sinai as "the Lord your God who brought you out of the land of Egypt. . . . You shall have no other gods before Me. . . . For I, the Lord your God, am a jealous God." (Deut. 5:6–9). This means simply that God will not tolerate divided allegiance. He is not the senior partner, the man upstairs, nor our co-pilot. He is God. We find our meaning in becoming His servants.

In contrast to the idols from which they had turned, He is "the living and true God." Living in contrast to the deadness of all idols. True in contrast to the falsity of the idols. A common characteristic of all idols is that they promise more than they can deliver—they are neither vital nor true. Whether your idol is money, government, sex, or whatever, you will discover this flaw in them all. Only God is living and true.

Waiting for Jesus. The final dynamic of their influence was their view of history. They were living with the assured conviction that Jesus would return. This had been the promise after the resurrection (Acts 1:11), and it was His victory over death that made the promise credible.

This doctrine of the second advent is sadly neglected in many churches today and even rejected in some. Unfortunately, in yet others it is majored upon in the form of predictions. The recovery of a dynamic view of the Second Coming of Christ must be a matter of high priority for us. The technical term for this is eschatology, from the Greek word, *eschaton,* meaning "last" or "last things." What is at stake in eschatology is not how to predict the end of the world, but how to understand what history is all about.

The second advent of Christ means that history is moving to a particular conclusion. That conclusion centers in the coming of Christ the King to establish eternally the Kingdom of God which began with His first advent. The Kingdom will be complete when, and only when, He comes again.

The inclusion of the concept of deliverance from "the wrath to come" is troublesome to those who are uncomfortable with the idea of a God of wrath. Such an idea is offensive to those who want only to stress the love of God. But the wrath of God is too prevalent throughout the Bible to be dismissed. God's wrath is not to be regarded as the anger and ire expressed in human temper tantrums. Rather, His wrath is the other side of His love. It is the necessary corollary of His love, reminding us that our choices do indeed have significant consequences. God's love and wrath are best seen as two sides of the same coin.

Problems pertaining to the eschatological beliefs of the Thessalonian Christians are dealt with by Paul at comparable length in the two letters (1 Thess. 4:13–5:11, pp. 80–89; 2 Thess. 2:1–12, pp. 116–25).

CHAPTER FOUR

Evangelism at Its Best

1 Thessalonians 2:1–12

Most of Paul's letters were written to respond to some attack that had been made against him or to correct some error in the local situation. Sometimes reading Paul's letters is like listening to one end of a telephone conversation. We're really not certain what the issue was that prompted the response.

Paul now moves into a direct defense of his conduct and ministry in Thessalonica. Apparently, both his motives and his methods of ministry had come under fire by some who wanted to discredit him and his ministry. The matter is critical, for if Paul or his ministry can be repudiated, then the very foundations of the church at Thessalonica—and everywhere else—can be undermined.

We can be grateful for these attacks on Paul, because they drew from him these magnificent letters. We learn more about the motives and methods of evangelism from these paragraphs in defense of his ministry than we would have if, perhaps, Paul would have tried to write a textbook on the theme. Here is practical reality, growing out of the heat of conflict.

THE BOLDNESS OF AUTHENTIC WITNESS

1 For you yourselves know, brethren, that our coming to you was not in vain.

2 But even after we had suffered before and were spitefully treated at Philippi, as you know, we were bold in our God to speak to you the gospel of God in much conflict.

1 Thess. 2:1–2

The first accusation with which Paul deals may have gone something like this: "Paul and his friends just move around from place to place and don't accomplish anything that does any real human good!" Paul responds with the fact, well known by the Thessalonians themselves, that his work there was not *"in vain."* The Greek word he uses is *kenōs.* It connotes something that is void of meaning or value.

The work and witness of Paul was anything but empty. His preaching and teaching were directed to very specific goals. Any thought that Christian evangelism is just a matter of words and forms has no place with Paul. Evangelism must always be focused upon the redemption and transformation of individuals. It's always a matter of life or death.

The ever present danger in professional ministry is that of routine and emptiness. How easy it is to get so accustomed to our regular rounds of preaching and teaching that we lose our sense of urgency. The renowned nineteenth-century pulpit orator Philip Brooks called upon a young preacher to preach "as a dying man to dying men." Whether preaching to a vast assemblage or leading a small Bible study group, let us pray that God would give us this passion for hurting and dying men and women! Christian witness reduced to routine performance is a travesty upon the Gospel—"the power of God to salvation for everyone who believes" (Rom. 1:16).

Greek has more than one word for *but,* and verse 2 begins with the strongest adverse word at Paul's disposal. The one Paul uses here, *alla,* makes the greatest possible contrast with the previous sentence. More than being *"not in vain,"* their preaching had been *"bold."* This boldness is all the more dramatic when seen in the context of what had happened to them just before coming to Thessalonica.

Their last stop had been in Philippi, a few miles northeast of Thessalonica, recorded in Acts 16:11–40. After a riot prompted by the conversion of a fortune-telling slave girl whose healing became an economic threat to her owners; they were thrown in jail and charged with being subversives. The magistrates had neglected to ascertain the fact that Paul was a Roman citizen. After a well-timed earthquake and the dramatic conversion of the Philippian jailer, this gross injustice to Paul, a Roman citizen, was duly noted in city hall. The magistrates offered to drop all charges and asked Paul to leave the city quietly.

Paul's sense of humor, as well as his sense of justice, came flashing forth in his reply: "They have beaten us openly, uncondemned Romans, and have thrown us into prison. And now do they put us out secretly? No indeed! Let them come themselves and get us out" (Acts 16:37). The late Herman Hickman, former Yale football coach, used to say, "If they are chasing you out of town, get up front and make it look like a parade." Apparently, Paul led the parade out of Philippi that day. Next stop: Thessalonica.

It's likely that Paul is now responding to a second accusation: "These people are jailbirds, disloyal to Rome!" He refers openly to the Philippian experience. He has nothing to hide. He makes it clear that in the midst of conflict, Christian witness still goes forth in boldness.

The word translated "bold" needs more than one English word to capture its double meaning. It describes both "a lack of fear" and "a full confidence in the message itself." Here are two additional marks of authentic evangelism.

The Good News of Jesus, the Gospel, must always be proclaimed without fear. The greatest fear that most of us face when contemplating Christian witness is the fear, not of persecution, but of rejection. The fear of being regarded as foolish or stupid all too easily cripples or paralyzes us. The fear of not being accepted too often imprisons us in silence. This kind of fear is grounded in a preoccupation with results. And in our calculation to produce results, we may distort the Gospel, telling people what they want to hear in order to get their positive response. A desire to win more people to Christ and to bring more people into our churches is certainly integral to the Gospel. But our evangelism must be designed, not to get results, but to be "bold in our God" in sharing the story of the Gospel.

At the same time, we can proclaim the Gospel with complete confidence in its power and validity. It is *the gospel of God."* It is not of human origin. It is not something that was developed by men and women of religious genius or special insights. It is God's plan for human salvation. It is God's way of bringing people into right relationships with Himself and with each other. We can trust this Gospel of God to change human lives and relationships.

I see it again and again as a pastor. In recent years, we've developed in our church a special program for people with alcohol-related problems. As a supplement to Alcoholics Anonymous, Al-Anon, and other programs, we've formed a fellowship for alcoholics and their families that focuses specifically upon our relationships with one another in Christ.

I first met my friend, whom I'll call Ted, more than ten years ago.

His story was like many I'd heard before. For more than twenty years, he'd been struggling with the disease of alcoholism. Two marriages, five jobs, and thousands of dollars later, he was still under its power. Though he'd tried A.A. before, he agreed to try it again. This time he became a recovering alcoholic and has now celebrated more than ten birthdays of his sobriety.

But after his eightieth birthday, he came to the growing conviction that there was even something greater than sobriety. Through prayer and the support of some caring Christians, Ted came to know more of the grace and peace of Christ. He came to experience the assurance of God's complete forgiveness for all of the sins and hurts of the past. He discovered the power of Christ to accept himself in a new way, knowing that God loved him not just because he was sober but because he was a child of God's grace. He has found complete acceptance by God and by his Christian friends—and he even knows that if he were to fail again that he would still be loved. Sometimes when I'm a little edgy or down, I get together with Ted because the sense of God's grace and peace flows through him. Ted is now one of our trained lay counselors, and what a ministry he has to others!

We have every reason to be *"bold in our God"* in our Christian witness. For the Gospel is the power of God to transform human life!

The Importance of Sincere Motivation

3 For our exhortation did not come from deceit or uncleanness, nor was it in guile.
4 But as we have been approved by God to be entrusted with the gospel, even so we speak, not as pleasing men, but God who tests our hearts.
5 For neither at any time did we use flattering words, as you know, nor a cloak for covetousness— God is witness.
6 Nor did we seek glory from men, neither from you nor from others, when we might have made demands as apostles of Christ.

1 Thess. 2:3–6

Paul continues his defense against the accusations designed by his foes to discredit his ministry. At least three of them are confronted in these verses, all of them having to do with his motivation. Some

had apparently accused Paul of being motivated by deceit, uncleanness, and guile (v. 3). Each of these is a serious charge, and all three
together are overwhelming. However, evangelism could be practiced
out of any or all of these motives.

The Greek word *plané*, translated *"deceit,"* really means "error." The
ultimate issue is always truth. The Gospel is either true or it is not.
Paul stakes his entire life on the truth of the Gospel. There's a tendency in our day to judge values by the wrong standard. "Does it
work?" is often asked more than "Is it true?" The test of the validity
of the Gospel is truth not pragmatism. Evangelism must be deeply
rooted in truth. The danger in preaching to attract an audience is
obvious. It is too readily disguised to provide solutions that work
rather than truth that is to be confronted. The acid test for every
sermon or Bible class must be: *Is it true?* If Christ is presented as a
means by which we can be successful, happy, or whatever, we are
betraying the Gospel of God. We are guilty of deceit and error even
though we may be successful in drawing followers.

The second charge refuted in verse 3 is *"uncleanness."* The word
used here refers primarily to sexual immorality. This accusation must
have come from the leaders of the synagogue, for the culture around
them was flagrantly permissive in matters of sexuality. The standards
set forth in the Scriptures of Israel were certainly out of step with
prevailing community standards. If Paul and his company could be
discredited in this arena, the Gospel could be rejected as another
pagan religion. Cult prostitution was not uncommon in those religions, with orgiastic rites as part of worship. Paul deals with sexuality
in more depth in 1 Thessalonians 4:1–12, but here he denies the accusation. Actually, his conversion to Christ raised his sexual standards, for Christ takes us beyond the letter to the spirit of the
standards (Matt. 5:27–30). Who can ever be the same after Jesus'
teaching about adultery in the heart?

The third charge is that Paul was motivated by *"guile."* The word
originally referred to catching a fish with bait, and thus came to
mean any method of deception to trap or catch another. Jesus, indeed,
had called those early fishermen in language that they well understood: "Follow Me, and I will make you fishers of men" (Matt. 4:19).
The metaphor was obviously intended to connote vocation and not
craftiness. There is no place for manipulation or trickery in evangelism. Paul made it clear: "But we have renounced the hidden things
of shame, not walking in craftiness nor handling the word of God

deceitfully" (2 Cor. 4:2). Guile, craftiness, and cleverness had no place in Paul's methods or ministry.

Having denied the allegations that his ministry was motivated by deceit, uncleanness, or guile, Paul now defends himself by citing three specific examples in verses 4–6. These three verses call us to integrity in our own preaching and teaching.

Paul makes it clear that the ministry of his company was not motivated by deceit, uncleanness, or guile, because they had not spoken "as pleasing men, but God" (v. 4). We've already seen that truth is the criterion for evangelism. In recent years, a science of "church growth" has been developed in which the factors that make churches grow are identified through actual studies of such congregations. Widespread correlations have been discovered with the assumption that the factors that have led to growth in many churches can be translated into principles capable of general application.

In my judgment, church growth methodology has both potential and peril. The potential is obvious, granted that our mission is to bring as many people as possible to faith and discipleship. Growing churches can represent the growth and expansion of the Gospel and the Kingdom of God. But it can also represent the effectiveness of clever marketing strategies.

To Paul, the ministry of evangelism had been entrusted to him by God, and it was to God alone that he felt accountable. To speak in ways pleasing to men and women may well produce a growing congregation, but the test is whether or not we are pleasing God. The classic description of what pleases God was given by the prophet Micah long ago: "Will the Lord be pleased with thousands of rams or with ten thousand rivers of oil? . . . He has shown you, O man, what is good; and what does the Lord require of you but to do justly, to love mercy, and to walk humbly with your God?" (Mic. 6:7–8).

This is not to say that pleasing God will keep a congregation from growing. It does mean that there is something much more important than numerical growth or success. We are called not to please people but God. If people are pleased by what is pleasing to God, there will be growth. But if they are not pleased by what pleases God, the mandate is to please God no matter what happens to the numbers.

Neither was their ministry guilty of deceit, uncleanness, or guile, because they did not *"use flattering words . . . nor a cloak for covetousness"* (v. 5). This sentence is difficult to translate clearly into English, but it seems to me that "flattering words" and "cloak for covetousness" are best taken together. The idea of flattery here is giving another a sense of comfort by speaking in order to achieve the speaker's own ends. The *"cloak for covetousness"* then becomes the description of the speaker's motive. Covetousness, indeed, includes desire for money, but it embraces the whole attitude of always wanting more: more money, more power, more adulation, more recognition, more, more, more!

Preaching and teaching can become a means of luring people into our covetousness. Preaching is a powerful force—for good or for evil. Paul appeals to God as his witness that his ministry had not been a cover to use people for his own aggrandizement.

Nor had their ministry been involved in deceit, uncleanness, or guile, because they did not seek glory from men (v. 6). Paul has stated one aspect of this in verse 4, but here his focus is upon his own feelings. There is an obvious inner satisfaction in being affirmed and praised for one's ministry. Paul denies that he ever preached in order to receive glory from others. That he has become one of the most highly praised Christian leaders of all times is a fact. But this was not his motive.

I tell my preaching students at Fuller Seminary that there are two kinds of sermons that may be judged by the response at the door. There are the "that was a great sermon" sermons, and there are the "good morning, Pastor" sermons. I'd much rather preach the former. But my commission by God is to preach for the glory of God—and that means both kinds of sermons.

I take the closing phrase of verse 6, *"when we might have made demands as apostles of Christ,"* to refer to the fact that Paul recognized certain rights of the preacher or teacher. The desire to have support and affirmation, acceptance and approval, is certainly legitimate; *but* whether or not one receives them, the call is to fidelity and integrity.

The demands are said to be those of *"apostles of Christ."* From this statement, some make a case for the ordained ministry as having a central place very early in the life of the church. The apostles are seen as having been given the full authority of Christ, which in turn was transmitted to the bishops. We shall deal with this subject in greater detail in conjunction with 1 Timothy 3.

Suffice it to say here that a strong case can be made that the apostle is simply "one who is sent." The commission was articulated in Mark 3:14, "Then He appointed twelve, that they might be with Him, and that He might send them out to preach." There is no evidence that this commission was to become a transfer of authority from one apostle to another. The essential task was preaching. Apostleship was not a position of power but a mandate to proclaim the Gospel. Paul was more conscious of his responsibility than of his authority.

THE ART OF GENTLENESS

I have my own image of Paul, as I'm sure you do. My basic feelings about him for a long time were somewhat foreboding. He seemed so stern and unbending, so unreachable and unfeeling. I was astounded the first time I read these words:

> 7 But we were gentle among you, just as a nursing mother cherishes her own children.
> 8 So, affectionately longing for you, we were well pleased to impart to you not only the gospel of God, but also our own lives, because you have become dear to us.
> 9 For you remember, brethren, our labor and toil; for laboring night and day so as not to be a burden to any of you, we preached to you the gospel of God.
>
> *1 Thess. 2:7–9*

At the climax of his impassioned defense before his critics, he reveals a most attractive warmth from deep within. He was a man of feelings, a man of warmth, a gentle-man! The very language of these verses oozes a sensitivity not often associated with Paul.

To describe his own gentleness, he uses the soft, warm picture of a mother nursing and cherishing her own children. Or perhaps the language suggests that Paul portrays himself as a nursemaid. We must pause for a moment and have a little fun with words.

The translation of verse 7 hinges upon two words, *ēpioi* and *nēpioi*. The first means "gentle" and the second means "babes." Which word was used by Paul? Since the preceding word ended in *n*, it's very possible that a scribal error in copying the text could have gone either way. Both are found in different manuscripts, and a settled decision is not possible.

The variance only enriches the sentence. If Paul used *ēpioi*, the picture is the gentleness of the mother nursing her baby. But if Paul used *nēpioi,* the translation could read, "we were like a nursing mother among you talking baby talk." Either way, the picture is one of tenderness and gentleness by the apostolic party to the Christians in Thessalonica. The attitude and style of the evangelist must be shaped by the needs of the hearers without sacrificing the essence of the Gospel.

There is a possibility that the word translated "affectionately longing for you" *(homeiromenoi)* actually was a special word of affection used in the nursery. If so, we have a further indication of the warmth and sensitivity of Paul. So deep was his affection that he affirmed his willingness to give himself for them. The word translated "lives" is *psuchē,* which really means the whole of one's personality. Paul and his friends were eager not only to give a message, but to give themselves as well. Blessed indeed are those whose evangelists are more than talkers. The willingness, and even eagerness, to give ourselves to others may well be the missing link in many of our evangelistic endeavors.

Paul had already embodied these words with his actions. He reminds them that he had labored and toiled among them. This presumably means that he earned his living making tents even while he preached and evangelized. His reason for this was his desire not to be a burden to them.

In all of this, we see Paul as a model of the true evangelist, passionately committed to the proclamation of the Gospel, yet a man of tenderness and gentleness.

THE NECESSITY OF INTEGRITY

> 10 You are witnesses, and God also, how devoutly,
> justly, and blamelessly we behaved ourselves among
> you who believe;
> 11 as you know how we exhorted, comforted, and
> charged every one of you, as a father does his own
> children,
> 12 that you would walk worthy of God who calls
> you into His own kingdom and glory.
> *1 Thess. 2:10–12*

Paul now concludes his defense by appealing to the witness of the Thessalonians, as well as of God, to the integrity of his behavior.

He insists his behavior, and that of his associates, was devout, just, and blameless. Whether he intended it or not, Paul gives us a concise definition of integrity. Many commentators outline this trilogy of qualities by noting that they were (1) devout in their behavior toward God; (2) just in their behavior toward the Thessalonians; and (3) blameless in their behavior toward themselves.

This distinction seems artificial, for each of these words relates to God, others, and self. Holiness, justice, and purity are the ingredients of integrity. Whatever the charges leveled against Paul and his colleagues, he had nothing to fear because of the comprehensive quality of their behavior in all dimensions.

If Paul was gentle like a mother, he was also firm like a father. Exhorting, comforting, and charging were also part of his apostolic ministry. The presence of comforting between exhorting and charging is cause for reflection. The demands of discipleship are rigorous. To be a committed follower of Christ is always costly. Failure is a regular part of the Christian life—there is no such person as a perfect Christian. Thus, comfort must always be in the midst of our ministry of exhorting and charging.

The goal of exhorting, comforting, and charging is clearly stated in verse 12: *"walk worthy of God."* This in no way contradicts our salvation by grace through faith. But having been met by the grace of God, we can only want all the more to walk in ways worthy of His love for us. God's call is rightly translated here in the present tense. God is always calling us, coming to us, loving us. That awareness makes our worthy walk all the more urgent.

God is calling us to His Kingdom and glory. The two seem to be synonymous here. The Kingdom of God was certainly the central theme of Jesus' teaching, deeply rooted in the Old Testament. The Kingdom is more than a concept; it is a present reality. It is neither political nor geographic; it is something that happens within us as we commit ourselves to God in Jesus. The Kingdom is here, and it is yet to come in its fullness. God is always calling us into His Kingdom and glory.

How grateful we can be to Paul's critics and attackers. In defending himself, Paul gives us a profound statement of what evangelism is. He ties together the strands of bold witness, sincere motivation, gentleness, and integrity. To blend each of these into our proclamation of the Gospel will guarantee fidelity to the God who calls us into His Kingdom and glory.

CHAPTER FIVE

The Power of Christian Relationships

1 Thessalonians 2:13—3:13

One of the most significant emphases in many Christian circles today is that of the power of relationships. It was in the mid-sixties that I was introduced to what has come to be called relational theology. The discovery of the importance of open, caring, supporting relationships in Christ has changed the quality of my life. The dynamics of enabling people to relate with one another in and through small groups has become the core of renewal in our congregation.

Life without regular involvement in a small group is inconceivable to me. It has been in the intimacy of close relationships in Christ that I have really come to experience God's love in and through the love of others. It is in the context of those relationships that I have been confronted and held accountable for growth in obedience and discipleship. It is in the give and take of honest sharing that I have found the freedom to examine some of my prejudices and fears. And it is in the climate of trust and support that I have been able to change both thinking and behavior when it has become clear that such change was essential for growth toward wholeness.

In this chapter, Paul gives us a beautiful picture of the central dynamic of Christian relationships in his own life and in the life of the early Christians. This was not written as a manual for developing small groups. Nor was it designed to instruct us how to develop or improve effective one-to-one relationships. But I find this section to be a powerful statement about not only the necessity, but also the exciting potential of relationships centered in the Lord Jesus.

Because there is so much emphasis on the importance of relationships in the culture around us, we must always point out that in Christian community we are pointing to something unique. For this is community that centers in Jesus Himself. Paul begins this section on relationships by clearly articulating this uniqueness.

THE BASIS OF CHRISTIAN COMMUNITY

13 For this reason we also thank God without ceasing, because when you received the word of God which you heard from us, you welcomed it not as the word of men, but as it is in truth, the word of God, which also effectively works in you who believe.
14 For you, brethren, became imitators of the churches of God which are in Judea in Christ Jesus. For you also have suffered the same things from your own countrymen, just as they did from the Jews,
1 Thess. 2:13–14

Paul is about to move into the warmest statement in any of his writings about the love and affection he felt for his brothers and sisters in Thessalonica. But he begins by establishing the basis for those relationships.

The basis is simply and clearly: the Word of God. In this magnificent statement, Paul declares: (1) that all Christian relationships must be established by receiving the Word of God; (2) that the Word of God is an active force; (3) that Christian relationships involve suffering and hardship.

The reception of the Word of God is the basis of Christian community. The Word of God is a phrase that means not only the written and spoken words found in the Bible, but also the Incarnate Word, Jesus Himself. While we may have many friendships and relationships based on other things, those relationships growing out of our acceptance of the authority of the Bible and the lordship of Jesus are like no others. I've become very close to a man in our congregation who received Jesus into his life about a year ago. This man has always had a lot of friends and enjoys human relationships. He has played golf with one group for more than twenty years, and that certainly develops significant relationships. But he tells me that he is discovering a quality in these new relationships with people in Christ that he never realized possible.

The Word of God is more than a collection of writings or even someone who lived long ago. It is an active force *"which also effectively works in you who believe."* This dynamism of the Word of God is stated eloquently by the writer of the book of Hebrews: "For the word of God is living and powerful, and sharper than any two-edged sword, piercing even to the division of soul and spirit, and of joints and marrow, and is a discoverer of the thoughts and intents of the heart" (Heb. 4:12).

This Word of God lives within us. It grows within us. It nurtures us, guides us, and corrects us, as we shall see in 2 Timothy 3:14–17. I feel strongly that small groups of Christians should always include some form of Bible reading or study and prayer in their times together. The essential thing that makes our groups different from all other group life is the Word of God. We are those who are brought together in receiving the Word, and we are guided, renewed, and energized by the Word.

And our relationships involve us in suffering and hardship. Paul affirms the Christians in Thessalonica for their suffering. To be sure, most of their suffering grew out of persecution from "their own countrymen." But I believe that there is also suffering inherent in relationships. Life is difficult. We are all sinners, and the basic word for sin in the New Testament is an archery term, "to miss the mark." For people who regularly "miss the mark," to relate in depth caringly is to take on pain and hardship. To impose our fantasies for a perfect, harmonious relationship on another is to demand an unreal relationship—and that becomes phony! Real relationships involve us in suffering. And what a liberating discovery it is that in suffering together we experience our deepest intimacies. That's why many of our folks call their groups "support groups."

THE CONTRARY FORCES

15 who killed both the Lord Jesus and their own prophets, and have persecuted us; and they do not please God and are contrary to all men,
16 forbidding us to speak to the Gentiles that they may be saved, so as always to fill up the measure of their sins; but wrath has come on them to the uttermost.

1 Thess. 2:15–16

Most of the suffering of the Thessalonian Christians came from the people around them who opposed violently their commitment to the Lord Jesus and their determination to follow and to worship Him. Persecution was fierce in Judean Palestine and in Thessalonican Greece. Here Paul speaks out against the persecution that Judean Christians suffered by Jews in the tradition of the Old Testament prophets. He sounds like Amos or Jeremiah, thundering forth the wrath and the judgment of God upon His disobedient Hebrew people.

Caution is in order here. Indeed, it was the Jews who killed Jesus, just as they had their own prophets. It was the Jews of the Mediterranean world of the first century who persecuted the Christians. And Paul's indignation lashes out at them in this passage as nowhere else in his writings. In fact, when he writes the Roman letter later on, he expresses compassion and care for his Jewish brothers and sisters. In Romans 9–11, he shows his belief and hope that God has not abandoned or rejected them.

We have no right to lay the sins of the Jews of the first century or any other century on Jewish people today. The history of anti-Semitism is the dark underbelly of Christendom. Sadly, Christians have all too often been in the vanguard of hate and prejudice towards Jews.

We can't rewrite the history of the first century and put all of the blame on the Romans. But we have no right to perpetuate age-old animosities. By the time Paul wrote to the Ephesians he had clearly come to the conclusion that all of these past divisions had been overcome by Jesus Himself. Ephesians 2:11–22 needs to be read in conjunction with this prophet-like statement of Paul. If anything, Paul is saying that we Gentiles have been brought into the true Jewish family in and through Jesus the Christ Himself.

Paul's letter to the Galatians also had a lot to say about this matter. He had certainly come to the conviction that the old prejudices were no longer possible in Christ: "There is neither Jew nor Greek, there is neither slave nor free, there is neither male nor female; for you are all one in Christ Jesus" (Gal. 3:28).

As there were forces opposing them as they lived out dynamic, Christian relationships, so there will be opposing forces working against us if we are faithful to the Gospel of God's love and justice. The cost of discipleship in American culture is becoming increasingly clear. Faithfulness to God's concerns for justice and righteousness, for the poor, and for the sacrificial pursuit of peace is going to bring us into persecution and rejection. But our responses must always be shaped by the Man on the cross who said, "Father, forgive them, for they know not what they do" (Luke 23:34).

There is a coming and going in all human relationships. Apartness as well as togetherness is essential to the growth of every relationship. It is this reality to which Paul now bears witness.

THE POWER OF SEPARATION

17 But we, brethren, having been taken away from you for a short time in presence, not in heart, endeavored more eagerly to see your face with great desire.

18 Therefore we wanted to come to you—even I, Paul, time and again—but Satan hindered us.

19 For what is our hope, or joy, or crown of rejoicing? Is it not even you in the presence of our Lord Jesus Christ at His coming?

20 For you are our glory and joy.

1 Thess. 2:17–20

You will recall that Paul's departure from Thessalonica was abrupt and unplanned (Acts 17:5–10). After the assault on Jason's house, Paul and Silas were shipped off to the next town, Berea, under cover of darkness. From the time of that hasty departure, Paul was filled with intense desire to return to them. This very desire attests to the power of their relationships.

In fact, the phrase *"having been taken away from you"* meant in Paul's language "having been orphaned." He saw himself as a mother (2:7) and as a father (2:11) to them. He also felt like one of their children. This is exactly what happens in Christian relationships. The movement from responsibility and caring to dependence and being cared for is an essential rhythm in group life. Whenever I become involved in a group with people in our church, I make clear at the outset my need for this rhythm. If they can accept me only as a father figure, I cannot experience genuine community with them. We all need to have relationships in which we can be children as well as parents. Paul felt like an orphan in his removal from the Thessalonians.

Though the orphan in him desperately wanted to return to his family, the power of Satan hindered him. A world filled with devils is not the conscious milieu of most healthy people today. But we do well to join with Paul in recognizing that "we do not wrestle against flesh and blood, but against principalities, against powers, against the rulers of the darkness of this age, against spiritual hosts of wickedness in the heavenly places" (Eph. 6:12). Martin Luther is quoted as saying: "If you don't believe in the Devil, it's because you've never tried to resist him." There is a battle going on. Indeed, Christ has won the victory, but the "mopping-up" operation will continue until He comes again in final triumph.

Though he was hindered from returning, Paul used the absence and separation creatively. In fact, the intense, emotional tribute that he now pays them probably resulted from the absence. Every relationship needs togetherness and apartness, presence and absence. As I write these pages, I am, of necessity, absent from those closest and dearest to me. But I find these separations to be opportunities for growth in my love and gratitude for them. Togetherness keeps us in touch with reality. Apartness allows us to idealize the relationship. We need both. I find that the togetherness that follows the separation is always very special. The rhythm is important to growth.

It was out of the separation that Paul could idealize the Thessalonians as his *"hope, joy, and crown of rejoicing"* (v. 19). Growing relationships in Christ give us hope for the future—they can only improve with age. They give us joy in the present that comes from knowing one is loved. And they are like the crown, the wreath of victory, or the festive garland. And all of this points to the day when we shall hug one another *"in the presence of our Lord Jesus Christ at His coming."* The word used here for Jesus' coming is *parousia.* This is the first reference in Christian writing to the Second Coming of Christ. This subject will be the theme of pp. 80–89 and pp. 116–25.

Note well the phrase in verse 17: *"taken away from you for a short time in presence, not in heart."* In true relationships, we are never apart.

From Berea, Paul moved south to Athens. What could be more lonely than being alone in a great metropolis, desperately wanting to be at home with those you love? So intense was his desire for the Thessalonians, Paul sent Timothy back to them to be in communication with them. In our day, Paul would have used the telephone. As we learned in the Introduction, Paul then moved on to Corinth, and this letter was written after Timothy had returned from Thessalonica.

THE CONTINUING NEED FOR SUPPORT

1 Therefore, when we could no longer endure it,
we thought it good to be left in Athens alone,
2 and sent Timothy, our brother and minister of
God, and our fellow laborer in the gospel of Christ,
to establish you and encourage you concerning your
faith,
3 that no one should be shaken by these afflictions;
for you yourselves know that we are appointed to this.
4 For, in fact, we told you before when we were
with you that we would suffer tribulation, just as it
happened, and you know.

1 Thess. 3:1–4

Paul's need to communicate with them was a result of his deep love for them. He was well aware that they were under intense pressure. Not only had the leaders of the synagogue forced him out of Thessalonica, they had pursued him to Berea as well. Though he had great confidence in them, he needed to know firsthand that they were standing firm in the midst of persecution.

Paul sent Timothy, commissioning him *"to establish [them] and encourage [them] concerning [their] faith."* The word Paul used for *"establish"* has the meaning of "strengthening." The verb comes from a noun meaning "a support." The word translated *"encourage"* is *parakeleō*, the term Jesus used to denote the Holy Spirit in John 14:16, 26. It means literally, "one called alongside to help."

The need for constant strengthening and support is an integral part of the Christian community. There's a tendency to portray the ideal individual as one who stands alone with no need for help. How sad! The Christian ideal is that of needing support. The recognition of need is the beginning of health. The acceptance of weakness is the beginning of faith.

One of the great discoveries in my Christian journey has been that I am always in need of individuals and groups for strengthening and encouragement—and I always will be. To know and accept that about each other is the basis for all growing Christian relationships.

Verse 3 concludes on a note that is difficult to accept. The idea of being "appointed" to suffer is a hard pill to swallow. Contemporary preachers are all too prone to present the Gospel as a way out of suffering, an antidote to pain. Not so in the New Testament. Afflictions are a necessary part of our growth by divine appointment. Jesus is the Good Shepherd who walks with us *through* the valleys of darkness. His cross becomes the theme of Christian discipleship. This is why our support for one another is so crucial.

PAUL'S NEED FOR HIS FRIENDS

This need for support was not just something that Paul preached for others. He made it clear that he needed it himself.

> 5 For this reason, when I could no longer endure it, I sent to know your faith, lest by some means the tempter had tempted you, and our labor might be in vain.
> 6 But now that Timothy has come to us from you, and brought us good news of your faith and love, and that you always have good remembrance of us, greatly desiring to see us, as we also to see you—
> 7 therefore, brethren, we were comforted concerning you in all our affliction and distress by your faith.
> 8 For now we live, if you stand fast in the Lord.
> *1 Thess. 3:5–8*

His concern for their well-being was paramount. This, we have seen, is at the heart of the meaning of *agapē* love. Again, the presence of "the tempter" must always be kept in mind. The report of Timothy had been good news for Paul. Not only were they strong in their faith and love, but perhaps the best news for Paul was their continuing love and care for him.

Again, he articulates his need to be with them. Any picture of Paul as a lone ranger without deep needs for a caring supporting network of relationships in Christ is permanently erased by this passage from his pen. He simply had to have the support of his brothers and sisters in Christ. This becomes all the more significant when you recall that he was only in Thessalonica for a couple of weeks (Acts 17:2). Christian relationships have a way of taking on great depth in a short period of time.

As a pastor in one suburban congregation for more than nineteen years, I've seen a lot of people come and go. The healthiest and happiest folks I see in the IBM (I've Been Moved) set are those who have learned to move into small groups quickly. Some people who have been with us only a matter of months bear witness to deep relationships that transcend distance and job transfers.

There's a powerful insight in verse 8. Paul literally found his life in the well-being of others. The "me" generation is trying to find life in self-fulfillment without realizing that lasting fulfillment comes through relating to the needs and growth of others. As we run out the options of trying to find our fulfillment by ourselves, I'm confident that we will rediscover this central fact of life. *"We live, if you stand fast in the Lord"* is a beautiful way of saying "I need you."

Your Joy Is My Joy

9 For what thanks can we render to God for you,
for all the joy with which we rejoice for your sake
before our God,
10 night and day praying exceedingly that we may
see your face and perfect what is lacking in your faith?
1 Thess. 3:9–10

In one sense, Paul had every reason to be proud of the good work he had done in Thessalonica. To have introduced the Gospel there in the course of a few days and to have planted a church that was now growing under persecution was no small achievement. Yet, for Paul, there could only be thanks to God. For Paul really believed and lived what he preached, that God alone was the source and sustainer of the life of the Christian community.

Again there is the profound witness to the power of Christian relationships in his words. Their joy is his joy. When they are strong, he celebrates. Their lives in Christ are inseparably intertwined.

Paul's Prayer for His Friends

11 Now may our God and Father Himself, and our
Lord Jesus Christ, direct our way to you.
12 And may the Lord make you increase and abound
in love to one another and to all, just as we do to
you,

13 so that He may establish your hearts blameless
in holiness before our God and Father at the coming
of our Lord Jesus Christ with all His saints.

1 Thess. 3:11-13

It cannot surprise us that this great section on relationships closes
with a prayer for them. Genuine Christian relationships are bound
together in prayer. Praying together in groups, praying together in
personal relationships, and praying for one another in our apartness
is the cement that bonds us in Christ.

Paul's prayer has two components: (1) that Paul will get back to
Thessalonica; and (2) that the Thessalonians will increase and abound
in love.

In praying specifically to get back to Thessalonica, Paul models
an important aspect of prayer. We are often more comfortable with
praying in general than with praying in specifics. To pray specifically
is to bring the details of our lives into God's presence. Paul expresses
his honest desire to God. But this does not mean that if he doesn't
get to Thessalonica his prayer has not been answered. Rather, Paul
is simply committing his desire to God for direction.

To pray in specifics is to open ourselves to God's direction and
control. Such prayer is based on the premise that we may or may
not be on the right track with our desires. It is not a demand for a
specific answer, but a search for God's guidance. This is far removed
from a concept which makes prayer into some kind of a shopping
list for God's magic provision.

How well I remember years ago working on some wiring in the
house with one of our infant daughters alongside. She decided that
she wanted the knife that I was using to strip the insulation from
the wire. Her desire took the form of a demand. But I happened to
be in a better position to know her needs. No matter what she thought,
having that knife was not in her best interests. With howling and
yowling she communicated her lack of confidence in my wisdom.
Don't we sometimes relate to our God and Father in the same way?

Let us not hesitate to bring all of our needs and all of our desires
to God. Then let us confidently follow His leading—whether or not
we get what we asked for.

We must not miss a profound point of theology in the first part
of this prayer. The facts that *"our Lord Jesus Christ"* is linked directly
with *"our God and Father Himself,"* and that the Greek verb translated

"direct" is in the singular, are a clear statement of Paul's belief in the deity of Christ. And this in the earliest writing of the New Testament! That Jesus is God incarnate is clearly the earliest of Christian beliefs.

The second part of the prayer is for the growth of their love. The word again is *agapē.* The source of this love is the Lord. We do well to keep in mind that *agapē,* self-giving love, does not come naturally. It is the gift and the work of God. There is an abundance of literature today witnessing to the frustration of trying to develop this kind of love apart from its only source, God Himself. It's a bit like trying to find water in the desert without a well. Apart from God, *agapē* love is unattainable.

Paul is not willing that such love be contained within the Christian community. It is to abound to one another *"and to all."* How easy it is for us in our groups and in our relationships to become exclusively involved in our own concerns and interests. This is the point where group life stagnates. Again and again, we are discovering that groups need to find avenues of service to others to sustain their vitality. The principle of self-giving love applies to groups as well as to individuals. Abounding love has no borders.

The purpose of this love is stated as the conclusion of Paul's prayer. Where love grows and abounds, our *"hearts"* will be established and strengthened in holiness. The "heart" in the Bible is a general term embracing our capacity to think, feel, and make decisions. It is probably best expressed by the idea of the whole person. The reality here is that the person who is growing in love in Christ is a person whose whole personality is growing toward wholeness.

"Blameless in holiness" is not a matter of achieving moral perfection. To be holy is to be set apart by God for His service. Holiness is not an attainment by the few—it is the act by which God sets each of us apart for Himself. In this action of God, we are blameless— accepted and loved by God to the very day of Christ's coming.

For a long time, I wondered why some commentators call 1 Thessalonians "the epistle of friendship." Having touched deeply this section in which the power of human relationships is so powerfully affirmed, I now agree with this designation. Here is a side of Paul not always portrayed. But more importantly, here is the way of life abundant— life in growing and dynamic relationships with God, with each other, and with those around us.

CHAPTER SIX

A Life that Pleases God

1 Thessalonians 4:1–12

The last three verses of chapter three could well have been a fitting conclusion to the letter. But before Paul can put it in the envelope, he must say more. What follows his *"finally"* are some of the most important things in the letter.

WALKING WITH GOD

1 Finally then, brethren, we urge and exhort you by the Lord Jesus, that as you have received from us how you ought to walk and to please God, you would abound more and more;
2 for you know what commandments we gave you through the Lord Jesus.

1 Thess. 4:1–2

It will become characteristic for Paul to conclude his letters with practical exhortations. To him, the Christian faith was always a blend of belief and behavior, words and works. There's a dangerous tendency in orthodox circles to focus on doctrine to the detriment of duty. Doctrinal conflict that neglects the duty to love one another becomes destructive of Christian community. At the same time, there's another danger in emphasizing behavior at the expense of doctrine. It can never be a case of either/or—it must always be both/and.

With the words *"urge"* and *"exhort,"* it is clear that these practical matters to follow are of supreme importance. The appeal is based upon the *"commandments we gave you."* Doctrine is the basis of goodness. And the doctrine comes "through the Lord Jesus."

The life of Christian discipleship is described as two things: *"to walk and to please God."* Walking was the most common means of moving about in the ancient world. The Hebrews were fond of referring to one's entire life as a walk. "Enoch walked with God" (Gen. 5:24), is the highest affirmation of the quality of his life. The same tribute was paid to Noah (Gen. 6:9). The people of God are commanded, "Ye shall walk in all the ways which the Lord your God has commanded you, that ye may live and that it may be well with you, and that ye may prolong your days in the land which you shall possess" (Deut. 5:33). In the best known of all Psalms, the psalmist portrays suffering and sorrow as a "walk through the valley of the shadow" (Ps. 23:4). The strength offered by the Psalm is that God is walking with us.

For all too many of us, life has become more of a run than a walk. One of the symbols of our age may well be the jogger. Books on running are big sellers, and at least a couple of experts on the subject have made vast fortunes. I believe in aerobics, and I too run at least three times a week, but lately I've taken up more walking. I'm coming to a growing sense of the need to think of life as a walk, rather than a run.

A casual stroll has become to me a symbol of solitude. It's a way of being alone and a way of reflecting. The mild physical activity frees the mind to focus on God. When I walk in our community, people frequently stop their cars to offer me a ride. The idea that one would walk just to walk would seldom occur to us goal- and destination-oriented folks. Even more amusing are the passing joggers with stereo headsets. At the very point where they might think and reflect, solitude is denied. Walking is an attitude more than an action. To practice walking could be one way of recovering a sense of our life as a walk with God.

To walk with God is to please God. Again, we are more likely to think that we are pleasing God in the fast pace of our many activities than in the slow and steady pace of solitude and service. One of the ways of pleasing that God called for in the Bible is to wait for Him. "Wait on the Lord; be of good courage, and He shall strengthen your heart; wait, I say, on the Lord!" (Ps. 27:14). In our age of instant gratification, we don't like to wait for anything. How quickly we want results. Someone said, "My trouble is that I'm always in a hurry, but God never seems to be." To please God is to walk with Him and to wait for Him. "Those who wait on the Lord shall renew their strength; they shall mount up with wings like eagles, they shall run and not be weary, they shall walk and not faint" (Isa. 40:31). There are times to soar and times to run. But most of life is walking—and waiting.

To live in this way is to please God. And in this, Paul would have us *"abound more and more."* Our life in Christ is never to be static. It is growth in abundance. It is the growing experience of God's infinite love. It is the expanding encounter of God's resources and our needs.

The walk with God that pleases God is now viewed in two basic areas of relationships: sexuality (vv. 3–8) and community (vv. 9–12).

THE MEANING OF SEX

3 For this is the will of God, your sanctification: that you should abstain from sexual immorality;
4 that each of you should know how to possess his own vessel in sanctification and honor,
5 not in passion of lust, like the Gentiles who do not know God;
6 that no one take advantage of and defraud his brother in this matter, because the Lord is the avenger of all such, as we also have forewarned you and testified.
7 For God has not called us to uncleanness, but in holiness.
8 Therefore he who rejects this does not reject man, but God, who has also given us His Holy Spirit.

1 Thess. 4:3–8

God wills many different things for each of us in different times, places, and situations. But one of the things He wills for us all is our sanctification. The root word for sanctification is *hagios,* the word for holy. To be sanctified is to be holy. The call to holiness is intricately woven into the fabric of the Scriptures. Peter captured this when he wrote, using Leviticus 11:44–45: "As He who called you is holy, you also be holy in all your conduct, because it is written, 'Be holy, for I am holy' " (1 Pet. 1:15–16).

If you were asked to describe your concept of holiness with a color, what would it be? Black? Gray? To many, *holy* connotes the idea of drabness or dullness. White? To others, holiness means absolute purity—no blotches or stains. I would color it blue or green, or even a warm tan. These are the colors that convey to me the beauty of God's creation. And holiness, sanctification, has to do with being very much in tune with the will of God for His creation.

The root meaning of the Hebrew word for holy was that of being "set apart." An object used in the worship service in the temple was said to be holy because it had been set apart for special use. People are said to be holy in the same sense of being set apart for the service of God. We shall see this sense of holiness expressed in 2 Timothy 2:20–21, in which certain household vessels, being set apart for special use, become the analogy of a person as "a vessel for honor, sanctified and useful for the Master."

The call to sanctification is not a call to stuffiness or drabness. It is a call to usefulness, to availability, and to fidelity. It is a call to an adventure of discovering what life is really intended by God to be. Color it bright and warm, the way God colored His world.

Paul's first specific appeal with regard to holiness is in the realm of sexual behavior. He begins here, not because sexual sins are necessarily the worst of all, but because they were among the most common. While we live in a society that is in the throes of trying to throw off sexual restraints, they lived in a society that had none. When Paul wrote to Christians in places like Thessalonica and Corinth, he was addressing first generation Christians right out of Greco-Roman culture. Historians concur that it was a society in which there were no restraints when it came to sexual mores.

Christianity's roots were Hebrew, not Greek or Roman. As such, the contrast in this realm was dramatic. The Law of Moses placed adultery and coveting the neighbor's wife strictly out of bounds. For centuries, the Hebrews practiced plural marriage even within the Law. Solomon with his "seven hundred wives, princesses, and three hundred concubines" (1 Kings 11:3) may have been the highest achiever, but such practice eventually was abandoned. The understatement of the ancient writer was that Solomon's wives "turned his heart after other gods" (1 Kings 11:4). While the Hebrews were a long time coming to monogamy, by the time of Jesus, standards of sexual and marital purity had been established which were absolutely foreign to the surrounding culture.

To understand this background of the early Christians is important. The reason Paul tackles the sexual question first is not difficult to see. The first thing a new, Gentile convert would have to confront would be the radical changes in sexual standards demanded by Jesus Himself (Matt. 5:27–31) and applied in the early church (1 Cor. 6:15–20). While this was not a frequent theme, either in the teachings of Jesus or of Paul, its importance cannot be minimized.

Increasingly, our culture is moving away from its Judeo-Christian heritage in this area, and the sexual revolution is an accomplished fact. Paul's counsel to *"abstain from sexual immorality," "to possess [one's] own vessel* [either one's body or one's wife] *in sanctification and honor,"* and *"that no one should take advantage of and defraud his brother in this matter,"* is likely to fall on deaf ears apart from those who in some way are responsive to God's call to holiness. Unfortunately, this counsel is not always taken seriously within the Christian community itself.

The simplest reading of the entire matter is that God has created us for intimacy with one another. One of the ways of sharing that intimacy is sexual intercourse. And that is designed by God to be used only in the context of a lifelong commitment of marriage. It needs to be said loudly, lovingly, and clearly that sexual loving apart from marriage is out of bounds, not because sex is bad, but because it is so good. Sex is holy. It is set apart for special use.

That this view is countercultural and regarded as antiquarian by many does not in the least invalidate its truth. The principles by which God's creation operates are neither determined nor discovered by the majority of the people surveyed, no matter how accurate the poll. The law of gravity is a description of the way things really are. We may all decide to defy it and jump off the cliff together, but we will all hit the bottom at the same time. We may achieve by consensus a rewrite of sexual standards in our generation, but the way God made things is the way things really are. If Jesus is right, it's not for us to write new rules.

Paul's final word in this section makes it clear that the bottom line is obedience to God. To reject Paul's appeals is not to reject mere human opinion but God Himself (vv. 7–8). I take Paul's reference here to the Holy Spirit as an appeal to the witness within us about the meaning of our sexuality. In our most honest and healthy moments, does not the Word of God ring true? *"God did not call us to uncleanness, but in holiness"* (v. 7).

Because of the nature of the sexually "liberated" world in which we live, we dare not conclude this section without remembering that the Gospel is ultimately redemptive. Jesus has come not to put us in bondage to rules and regulations, but to set us free. Much that is offered in the name of sexual freedom only leads us to greater bondage. The Christian standard confining sexual loving exclusively to marriage may appear to be bondage, but in reality it is a way to freedom—the freedom to enjoy one's sexuality in the way intended by God.

Perhaps the ultimate myth in need of greater examination is that one cannot have a fulfilling life without occasional or regular sexual experience. Was Jesus unfulfilled? Or wasn't he truly human? My understanding of sexuality has been enriched by some who have chosen a life of sexual abstinence as a part of their religious vocation. Protestants can learn much from them. We must not readily assume that religious celibacy is grounded in the belief that sex is sinful. In reality, celibacy in Roman Catholic tradition has its roots in Paul's letter to the Corinthians. Paul exalts singleness as a means of Christian service: "He who is unmarried cares for the things that belong to the Lord—how he may please the Lord. But he who is married cares about the things of the world—how he may please his wife" (1 Cor. 7:32–33). The same application then follows for women (not one of the most widely quoted passages of Paul).

Thomas Aquinas defined celibacy as a vacancy for God. It is seen as a conscious decision to keep that area of one's life open for God and available for the service of God. Not only does the celibate witness to us that life can be fulfilling without sexual experiences, but of greater importance, that each of us needs to have an inner core of our being reserved for God. Preoccupation with sex, be we single or married, can become another thing that crowds God out of our lives.

The Gospel is indeed redemptive. It can liberate us from a consuming and disproportionate concern with sex. And it can bring us forgiveness and healing when we have misused sex, hurting ourselves and others. In our time the need is to communicate our biblical understanding of sex as the good that it really is.

The second theme dealing with the walk that is pleasing to God is Christian community, life together. While salvation is always personal, it is never private. The distinction between personal and social ethics can be misleading. Some would say that Paul has treated the personal ethics of sexuality and now moves to social ethics. I insist

LIFE TOGETHER

9 But concerning brotherly love you do not need
that I write to you, for you yourselves are taught by
God to love one another;
10 and indeed you do this to all the brethren who
are in all Macedonia. But we urge you, brethren, that
you increase more and more;
11 that you also aspire to lead a quiet life, to mind
your own business, and to work with your own hands,
as we commanded you,
12 that you may walk properly toward those who
are outsiders, and that you may lack nothing.

1 Thess. 4:9–12

This section is characteristic of Paul. It begins with an affirmation
and moves to an exhortation, probably addressing some conduct that
Paul felt needed correcting. The affirmation begins warmly: *"You have
no need that I should write to you,"* for, as he goes on to say, they are
quite accomplished in brotherly love both in Thessalonica and all
Macedonia. In the middle of verse 10, however, comes the *"but"* leading into the apparent confrontation and correction.

This is a good model to follow. Regularly, my reaction to constructive criticism depends upon how it is given. When someone comes
to me in negative anger, I tend to react defensively. But when one
begins with an affirmation, I'm more likely to be open and responsive.
It happened to me both ways at the door after church the other
Sunday. One man came out breathing fire over a statement I had
made in the sermon, "Of all the stupid things I've ever heard! What
on earth did you mean by that?" If he intended that as a question
for clarification (and he may have), that's not what he got! What
he got was a defensive statement affirming my belief in what I had
said. Within minutes, another man approached me, "Pastor, that was
a most interesting and challenging sermon. I'm sure it took a lot
of courage for you to say what you did. But, did you really
mean . . . ?" What a difference! I went to great length to clarify

my position and to affirm him in his right to disagree. Admittedly, I should have had the maturity and grace to respond to both men with the same care and sensitivity. But I didn't that day.

There is no better way to confront and to reprove than by beginning with affirmation. And by affirmation is not meant insincere flattery. We frequently create the climate, and thus the response to our criticism, by the way we make it. Paul's consistent pattern was to preface criticism with praise. It certainly made a thoughtful and positive response more likely.

Now, what was the problem? Often, in reading Paul's letters, we have a situation not unlike Johnny Carson's "Karnak" routine. The all-knowing Karnak is given the answer and then must reply by giving the question. How do we re-create the situation that Paul was confronting? Sometimes, by reading opposites into the words of the passage.

In verse 11, he calls them to *"aspire to lead a quiet life, to mind [their] own business, and to work with [their] own hands."* It is fair to assume that had they been doing these things, his instructions would have been unnecessary. Thus, it is likely that Paul was responding to reports that they were *not* leading quiet lives, that they were butting into each other's business, and that they were not willing to work. But this does not square with the picture that we have of them in the letter thus far. Everything has portrayed them as caring, loving, dedicated people.

What could have gone wrong? The clue perhaps comes in looking ahead in the letter. Most of the remainder of the letter will deal with what were some serious errors in their understanding of the return of Christ. In this, the earliest of Paul's writings, more emphasis is placed upon this theme than in any others. Apparently, in the early years of the young churches there was a widespread belief that Jesus would return very soon, certainly within their lifetime.

As speculation flourished and grew, many aberrations developed. Perhaps many of them quit their jobs to "wait" for the expected event. Others, very likely, were busy stirring up excitement with the latest "signs" of His coming. Still others became just plain meddlesome and obnoxious. What better counsel under such circumstances? People who lead a quiet life, who mind their own business, and who work with their own hands provide the material out of which genuine Christian community is shaped. Efforts to experience life together based upon frantic activity, probing into other's business, and exploiting the work of others are doomed to failure.

Two products of Christian community are set forth in verse 12. Life together as intended by Christ is a strong witness to "outsiders." I see this again and again. When there are situations in which the people of the church really care for and support one another, I discover people more interested in what is being said from the pulpit and in the adult education classroom.

The second product of Christian community is a certain sufficiency: *"that you may lack nothing."* Experiencing this kind of community is virtually impossible in our situations. The ideal of a community in which each person has no unmet physical needs is probably most closely realized in the Roman Catholic orders. In affluent suburbia, we are strongly committed to our rights to private property and personal possessions as our own. We can experience a kind of community based upon charitable giving, out of what we can afford to give. And through this system, we do an impressive amount of good things for needy people. But we sacrifice the real possibility of a genuine community in Christ. Having the ideal before us at least calls us to a different way of thinking and living.

In this short section, we have a beautiful picture of the life that pleases God. We walk with Him as men and women, created for fullness of life—in our sexuality and in our relationships. The life that pleases God is life in the Body of Christ.

CHAPTER SEVEN

The Second Coming of Christ

1 Thessalonians 4:13—5:11

As with the previous section, we are dealing here with questions that had arisen in Thessalonica about the return of the Lord. The promises of Jesus were unmistakably clear. One of the better known is in John's Gospel: "In My Father's house are many mansions; if it were not so, I would have told you. I go to prepare a place for you. And if I go and prepare a place for you, I will come again and receive you to Myself; that where I am, there you may be also" (John 14:2–3). The disciples had also received the dramatic message after His ascension: "This same Jesus, who was taken up from you into heaven, will so come in like manner as you have seen Him go into heaven" (Acts 1:11).

There's bound to be speculation about this kind of promise, and it began early in the life of the church. In this, his first letter, Paul addresses three questions troubling the Thessalonians.

1. What happens to those who die before He comes? (4:13–18)
2. How can we know when He will come? (5:1–3)
3. How should we live while we await His coming? (5:4–11)

In the light of their belief that Christ would return very soon, grief at the death of a loved one was compounded by the fear that he or she had thus missed the glorious event.

WHAT OF THOSE WHO HAVE DIED?

13 But I do not want you to be ignorant, brethren, concerning those who have fallen asleep, lest you sorrow as others who have no hope.
14 For if we believe that Jesus died and rose again,

so also God will bring with Him those who sleep in
Jesus.

15 For this we say to you by the word of the Lord,
that we who are alive and remain until the coming
of the Lord will by no means precede those who are
asleep.

16 For the Lord Himself will descend from heaven
with a shout, with the voice of an archangel, and with
the trumpet of God. And the dead in Christ will rise
first.

17 Then we who are alive and remain shall be caught
up together with them in the clouds to meet the Lord
in the air. And thus we shall always be with the Lord.

18 Therefore comfort one another with these words.

1 Thess. 4:13–18

We do well to begin any discussion of this subject by checking
our vocabulary. "Second coming" and "end of the world" are not
properly a part of the vocabulary of the Bible. Their popular usage
has grown out of the need to express technical terms in everyday
language. The most commonly used term to describe Christ's return
is *parousia*. We saw the first occurrence of it in 2:19 and then again
in 3:13. Its common use meant "presence" or "appearing." Because
it was sometimes used of the visit of royalty, it naturally became
the appropriate word to refer to Christ's Second Coming.

The *parousia* was identified with the Old Testament's Day of the
Lord. To the Hebrew, all of history consisted of two ages—the present
age and the age to come. The end of this present age and the beginning
of the age to come would be inaugurated with the Day of the Lord.
That day would end this sinful, fallen age and usher in the golden
age and the eternal abolition of sin, suffering, war, and death. It
would also mark the final judgment of God. To the early Christians,
the Day of the Lord and the *parousia*, the second coming of Christ,
were one and the same. They both mark the event that will be the
end of this age, the end of the world.

The early Christians had good reason to believe that Christ's return
would be within their lifetimes. At least there was no compelling
reason *not* to believe so. I've often heard folks argue that since those
first-century Christians were so mistaken in their view of Christ's
return, they might well have been wrong in the idea that He would
ever return. Nonsense! It's not a case of being right or wrong about

the fact of Christ's return. It's a case of believing Jesus' own promise. Paul will confront the error of speculating about the time of His return in the next section.

The fact that the Thessalonians were mistaken in their belief that Jesus would return in their lifetime has nothing to do with the fact that Jesus Himself promised that He would come again.

They were mistaken, and their erroneous belief gave rise to great anxieties. As time went on, more and more of their friends and loved ones died. With each death there was not only the normal bereavement, but also the fear and remorse in knowing that their loved one had indeed missed out on the *parousia* by virtue of having died too soon.

As is often the case, their error becomes our gain. Some of the greatest insights in Paul's letters come to us through his confrontation of false and erroneous beliefs and practices in the early church. Because of their mistaken views concerning the *parousia*, Paul has written what is perhaps the most significant paragraph of this letter. He brings them assurance, declaration, and comfort.

Assurance. Paul's pastoral heart instinctively enters into their grief. He does not belittle their sorrow, but he assures them that they need not sorrow as others who have no hope. Every pastor knows the awkward feelings that arise when called into a death situation where there is no evident faith in Christ. Paul will later write to the Corinthians: "If in this life only we have hope in Christ, we are of all men the most pitiable" (1 Cor. 15:19). Our hope is unlike any other hope for it is grounded in the fact of Christ's victory over death through His resurrection. Our sorrow, therefore, is unlike other sorrow for it is embraced by our hope.

The language of Paul is tender in its assurance. The picture of death as sleep is not unique to Christianity, but where else can you find the strong assurance of believing that your loved ones are asleep in Jesus? How different from the modern view of death which guides us through various "stages" of death and dying from denial to acceptance. The end result is to experience death as natural and peaceful. All of this is helpful, and it's comforting to know that death is rarely traumatic. We must learn to accept death as the ultimate experience for each of us. But the Christian view goes way beyond mere acceptance. "To be absent from the body and to be present with the Lord" (2 Cor. 5:8) is to be "asleep in Jesus." This is our view of death and dying.

Being asleep involves future awakening. The point of sleeping is to wake up fresh and renewed. Now Paul presents the resurrection of Jesus as the guarantee that the dead shall return with Jesus in the *parousia*. This leads to the most vivid description we have of that day.

Declaration. Paul begins his declaration of verses 15–17 with an appeal to the authority of *"the word of the Lord."* This can mean one of three things. He could be basing this teaching upon a passage like Matthew 24:31, but there are no sayings of Jesus recorded in the Gospels which give the details that are here. Or, he could be giving us a statement of Jesus not recorded in the Gospels, as in Acts 20:35. Or, he may feel that the Lord has given him a clear word on this matter through the Holy Spirit, as in 1 Corinthians 2:13. To Paul, this teaching rests on the authority of Jesus, and there's certainly nothing in the Gospels that contradicts this possibility.

Paul allays their fears about those who have died by insisting that the dead will participate in the *parousia* first! They are already with Him, and they will precede us. His use of the phrase *"we who are alive and remain until the coming of the Lord,"* could well indicate a belief that he will be among the "we." While we cannot know whether he did, I reject the criticism that Paul was "mistaken," on the same grounds stated earlier. He certainly never engaged in any speculation about dates, and he never made any predictions in his letters. I see him as a model for us. We would do well to live more in the consciousness of the *parousia* than we are inclined to do. Every generation of Christians is called to live in the hope of His coming, not in fear and forecasts, but with the undergirding sense that this is what history is all about.

In January 1965, we had just moved from our pastorate in Buffalo to the La Canada Presbyterian Church in Southern California. At the same time, my closest friend, Donn Moomaw, had just moved to the Bel Air Presbyterian Church nearby. We were both delighted with the prospects of living near each other for the first time ever. During the first week, we got together for a game of golf. The anticipation of our future together was high. After we had teed off, walking down the first fairway, Donn said to me, "Do you really want the Lord to come right now?"

In my experience, wanting the Lord to come is different from living in the hope of His coming. On a beautiful, winter day in a warm climate, playing golf with one's best friend, looking forward to new challenges and opportunities, I can't say that I really wanted the Lord to return.

There have been other times, however, when I have wished for His coming. I recall a very low time when I was faced with a very difficult situation that brought into question my continuation in pastoral ministry. I remember well driving down the highway one night, thinking of steering into a concrete abutment. Through my scalding tears, thinking of the possibility of suicide, I cried out, "Lord Jesus, please come!"

Whether I want Him to return depends a great deal on how I feel about my life and work at a given time. But while those desires ebb and flow, I can consciously live in the awareness that some day He will come—not on the basis of my needs and desires, but by the will of God.

Paul's description of the Day of the Lord is shaped by the picturesque imagery of a style of writing common from about 300 B.C. to Paul's day. It is called apocalyptic writing, and, like poetry or prose, has a style of its own. *Apocalypse* means "the unveiling or revelation of that which is hidden or mysterious." It abounds in vivid imagery, symbolic numbers and codes, and is not intended to be taken literally at all points. Among examples of this style found in the Bible are the Books of Daniel and Revelation, and sections of the Gospels such as Matthew 24 and 25. The language here is not that of a literal news account, but the language of vision and hope.

There is no language to describe the indescribable wonder of that great day. What is important is not the imagery but the reality. The reality promised throughout the Scriptures and proclaimed by Jesus is that history is moving toward its appointment with God. Jesus will return. And with Him those who are asleep in Him. We shall be joined with them and the Lord. *"And thus we shall always be with the Lord"* (v. 17).

Comfort. With the assurance and the declaration there is comfort. The Greek word is *parakaleō,* a word meaning "to call one alongside." It is the word used also of the Holy Spirit. In times of grief and bereavement, we need to call someone alongside for support and strength. The comfort that comes in this assurance and declaration is our great legacy from Paul. There is no greater joy than to be called alongside one in grief, to touch the sufferer with these words, and to experience together the beginning of healing and hope.

From the lofty heights of the apocalyptic vision of the *parousia,* the Day of the Lord, Paul now descends to the dusty plain of a persistent and unproductive question, "When will He return?" It's most likely that the speculators were as present then as they are now.

WHEN WILL HE RETURN?

1 But concerning the times and the seasons,
brethren, you have no need that I write to you.
2 For you yourselves know perfectly that the day
of the Lord so comes as a thief in the night.
3 For when they say, "Peace and safety!" then
sudden destruction comes on them, as labor pains on
a pregnant woman. And they shall not escape.

1 Thess. 5:1–3

Predictions about the end of the world and the coming of Christ are not unique to our time. In every age there have been those who interpret the "signs of the times" as indicating Christ's soon return. The matters concerning the end times are called eschatology, from the Greek word *eschaton*, "last things."

There were those in Thessalonica who had concluded that Jesus would surely come most any day. As we saw in 1 Thessalonians 4:9–12, some were apparently stirring up all kinds of excitement and others had quit their jobs to await the event. The pattern has been repeated again and again.

Paul's opening sentence is a reprimand. *"You have no need that I should write you"* must have been said with a groan of annoyance. To emphasize his anguish, he continues, *"you yourselves know perfectly. . . ."* These are the words of a troubled parent. "How many times do I have to tell you?"

There's only one thing for sure that can be said about the coming of Christ. It will be like "a thief in the night." This figure of speech does not liken the Lord to a thief, but is only intended to underscore once and for all that no one can know when He will come.

What amazes me most about the purveyors of prophetic schemes is their flagrant disobedience to the Scriptures and to Jesus Himself. In the clearest way Jesus said, "But of that day and hour no one knows, neither the angels who are in heaven, nor the Son, but only the Father. Take heed, watch and pray; for you do not know when the time is. . . . the master of the house is coming. . . . And what I say to you, I say to all: Watch!" (Mark 13:32–37). After His resurrection, the disciples asked Him the perennial question about the time of the restoration of the Kingdom—the Day of the Lord. Again his emphatic answer: "It is not for you to know the times or seasons which the Father has put in His own authority" (Acts 1:7). Paul is simply reinforcing Jesus' strong prohibitions against making predictions and forecasts regarding His coming. To do so is to place oneself in clear disobedience to Jesus Himself.

His coming will be a total surprise to those who are forever doing business as usual, saying, *"Peace and safety!"* The reference here seems to be to those who place all of their eggs in this world's basket and live as though they could build the Kingdom of God here on earth without His coming. To live in expectation of His coming does not mean that it will not surprise us. I choose to think of it as living with the certainty that it will surprise us—for it is not given to us to know, and we're told not to speculate.

Thus there are two extremes to be avoided. One is the arrogance of pretending to have some special knowledge about the future and His coming, even if it claims to be based upon the Bible. The other is to live apart from the continuing awareness that on the day of God's choosing, He will come!

Once we have truly accepted the fact that we cannot know and we are not to speculate about when He will return, the question arises as to how we are to live in this expectation and hope.

How, Then, Shall We Live?

4 But you, brethren, are not in darkness, that this Day should overtake you as a thief.

5 You are all sons of light and sons of the day. We are not of the night nor of darkness.

6 Therefore let us not sleep, as others do, but let us watch and be sober.

7 For those who sleep, sleep at night, and those who get drunk are drunk at night.

8 But let us who are of the day be sober, putting on the breastplate of faith and love, and as a helmet the hope of salvation.

9 For God has not appointed us to wrath, but to
obtain salvation by our Lord Jesus Christ,
    10 who died for us, that whether we wake or sleep,
we should live together with Him.
    11 Therefore comfort each other and edify one
another, just as you also are doing.

1 Thess. 5:4–11

In stark contrast to those who will be utterly surprised and destroyed by His coming, Paul portrays Christ's own as *"sons of light
and sons of the day"* (v. 5). The drama of this metaphor has been weakened by the advent of electricity. You have to imagine what it would
have been like to live in a world without electricity and light bulbs
to feel the impact of this language.

During a recent retreat with our Session at a nearby hotel, there
was a complete power failure for more than forty-five minutes—no
lights, no telephone, and it was a while before anyone located candles
and flashlights. Needless to say, everything came to a halt until the
lights came on again.

Those living in darkness are portrayed as sleeping and as being
drunk. In this case sleep and drunkenness picture someone who is
not in touch with or in control of his or her own life. When we
are asleep, we are pretty much out of touch with the world around
us, except for our dreams. The drunk has lost control of his or her
ability to make wise decisions and to coordinate responses. People
who do not live in expectation of Christ's coming are likened to
sleepers and drunks—not really in touch with present or ultimate
reality.

Living in the light of Christ's promised return is like living in
the light and in sobriety. Sobriety and light go together. These words
have become especially important to me through a growing number
of friendships with alcoholics who have come to sobriety. We do a
great deal of work through our congregation with people having alcohol problems. No one is more radiant than the person who has found
continuing sobriety after years of drunkenness. This is just as true
for the spouse or friend as for the drinker. The other evening, I asked
the wife of one of our alcoholics who came to sobriety two years
ago how everything was going. Tears cascaded down her cheeks as
she said, "It's like we've moved from hell to heaven!" And they
have!

87

God created us to live in the light and in sobriety. And to live as children of the day is to live with the continual and growing expectation of Christ's coming.

Even as Paul thinks of life in the light and in sobriety, he is gripped with the reality that our life until Jesus comes will be a battle. And we gird for the battle with Paul's favorite trilogy—faith, hope, and love.

Faith and love are here presented as our breastplate, and hope is presented as our helmet. Paul will later develop this metaphor of the armor in fuller scope in Ephesians 6:10–20. There, the breastplate is righteousness, the helmet is salvation, and neither hope nor love is included. Thus, the imagery should not be pushed too far. But what a strengthening and reassuring picture as we face difficulty and opposition because of our walk with God. Faith, love, and hope— our breastplate and our helmet!

Paul concludes this delightful section with a final word of comfort for them and for us (vv. 9–11). The basis of our hope is God's appointment of us, not to wrath, but to salvation. To say that we "obtain" salvation by our Lord Jesus Christ does not place it within the realm of human achievement. It is, first and last, the gift of God by His grace through Jesus Christ. We obtain it simply in the sense of coming to Christ to receive it.

It is Christ's death for us that transforms our deaths into sleep. And His death is the ground for our life together in Christian community. And here the message comes full circle, back to the first of the three questions. Those who have died physically are alive with the Lord. They have left us for a little while, and they are now with Him. And some day—that day—we shall all be together again.

Until that day, we shall continue to live with Him, and on this side we shall comfort and edify one another. To edify has to do with building an edifice. We have the privilege of building together this temple of God in which we are living stones (1 Pet. 2:4–5).

We can be grateful, indeed, for the errors of those Christians in Thessalonica. We would all be poorer in our knowledge and hope of our glorious future without their need to be corrected by Paul.

And now we march forward in hope, even in a world living under the cloud of possible nuclear annihilation. We look to a new heaven and a new earth where "He will dwell with them, and they shall be His people, and God Himself will be with them and be their God. And God will wipe away every tear from their eyes; there shall be no more death, nor sorrow, nor crying; and there shall be no more pain, for the former things have passed away" (Rev. 21:3–4).

And so shall we ever be with the Lord.
Amen.

CHAPTER EIGHT

Life in the Church

1 Thessalonians 5:12–28

Paul now brings his first letter to a close by bringing together a number of matters relating to their lives together in the Christian community. While some of these related to specific issues then and there, the entire section provides us with timeless counsel for life in the church.

The most likely reading of the situation is that the leaders of the congregation had rebuked some of the members for error or misconduct. Perhaps they had dealt firmly with those who had stopped working to wait for the expected *parousia*. For whatever reasons, Paul urged an attitude of support and respect.

RESPECT FOR LEADERS IN THE CHURCH

12 And we urge you, brethren, to recognize those who labor among you, and are over you in the Lord and admonish you,
13 and to esteem them very highly in love for their work's sake. Be at peace among yourselves.

1 Thess. 5:12–13

If, indeed, the elders of the church had confronted some of the brothers and sisters regarding some errors in thought or practice, it's most likely that their efforts were met with resistance and rejection. That's why church discipline is virtually nonexistent in most of our fellowships. For most of us, nothing is more unpleasant than being cast in the role of disciplinarian or enforcer. But the health of a congregation depends upon some degree of commitment to certain standards of doctrine and conduct. Paul's appeal to the congregation, perhaps divided in its support of the leaders who had exercised discipline, is designed to restore a sense of peace and harmony.

This passage has special interest in that here, in the earliest New Testament writing, is an indication of some form of organization in the early church in which there are officers with authority for leadership. By the time we get to Paul's last letters (1 and 2 Timothy), we will see that those officers and their duties are much more clearly delineated. But here there is obviously some form of organization of officers in the church. From the model of the Jewish synagogue, it should not surprise us that elders were appointed from the earliest times (Acts 11:30; 14:23). We do not know at this point how they were chosen or exactly what their responsibilities were, but there is every reason to believe that elders were functioning by the time this letter was written.

Three functions of these elders are recognized: (1) *"who labor among you"*; (2) who *"are over you in the Lord"*; (3) who *"admonish you."*

"Labor" is the word for hard work. Leadership in the church is not a matter of privilege. It is hard work, never merely a place of honor. It is diligent, often self-sacrificing effort. In a time when clergy are often given special treatment and privileges, it is well for us to keep in mind that leadership in the church is hard work.

The second function of leadership designates some measure of authority. The Greek word literally means "to take the lead." It is the same word used in Romans 12:8 and translated there "he who leads." Too often, authority is seen as power rather than responsibility. In the church we must resist this error. The authority given to leaders is not a matter of personal power, but of moral responsibility to lead and to guide. Thus, this is the only one of the three functions with a qualifier, *"in the Lord."* Only as the leader is under the Lord's authority is he or she fit to lead the people.

The third function is admonishing. This is one of those fascinating compound words used only in the New Testament by Paul. It means, literally, to "put in mind." This was the word used by Paul in his address to the Ephesian elders reminding them that he had warned them day and night for three years (Acts 20:31). It carries not only a sense of warning but of instructing as well.

Here, then, is the earliest description we have of the responsibilities of Christian leaders in the church—to labor, to lead, and to teach. These continue to be our primary tasks as leaders.

The people in the church are called to respond to such leaders in two ways: (1) to recognize them, and (2) to esteem them very highly in love.

To "recognize" is a translation of the word "to know." Here the word for "know" is used in the sense of "knowing the worth of" or of "respecting." The leader is worthy of respect, not by virtue of the title or the office, but by virtue of the quality and fidelity brought to laboring, leading, and teaching.

This is quite clear in the second admonition "to esteem them very highly in love." The esteem called for is a response to the work that is done: *"For their work's sake."* As I teach future pastors in the seminary, I can't stress this too strongly. Once we are ordained, we stand in a different relationship to people. Many of them bring us a great deal of respect and esteem by virtue of the office that we hold. But great caution must be exercised in our self-image, lest we forget that the esteem and love that we receive is based upon the Lord's work that we are called to do and not upon any particular merit within us.

Such attitudes and relationships among and between the leaders and the people in a congregation produce *"peace among yourselves."* This peace, then, is not the result of the absence of conflicts or disagreements, but the positive achievement of mutual respect between leaders and people.

DISCIPLINE IN THE CHURCH

14 Now we exhort you, brethren, warn those who are unruly, comfort the fainthearted, uphold the weak, be patient with all.
15 See that no one renders evil for evil to anyone, but always pursue what is good both for yourselves and for all.

1 Thess. 5:14–15

This section was likely addressed to some problems that had grown out of the exercise of church discipline. Paul here gives six timeless principles for discipline in the Christian community.

It is important to notice that the responsibility for these areas of discipline is placed upon the entire community and not just upon the church officers. It is the "brethren" who are addressed, just as they had been in verse 12. Thus, while the responsibility for these disciplines is a part of the work of the leaders, it must always be seen as a responsibility shared by the entire fellowship.

The first group singled out by Paul is the *"unruly."* The brethren are to "warn," the same word translated "admonish" in verse 12. The word *"unruly"* occurs only here in the New Testament and would be used of a soldier who had stepped out of the ranks. It was also used to describe disorderly behavior. While we tend to idealize "New Testament Christianity," those early Christians, too, had their disorderly and unruly folks to deal with. Here was a call to confrontation in the form of admonition and warning.

Then there are those who are quite the opposite of the unruly. They are the *"fainthearted."* Paul again uses a word that occurs only here in the New Testament. It means, literally, "little souls." The King James Version translated this "feebleminded," but this is much too harsh. The reference is to those in every group of people who become easily discouraged or frightened. Perhaps in Thessalonica there were folks who had become frightened and discouraged because loved ones had died and missed the *parousia.* They are to be comforted. This is the word used in John 11:19, describing the comfort that friends were bringing to Mary and Martha after the death of Lazarus.

To see comforting the fainthearted as a part of church discipline becomes a positive emphasis in an area of church life often regarded only as negative. Comforting those who have come on undue fear and discouragement is just as much a part of our responsibility to one another as is the warning of the unruly. I saw this recently in the case of a person whose spouse had decided to initiate a divorce. He felt unworthy to continue in the church because he had been such a failure as a husband and father. He had lost much of his sense of self-worth. Through the comfort and support of some men in a small group, he's finding the strength to continue in the fellowship.

Yet another group of people within the fellowship are the *"weak."* Presumably, the reference is to moral and spiritual weakness. There always seems to be a more prominent place in the church for the strong than for the weak. Yet the church is to be the place where the weak can be upheld. How tragic when churches become groups that are quick to judge and condemn the weak. I wish we could have a sign over our church door, "The weak are welcome here!"

The word to *"uphold"* the weak paints a beautiful picture. It comes from a word meaning "to hold before or against." It is the picture of a person keeping oneself face to face with someone, holding on to them. Instead of rejecting or belittling the weak, the Christian fellowship should be the place where a "buddy system" can be developed for them. When I was first learning to swim at a summer camp, I was assigned a "buddy" who was a strong swimmer. I was not allowed to swim out in the lake without my "buddy." What a source of joy it was the following summer to be a "buddy" to a beginning swimmer. Could not our small groups and church fellowship operate on the "buddy system"? Some folks have a hard time staying afloat on the treacherous waters of life. With a "buddy," they just might make it!

In case he missed anyone, with the categories of the unruly, the fainthearted, and the weak, Paul has a word for *"all."* And that word is "patience." We have already seen one of the Greek words for patience, *hupomonē*. It has to do with patience in stressful events. Here is the other word, *makrothumia*, which is patience with people—patience that does not retaliate. It is a picture of self-restraint in contrast to wrath or revenge. Church discipline must always be tempered with this kind of patience. Too often, discipline is exercised as a means of getting even for real or imagined wrongs. Patience is willing to go the extra distance with the goal of restoration and reconciliation.

The last two admonitions may well express how that patience comes into play. It begins by the adamant refusal to render evil for evil to anyone. Rendering evil for evil creates the classic lose-lose situation. You insult me. I insult you. We both lose. On the global scale, the two superpowers have now developed the ultimate model of the tragedy of evil for evil. You fire your nuclear warhead; I fire mine. We all lose. How do you break the cycle? One party has to risk a new approach.

And that is portrayed as pursuing *"what is good both for yourselves and for all."* This is about as close to a definition of *agapē* as you'll ever find. In the potential evil-for-evil situation, what is good for one is good for both. Whatever risks are taken to break the cycle should be based upon what is good for oneself. This is a point often missed, but Paul's order is profound. He starts with what is good for *"yourselves."* If I respond to the insult or the attack by asking what is best for me, and pursue that with some measure of long-range common sense, what I come up with will have the highest potential for both of us.

To see and practice life together in the church through the wisdom of these six principles could restore healthy and creative church discipline to our congregations.

STANDING ORDERS FOR THE CHURCH

16 Rejoice always;
17 pray without ceasing;
18 in everything give thanks; for this is the will
of God in Christ Jesus for you.

1 Thess. 5:16–18

These three verses have been called by some "the standing orders of the church." They are in the imperative mood, forceful commands directing our attitudes and actions. The very use of the imperative forces us to regard rejoicing, praying, and giving thanks as things other than feelings. We all know that feelings cannot be commanded. Telling your spouse not to feel angry or your child not to feel badly seldom leads to a happy evening at home. But behaviors can be called for. And that's what Paul is doing.

"Rejoice always." This is not the same as commanding one to feel happy at all times. Feeling happy is the natural response to experiences that bring us rewards. Please don't ask me to feel happy when I've just smashed my thumb with the hammer or even when I've just lost the tennis match. But neither smashing my thumb nor losing my tennis match need have anything to do with my joy and rejoicing in life.

Thus, throughout the Bible, we are called to joy and rejoicing in our sufferings. I can't make any sense of this without distinguishing between joy and happiness. I've long since accepted the fact that I cannot be happy at all times. But I'm satisfied that there can always be a basic joy in my life.

The basis of that joy is Jesus Himself. For in Him, I am able to distinguish between appearances and reality. Joy is tied to reality, not merely to appearances. This is so clear when I am with a family at the time of the death of a loved one. I was called by the sheriff in the middle of the night, informing me that the son of one of our families had just been killed in an automobile wreck. To them, at 3:00 A.M., the appearances were stark. The loss of a son. The shattering of the family. The grief. The remorse. It was not a time to call for happiness. But as the months have gone by, reality has transcended appearances. The reality of life eternal in Jesus Christ is central in their minds and hearts. The reality of God's love and presence through their grief is more than a slogan. The appearances were all very real, but the ultimate reality is Jesus Himself. And in this, they rejoice.

Even in the little things that make up most of our lives, the same truth is our hope. For a time, the smashed thumb and the lost tennis match appear to be terrible things. But the reality shines through in the light of God's love. The thumb will heal, and if not, I still have all of my other fingers. The tennis match remains lost, but I have the health and the leisure to play again, win or lose.

There is a perspective on life in Jesus Christ that enables us to rejoice always, even when we are unhappy. And this is something we can choose to do, whatever the tone of our feelings. It really becomes a matter of obedience.

"Pray without ceasing." As with the first command, we need to untangle some definitions and assumptions. Obviously, to pray without ceasing means something other than saying prayers, or the command is an impossibility. J. B. Lightfoot clarifies this point in his oft-quoted "It is not in the moving of the lips, but in the elevation of the heart to God, that the essence of prayer consists."

But having made the distinction between saying prayers and praying with the heart, the question of unceasing prayer demands deeper reflection. To pray without ceasing establishes prayer, not as a part of the Christian life, but as all of it. To pray day and night, in good times and in bad, without cessation or interruption, is not the experience of most people I know. Is this just a high ideal to be achieved by a few spiritual superathletes, or is it within the reach of ordinary folks like us?

For a long time, I experimented from time to time with the "Jesus Prayer." This was the discovery of a Russian peasant in the nineteenth century who learned a simple prayer that, when repeated hundreds of times each day, became to him an unceasing pattern of prayer. The Jesus Prayer is a beautiful summary of the Gospel: "Lord Jesus Christ, Son of God, have mercy on me, a sinner." While I love this prayer and find that it enriches my days when repeated often, it seems to have worked better for the Russian peasant wandering through the countryside than it does for me in the fast pace of the freeways.

The question still remains. How do I pray without ceasing? I wish I could tell you that I've achieved this in daily practice. I haven't. But I'm growing, and I've been helped greatly by a chapter in Henri Nouwen's book, *Clowning in Rome* (New York: Image Books, 1979). In the chapter entitled "Prayer and Thought," he ties the concept of unceasing prayer to one of the things going on within us at all times, namely thinking. Consciously or unconsciously, all of us are engaged in unceasing thought from birth to death. The brain is always active. The flat brain wave is the final sign of death. Sleep and dream studies indicate that our mind is always active during sleep.

Nouwen points out that our unceasing thoughts are both sources of joy and sorrow. Sometimes our minds wander when we desperately need to concentrate. Sometimes they keep us awake when we are in need of sleep. And yet our deepest joys come through our awareness and our thoughts. "Our thoughts are indeed the cradle where sorrow and joy are born. With an empty mind our hearts cannot mourn or feast, our eyes cannot cry or laugh, our hands cannot wring or clap, our tongue cannot curse or praise" (p. 69).

Nouwen encourages the goal of converting our unceasing thinking into unceasing prayer. This does not mean that we learn to direct our minds constantly to God. It means, rather, "to think and live in the presence of God" (p. 70). This means to live with a growing awareness that God is always present. It is to grow in our openness to God—to bring consciously all of our words and deeds into His presence.

I think of the analogy of love. When one is truly in love with another, there is an unceasing awareness of the other. This does not mean that one is consciously engaged in thinking of the other, but the "presence" of the other is constant. All decisions are made with the beloved in mind. All of life is oriented around this great love.

And so it can become in our lives with God. Such a constant awareness will require certain disciplines of prayer. Universal experience makes it quite clear that daily periods of intentional prayer, reflection, and meditation are essential to establish the climate of unceasing prayer for the rest of the day. The place of daily Scripture reading also is well established as an essential discipline. I find it helpful to begin each day with some statement of Jesus to be reflected upon consciously during the day. Nouwen finds the daily Eucharist, a practice perhaps all too foreign to us Protestants, as essential to the climate of prayer in his life.

It's long past time for us to issue an urgent call for unceasing prayer as an object for our attention and discipline. Such prayer means nothing less than practicing the presence of God in everything that we do.

"In everything give thanks." This is the third command, and it certainly grows out of the first two. Joy and unceasing prayer flow forth in a constant stream of gratitude. I'm not in agreement with the interpretation of this phrase that calls us to praise and thank God for literally everything that happens. I can't imagine God being thankful for everything that happens. Things that happen because of the selfishness or sinfulness of ourselves or others need to be changed, not accepted. I prefer to thank God for being God and to focus on Him rather than on the things that happen.

The great drama of the Bible centers in the belief that God is at work for good in the lives of His people, no matter what. There was nothing good in Joseph's brothers selling him to the Ishmaelite traders. There was nothing good about the injustices he experienced from Potiphar's wife. But, in retrospect, Joseph could say of it all: "You meant evil against me; but God meant it for good" (Gen. 50:20). This belief is articulated powerfully by Paul: "And we know that all things work together for good to those who love God" (Rom. 8:28). Our translation tends to make "all things" the subject rather than "God." A better translation is that "in everything, God is at work for good." We must never forget that God is at work in and through, and often in spite of the "things."

While I may not be able to give thanks for all of the things that happen, I can give thanks in everything for the confidence that God is always present and is always at work for good.

To rejoice always, to pray without ceasing, and to give thanks in everything *"is the will of God in Christ Jesus for you"* (v. 18). I read recently of a pastor who built a large room on top of a high tower behind his church. He climbed the pole, moved into the room, and said he wouldn't come down until God made clear His will for his life. Perhaps we should send these three great commands to that pastor on his perch.

Obedience to these three commands is difficult. But Christ calls us to a life of joy, prayer, and gratitude. Nothing worthwhile is ever easy, but the rewards of obedience to these commands are rich and full.

LIFE IN THE SPIRIT

19 Do not quench the Spirit.
20 Do not despise prophecies.
21 Test all things; hold fast what is good.
22 Abstain from every form of evil.

1 Thess. 5:19–22

Life in the church is life in the Holy Spirit. The promise of Christ before His ascension was the gift of the Holy Spirit to the believers (Acts 1:8). Too many Christians are like those in Ephesus who had "not so much as heard whether there is a Holy Spirit" (Acts 19:2). The Holy Spirit is God present and active. Here, caution is in order as we walk the tightrope of affirming God as One and God as Trinity. Historically, and, we insist, biblically, we affirm God as Father-Son-Spirit, Trinity, but always One God. Christianity is never a Jesus religion nor a Holy Spirit religion. There's a natural tendency for those who do not learn of the Holy Spirit until later in their Christian journey to overemphasize the Spirit at the expense of the Oneness of the Triune God.

When this happens in a given church, a reaction often occurs in which the Oneness of God is affirmed at the expense of the Trinity. But when the presence of God the Holy Spirit is denied or resisted, it's as though the power has been turned off. Without the sense of a Father-Son-Spirit God who is alive, present, and active, God tends to become little more than an object of thought and discussion, a "vague, oblong blur."

Thus, life in the church must always be focused upon the gifts of the Holy Spirit. Paul's three great passages on the gifts of the Spirit are basic to our understanding and experience (1 Cor. 12–14; Rom. 12; Eph. 4). Apparently, in the church at Thessalonica, there had been some excesses in the expression of some of the gifts of the Holy Spirit, and a negative reaction had resulted. This is not unusual, and while such aberrations must be confronted, so also must excessive reactions.

Paul's wisdom in addressing such problems is remarkable. In four brief statements, he gives the necessary guidelines for them and for us. Two of them seem to be related to the reactors. Two of them to the exessive enthusiasts.

To those who would stifle the "Holy Spirit enthusiasts," his directives are: (1) "Do not quench the Spirit." (2) "Do not despise prophecies." The Holy Spirit is often pictured in the Bible as fire. The classic portrayal is the appearance of "divided tongues, as of fire" sitting upon each of them in their gathering on the day of Pentecost after the Ascension (Acts 2:1–4). To deny or resist the gifts or working of the Holy Spirit is likened here to quenching the Spirit. Perhaps the most commonly used bucket of water is the ancient shibboleth, "But we've never done it that way before."

Apparently, the gift of the Spirit most rejected by the reactors was prophecy. We're at a disadvantage, because we don't know what form the gift took, nor why some of them had come to "despise" the prophecies. When he later wrote to the Corinthians about some of the problems surrounding the exercise of spiritual gifts there, Paul elevates the gift of prophecy to a place only below love itself (1 Cor. 14:1–5). He contrasts prophesying with speaking "in a tongue." Speaking in tongues is portrayed primarily as edifying the individual, while prophecies are seen as edifying the church.

The clearest definition of prophesying is given in 1 Corinthians 14:3: "He who prophesies speaks edification and exhortation and comfort to men." It seems likely that prophecies were spontaneous utterances in the gatherings of the congregation in which the Holy Spirit was regarded as addressing the believers through the one speaking. The emphasis was not upon prophecy in the sense of predicting the future, but rather in the sense of a word of exhortation or encouragement. These words would be crucial, especially in a time before they had the letters of Paul and the rest of the New Testament in written form, and in a time when most of them couldn't read.

But such gifts have a way of being distorted and abused because of the emotional complexities present in every one of us. Divisions between the reactors and the enthusiasts only compounded the difficulties. Having confronted the reactors in their quenching of the Spirit and despising of prophecies, Paul now has two words for the enthusiasts: (1) *"Test all things."* (2) *"Hold fast what is good. Abstain from every form of evil."*

The exercise of spiritual gifts always needs to be tested. This is necessary because of the human elements ever present in all that we do. The gifts of the Spirit can always be tainted and corrupted by our own conscious and unconscious needs and patterns. Testing implies a standard of measure. Our last high school-aged daughter has just taken her Scholastic Aptitude Test. She is being tested against the norm of thousands of other students in order to predict the likelihood of her success in college academic work.

What is the standard for testing spiritual gifts? The Scriptures. The Bible provides the norms and the standards by which we are to measure our doctrines and our practices. To be sure, our interpretations of these will differ, but everything is to be tested in the light of the Scriptures.

The testing reveals what is good and what is evil. The appeal is to *"hold fast"* the good and to *"abstain"* from the evil in all of its forms.

As with most treasured truths, there are extremes to be avoided in our experience and use of the gifts of the Holy Spirit. On the one hand, we are to be open to the Holy Spirit, seeking His guidance, direction, presence, and power. At the same time, we are to discern and test the fine line between human spirit and Holy Spirit. And all of this is to be done in a spirit of love and care for one another in our life together.

The message of the letter is now concluded. And the Apostle, in what has become an honored tradition in Christian history, closes with a benediction—a prayer for the well-being of the people—and some final requests.

AND IN CONCLUSION

23 Now may the God of peace Himself sanctify you completely; and may your whole spirit, soul, and body be preserved blameless at the coming of our Lord Jesus Christ.
24 He who calls you is faithful, who also will do it.
25 Brethren, pray for us.
26 Greet all the brethren with a holy kiss.

27 I charge you by the Lord that this epistle be read
to all the holy brethren.

28 The grace of our Lord Jesus Christ be with you.
· Amen.

1 Thess. 5:23–28

Of all the benedictions in Paul's writings, this seems to be the
least used. How unfortunate! *"The God of peace"* suggests the ancient
Hebrew *shalom* ("peace"), that magnificent word used to summarize
all of God's gracious goodness to us. This benediction reminds us
that our sanctification—our being set apart for His service—is ultimately the achievement of God Himself. And it is wholistic, involving
every part of our very being. To use this lofty benediction of *"your
whole spirit, soul, and body"* as the basis for a technical argument for
the trichotomous nature of human personality distorts its intention.
Here is a word of praise and worship, not a clinical discussion. It is
the whole of our being that will *"be preserved blameless at the coming
(parousia) of our Lord Jesus Christ."* And all of this through the faithfulness of God who both calls us and does His work of sanctification
in us.

This is indeed a benediction that deserves much more use in our
worship gatherings.

Before he completes the benediction, Paul has three final words
of request and charge: (1) *"Pray for us."* (2) *"Greet all the brethren with
a holy kiss."* (3) Read this epistle to all.

The request for prayer was more than a cliché. Paul made clear
again and again his need for the constant prayers of his friends. It's
a source of great strength to me to know that I have friends who
pray for me regularly. It's also a continuing challenge to know that
I have many friends who count upon my prayers.

The "holy kiss" was a customary way of greeting. The custom
still prevails, more in other cultures than in ours, of greeting with
a kiss on each cheek. Hugging has become a more common greeting
in many of the circles I move in, and I find it generally much more
meaningful than a handshake. I don't hug everyone who comes out
the door on Sunday mornings. The handshake still has its place. But
more and more I find the hug and the kiss on the cheek a beautiful
way of expressing genuine love and respect for brothers and sisters
in Christ.

The charge to read the letter publicly would be a guarantee

that the concerns of the letter would be heard by the entire congregation so that those who could not read would likewise receive its message. This practice of reading the letters aloud may have had a great deal to do with their ultimate incorporation into the canon of the Scriptures.

And now—the completion of the benediction, and the fitting final words of this magnificent letter:

The grace of our Lord Jesus Christ be with you. Amen.

Introduction to 2 Thessalonians

Why a second letter? Probably because the first letter did not accomplish everything Paul had hoped. No new subjects are introduced in this letter. The central issue is that of errors with regard to their views of the *parousia*, the expected return of Jesus. If anything, things had gotten worse since he had written the first letter. Now, some were teaching that it had already happened, and even claiming that such teaching had come from Paul himself. The loafers and busybodies continued their inactivity and destructive behavior, in spite of what Paul had written.

There's good reason to believe that this letter was written within a few weeks of the first epistle. If so, it's possible that Timothy and/or Silas had delivered the first letter, stayed there a short time, and returned to Paul in Corinth with more good news and bad news. So Paul writes again in response to both.

An Outline of 2 Thessalonians

I. Faith, Hope—and Endurance: 1:1–12
  A. Hello, Again: 1:1–2
  B. The Contagion of a Growing Faith: 1:3–4
  C. Joys and Sorrows in God's Final Judgment: 1:5–10
  D. Paul Prays Again: 1:11–12
II. The Return of Christ: 2:1–12
  A. The Error to Be Avoided: 2:1–2
  B. The Apostasy and the Man of Sin: 2:3–5
  C. The Restrainer: 2:6–7
  D. The Coming and Triumph of Christ: 2:8–12
III. Strength for Today: 2:13—3:5
  A. The Gospel in Summary: 2:13–17
  B. A Request for Prayer: 3:1–2
  C. Great Is Thy Faithfulness: 3:3–5
IV. The Dignity of Work: 3:6–15
  A. The Tough Question of Church Discipline: 3:6, 14–15
  B. The Example of the Apostles: 3:7–9
  C. The Command of the Apostles: 3:10–13
V. The Final Benediction: 3:16–18

CHAPTER ONE

Faith, Hope—and Endurance

2 Thessalonians 1:1–12

HELLO, AGAIN

1 Paul, Silvanus, and Timothy,

To the church of the Thessalonians in God our Father
and the Lord Jesus Christ:

2 Grace to you and peace from God our Father
and the Lord Jesus Christ.

2 Thess. 1:1–2

The greeting in this letter is identical to that in the first, with
one exception. Here the reference is to *"God* our *Father."* This simply
makes much clearer that Paul is emphasizing God as the father of
believers rather than the father of the Lord Jesus Christ.

You may wish to review the first chapter of this commentary on
1 Thessalonians, in which we have dealt with this greeting in detail.

The only difference is the context. Now Paul is writing this second
letter because the first did not succeed fully in correcting the errors
which he had addressed. If anything, this letter begins with remarkable restraint if such was the case.

THE CONTAGION OF A GROWING FAITH

3 We are bound to thank God always for you,
brethren, as it is fitting, because your faith grows
exceedingly, and the love of every one of you all
abounds toward each other,

107

4 so that we ourselves boast of you among the
churches of God for your patience and faith in all your
persecutions and tribulations that you endure,

2 Thess. 1:3–4

Here we begin another of those long, irregular sentences characteristic of Paul, indicating the likelihood that he dictated his letters. Verses 3 and 4 are a strong affirmation of the Thessalonian Christians. As we have seen in the first letter, this affirming style of Paul is customary. And it is all the more significant here because he has strong reasons to be angry with them. But he stays with his approach of affirming what can be affirmed before his confrontation and exhortation. A good practice for us all!

Paul expresses gratitude for two things, both of which he had written in the first letter: for their growing faith, and for their love for each other. His gratitude begins with an extra affirmation in the words *"We are bound."* This phrase suggests that they had not felt worthy of his praise. The subsequent phrase, *"as it is fitting,"* is a way of assuring them that this is not hollow flattery, but a genuine affirmation due them.

His appreciation for their increasing faith grows out of the concern expressed in 1 Thessalonians 3:10 for something that was "lacking" in their faith. Nothing brings greater joy to a pastor or leader in the church than the evidences of change and growth. The continuing problem to the leader is the normal slowness of growth. As I look back over nineteen years of pastoral ministry in one congregation, I can see evidences all around me of profound changes in people and in the church. But I'm aware that in the daily rounds the change is not as evident. On the door frame in our laundry room are a lot of pencil marks and dates with the initials of each of our girls. I can recall their frustration time after time when they stood up to the last mark only to discover they hadn't grown! But over the years, the marks did indicate growth, only not as fast as they wanted. And that's the way it often is in Christian leadership. The pace of growth is rarely as rapid as we wish it to be.

The second expression of gratitude was for their love for each other. This, too, represented a special joy to Paul. It was this for which he had prayed in the first epistle (1 Thess. 3:12). The idea of love abounding has a sense of special freedom, suggesting to me a picture of a child happily bouncing a ball.

Because of his gratitude for their *"exceedingly"* growing faith and abounding love, Paul has taken the liberty of bragging about them to others. Happy, indeed, is the church leader who can boast of the faith and love of the people of a church. And what impressed Paul the most was their *"patience and faith"* in all the persecutions and tribulations that they were enduring.

We detect a relationship here to Paul's favorite trilogy of faith, love, and hope which we examined in chapter 2 of 1 Thessalonians. Here it is patience that follows faith and love. Yet patience is always tied to hope. *"Patience"* here is our old friend, *hupomonē,* the word that means much more than passive endurance or survival. It is that active word in which one is seen not only as enduring, but also of taking the trial or suffering and using it in positive and creative ways.

Here are the signs of a contagious group of Christians. A growing faith, abounding in love, that transforms persecutions and tribulations into occasions for joy, is bound to make an impact on the world around it, including other churches.

JOYS AND SORROWS IN GOD'S FINAL JUDGMENT

5 which is manifest evidence of the righteous judgment of God, that you may be counted worthy of the kingdom of God, for which you also suffer;
6 seeing it is a righteous thing with God to repay with tribulation those who trouble you,
7 and to give you who are troubled rest with us when the Lord Jesus is revealed from heaven with His mighty angels,
8 in flaming fire taking vengeance on those who do not know God, and on those who do not obey the gospel of our Lord Jesus Christ.
9 These will be punished with everlasting destruction from the presence of the Lord and from the glory of His power,
10 when He comes, in that Day, to be glorified in His saints and to be admired among all those who believe, because our testimony among you was believed.

2 Thess. 1:5–10

This section begins in the middle of a long sentence, but moves into a separate theme: the divine punishment of the unjust and the rewarding of the faithful. Paul sees their faith, love, and endurance as *"manifest evidence"* of God's righteous judgment. It is not the persecutions and tribulations that are the proofs of God's righteousness. In the deepest sense, they could be regarded as contradictions of a righteous universe. But the fact that such things can be overcome by faith, love, and endurance is the manifest evidence to which Paul appeals. There is an underlying theme that our sufferings are part of the process by which God counts us worthy of His Kingdom. Just as righteousness is imparted to us by God through faith in Jesus, so worthiness of the Kingdom is declared to us by God through our sufferings for His Kingdom. We must make clear the distinction between suffering in order to gain the Kingdom and God's declaration of our worthiness through the suffering. Nowhere is the former even implied by Paul. We cannot leave this statement without recognizing that the *"manifest evidence"* of God's righteous judgment through their faith, love, and endurance is not intended to be a "proof" in the sense of a mathematical exercise.

What follows, beginning with verse 6, is a passage of great difficulty for those who wish to avoid the haunting questions of eternal punishment and hell. I have before me one respected commentary which makes no comment on verses 6 through 9. I might wish to place these verses in the category of "things I wish Paul hadn't written." I also have a list of things I wish Jesus hadn't said. We begin a section like this by pointing out that the Scriptures were not written to tell us what we want to hear. They are given to us to reveal the truth. And in this case, the truth may not be to our liking.

There are three basic issues presented in verses 6–9: (1) divine retribution, (2) eternal punishment, and (3) the glorification of Christ.

Divine retribution. Two rewards are set forth—to the troubler of the faithful, tribulation; to the believers who are being troubled, rest. The rewards are not meted out during this life, but when the Lord Jesus is *"revealed."* Here, the word is not *parousia* but *apokalupsis,* another word used to denote the Second Coming. *Apokalupsis* is rightly translated "revelation or revealing" and portrays the return of Christ as the "revealing." The title, of course, of the last book of the New Testament is *Apokalupsis Iōannou,* A Revelation of John.

We err if we think of divine retribution as an activity of God in the present age. Many evil people prosper. Many good people suffer. Christians in many times and places experience nothing but persecution and suffering, while their oppressors, the rich and powerful, live sumptuously. Take the current example in Uganda. Idi Amin engaged in widespread persecution and slaughter of countless thousands of believers. To be sure, he has fallen from power, but still lives lavishly in Syria. The Christians of Uganda continue to suffer incredible deprivations because of his madness. There is no sense in which divine retribution can be regarded as having fully happened.

The teaching here points beyond the return of Christ to the full establishment of the Kingdom of God. The righteous, those in Christ, shall be rewarded with rest and glory. The evil, *"those who do not know God,"* and *"those who do not obey the gospel,"* shall receive *"tribulation"* and *"vengeance."*

To be sure, many of us do not like to think in terms of divine retribution. The thought of God returning evil for evil in a realm beyond this life is not our idea of good news. But we have to look at the alternative. What kind of a world is it if our actions have no lasting consequences? If you grant that life does not end with death— that life is eternal—can you make sense out of a universe in which everyone receives the same reward, irrespective of their lives here? Can God be just and reward Idi Amin and St. Francis just the same? Are there no lasting consequences to our actions over a lifetime? Do Adolf Hitler and Billy Graham receive the same welcome?

The God of the Bible, present with us in Jesus Himself, is the God who takes us seriously. Our lives do matter, and our behavior does have lasting consequences. And Paul did not dream this up out of some sadistic urges. It was Jesus Himself who taught this quite early. Nowhere was He more specific than in His portrayal of the final judgment in Matthew 25:31–46. Those who had fed the hungry, clothed the naked, sheltered the strangers, visited the sick and the prisoners were rewarded. Those who had ignored and neglected such acts of kindness were sent away.

Divine retribution is another way of saying that this life is significant. Our actions have lasting consequences. What we do in this life might be likened to the introductory measures of an endless symphony.

Eternal punishment. The second element of bad news in this section is eternal punishment. *"Those who do not know God,"* and *"those who do not obey the gospel of our Lord Jesus Christ . . . shall be punished with everlasting destruction from the presence of the Lord."* Let us quickly come to Paul's rescue and recall that he was only transmitting what Jesus had clearly taught. The last word of the scene portrayed in Matthew 25 was

"and these will go away into everlasting punishment, but the righteous into eternal life" (Matt. 25:46). In the parable of the rich man
and Lazarus the picture is reinforced (Luke 16:19–31).

The philosophical argument for eliminating hell and eternal punishment has great emotional appeal. It is based upon the thought that
God's love cannot be defeated, and that somehow His love will find
a way to redeem every last sinner from hell. To hold this view, one
not only has to accept the fact that it is contrary to what we are
taught by Jesus Himself, but one has to ignore the pervasive power
of human sin and rebellion. It is my conviction that hell is a matter
of choice. One can only get there by pushing God's love aside. Paul's
phrase in verse 8 *"those who do not know God"* does not imply passive
ignorance. It refers to those who have neglected and refused the
knowledge of God that has been given to them, even though they
may not have knowledge of the Gospel of Jesus Christ. This was
developed in greater detail in his later letter to Rome (Rom. 1:18–
32).

Eternal punishment is never indicated in the Scriptures as meted
out because of mere ignorance. It is a result of disobedience. And
again we are back to the reality that our behavior does have lasting
consequences.

The language describing heaven and hell, of necessity, is always
figurative and pictorial. We cannot know what they are like in terms
of our earthly categories. They transcend all of our experience and
knowledge. But perhaps Paul gives us the closest thing possible to
a description of hell in the words of verse 9, *"punished with everlasting
destruction* from *the presence of the Lord and* from *the glory of His power"*
(emphasis mine). Separation from the Lord's presence and glory is
the ultimate punishment. And one chooses in this life to be present
with God or to be separated. C. S. Lewis, I think, suggested that
one who had chosen to be separated from Christ in this life is simply
given the freedom to continue in that choice. In that sense, heaven
or hell begins in this life. In death our choices are sealed.

The glorification of Christ. And now we move to the good news. What
joy is portrayed on that Day of the Lord *"because our testimony among
you was believed"* (v. 10). It's as though Paul is anticipating that happy
reunion when he shall be forever reunited with those Christians in
Thessalonica to whom he cannot now return. And all of the glory
on that day will focus on Jesus! He will be: (1) *"glorified in His saints,"*
and (2) *"admired among all those who believe."*

Here are two fascinating ideas. The thought of the glory of Jesus being seen in His saints suggests that we shall be reflectors of His brightness. What a future for each of us! To be with Him and each other on that day when His very glory will be seen shining in us!

The admiration of Jesus among all those who believe probably reflects a meaning of "admiration" no longer connoted in English usage. The root of the Greek word gives a sense of "marveling" or "wondering at." Thus, the New English Bible translates "to be adored among all believers." Phillips uses "It will be a breath-taking wonder to all who believe." Another dramatic picture of our future! To be a part of an awe-inspired assembly caught up in wonder, love, and praise!

Paul has faithfully delivered the bad news and the good news. The stark awfulness of the bad news makes the good news even better. God's offer of the good news is to every single human being. No one need live by the bad news. And that's the Good News!

PAUL PRAYS AGAIN

> 11 Therefore we also pray always for you that our
> God would count you worthy of this calling, and fulfill
> all the good pleasure of His goodness and the work
> of faith with power,
> 12 that the name of our Lord Jesus Christ may be
> glorified in you, and you in Him, according to the
> grace of our God and the Lord Jesus Christ.
>
> *2 Thess. 1:11-12*

As with the first letter, Paul continues what is to become his practice of incorporating prayers in his correspondence. In these prayers we see the personal side of the Apostle.

The opening word *"therefore"* points back to the preceding section. Thus Paul's prayer for the quality of their lives grows out of the bad news and good news connected with the Day of the Lord. The fact that our behavior does have lasting consequences is all the more reason for Paul to pray that it will be pleasing to God.

Like many of Paul's prayers, this one consists of some beautiful phrases, tightly woven together. The "bottom line," as it were, is stated first. The end of all Christian faith and life is to be counted *"worthy"* by God. This is never to be understood in the sense of earning God's approval by our goodness or efforts, but rather in the sense of pleasing Him in response to His love for us.

Certainly, every human parent experiences this. We have been blessed with children who, for the most part, behave in ways that bring us joy and pleasure. We have always tried to assure them that we love them whether or not they behave according to our desires and standards. Knowing that their behavior is not motivated by the fear of losing our love, makes it all the more meaningful to all of us. Happy, indeed, is the parent whose child can be counted worthy of the love of that parent. And happier still the child.

And this always leads me to the amazing thought that you and I can bring pleasure to God. Just think! When we live in such a way that God can count us worthy of the love that He bestows upon us, we bring Him joy and pleasure! This, to me, is the highest motivation for trying to please God. Not trying to earn His love—it is already given. Not afraid of losing His love—He will never leave us or forsake us. But just trying to live in ways that say "Thank you, Father, for loving me and counting me worthy."

The second part of the prayer is an absolute delight! It says that God will fulfill *"all the good pleasure of His goodness and the work of faith with power."*

Here is a beautiful portrait of the Christian life. The first phrase is difficult to translate into English. Placing *"His"* before goodness is an addition by the translator. The literal reading of the original text is simply "every good pleasure of goodness" or "every good desire of goodness." In the first case, a beautiful thought is expressed that goodness brings its own pleasure. Why is this so difficult to learn? There is a rich satisfaction in doing and being good. Loving acts, gracious words, thoughtful affirmations all have a way of bringing *"the good pleasure of goodness."*

The second translation suggests another facet of the power of goodness. Goodness has a way of creating its own desire for more goodness. It is contagious. The more one experiences goodness, the greater the desire.

"The work of faith with power" is the natural product of every good pleasure or desire of goodness. In 1 Thessalonians 1:3, we were first given by Paul this phrase *"the work of faith."* I choose to read the word for work *ergon* as emphasizing work as vocation. Paul is thus praying that their goodness and their faith will be the hallmark of

their sense of vocation. The power for all of this is given to us by the Holy Spirit.

The end result? The mutual glorification of Jesus Christ in us, and we in Him. Isn't it remarkable that these go together! When Christ is glorified in our desire for goodness and works of faith, then we are glorified in Him. And all of this by the grace of God and Christ. It is this sense of God's grace as the source of every goodness in life that should be the constant antidote to all proclivity toward self-righteousness.

CHAPTER TWO

The Return of Christ

2 Thessalonians 2:1–12

This section is the heart of the letter. It is most likely the reason for the letter. It focuses on some errors in their thinking regarding the *parousia*, the return of Christ. Just as this subject was the central issue in the first epistle, so it is here also. We can't minimize the importance of the fact that the Second Coming was so central a theme in the first letters of Paul. While the affirmation of belief in the Second Coming is clearly present in his later letters, the questions about the details, as in the Thessalonian letters, are no longer addressed.

Some suggest that this is because they gave up on Christ's coming as more time went by. But there's no evidence to support that. It seems, rather, that they learned to live with the reality that no one could know the time of His coming. Once that had been established and accepted, it was clearly unproductive to live with frantic expectations. The doctrine of the *parousia* becomes an established and settled part of the faith and a source of comfort and strength. Paul concluded his greatest chapter on the resurrection and the ultimate triumph of Christ with words that should set the tone for every discussion of the last things: "Therefore, my beloved brethren, be steadfast, immovable, always abounding in the work of the Lord, inasmuch as you know that your labor is not in vain in the Lord" (1 Cor. 15:58).

The passage before us, 2 Thessalonians 2:1–12, is undoubtedly one of the most difficult in all of Paul's writings. It has given rise to more speculative and diverse interpretations than any other section of Paul's letters. The main reason for this is that he writes to reinforce some things he had already taught them (1:5), and we are thus cast

116

into the role of listening to but one end of the telephone conversation. We do not know what it was that he had taught them, and we do not know for sure what error he was correcting.

One error he had addressed in the first letter (4:13–18) was the teaching of some that those who had died would not participate in the *parousia*. Another error seems to have been that some were predicting the event (5:1–11). Here, the error seems to be that some were teaching that the Day of the Lord had already happened.

In reading and studying this passage, we do well to maintain the awareness that it has been a source of conflict for centuries and that many sincere Christians have differed substantially in its interpretation.

THE ERROR TO BE AVOIDED

1 Now we ask you, brethren, by the coming of
our Lord Jesus Christ and our gathering together to
Him,
    2 not to be soon shaken in mind or troubled,
neither by spirit, nor by word, nor by letter, as if from
us, as though the day of Christ had come.

2 Thess. 2:1–2

The very form of his plea and the solemn use of the full title *"our Lord Jesus Christ"* indicates that what follows is of extreme importance. It is clear that the subject of the Second Coming had become a source of tension and disruption, just the opposite of what it should be. They were *"shaken in mind"* and *"troubled"* by whatever the false teaching was.

It had apparently come through three channels, *"by spirit or by word, or by letter"* (v. 2), and had indicated that the day of Christ had already come. This could have meant that a process had already begun which would bring Christ's actual coming at any moment and certainly within a very short time.

The reference to *"spirit"* probably indicates that some of this teaching had come in the form of prophecy, utterances in public worship purporting to be given by the Holy Spirit. Recall that Paul had urged them not to quench the Spirit and not to despise prophecies (1 Thess.

5:19–20). It's likely that such expressions were a regular part of the gatherings of the believers in Thessalonica. But Paul had also urged them to test all things and to hold fast to the good (1 Thess. 5:21). Here the issue could well be that any "prophecy" which created the troubling and shaking of their minds could not be of the Spirit. The product of Spirit-directed prophecies concerning the Second Coming is comfort (1 Thess. 4:18), building up (1 Thess. 5:11), and motivation for good words and works (2 Thess. 2:17).

In addition to prophecies, there had also been "words." This is probably a reference to teaching that did not purport to be generated directly by the Holy Spirit, but came in the form of normal discourse and dialogue.

A third form of the false teaching must have come in some kind of a letter claiming to have been from Paul. He denies responsibility for any such letter.

It would have helped us greatly in subsequent interpretation if Paul had described the erroneous teaching in more detail. But we need to remember that Paul had no way of knowing that this personal correspondence would some day be regarded as the Scriptures. The recipients in Thessalonica knew what he was talking about, and we can only wish that we shared their knowledge.

Before moving into the passage, there is an interesting example of doctrinal development connected with verse 1. There are two phrases in the verse relating to the Second Coming. The first is *huper tēs parousia*, "(concerning) the coming," and the second is *hēmon episunagōgēs ep auto*, "our gathering together to Him." Both of these phrases are generally interpreted as referring to the coming of Christ, with the latter emphasizing the thought of 1 Thessalonians 4:17, in which both those in Christ who have died and those still living will be "caught up together" to meet the Lord and "always be with the Lord."

J. N. Darby, around 1830, introduced the idea that those two phrases refer to two different events. Thus there came into his interpretation the scheme in which there is a "rapture" portrayed in the second phrase which occurs before the Second Coming. This view of the rapture, Jesus coming *for* His own, followed (perhaps much later) by the Second Coming, Jesus coming *with* His own, became the cornerstone of a school of thought called dispensationalism. This system is set forth in such places as the notes of the Scofield Bible and has been popularized in more recent years by Hal Lindsey's writings.

THE APOSTASY AND THE MAN OF SIN

3 Let no one deceive you by any means; for that
Day will not come unless the falling away comes first,
and the man of sin is revealed, the son of perdition,

4 who opposes and exalts himself above all that
is called God or that is worshiped, so that he sits as
God in the temple of God, showing himself that he
is God.

5 Do you not remember that when I was still with
you I told you these things?

2 Thess. 2:3–5

We do well to start this section by underscoring verse 5. Not only
are we unable to reconstruct fully the error being addressed, we don't
really know what Paul had taught them about *"the falling away"* and
"the man of sin" when he had been with them. This makes it certain,
at the outset, that we are going to have some unanswered questions,
not only at the beginning, but at the end of our study as well.

There are two themes in this passage which demand our attention.
The first is *"the falling away."* The word is *apostasia,* the "apostasy."
The word means basically a "rebellion." It can mean either a rebellion
that is political in nature, such as the overthrow of a government,
or a religious heresy, such as referred to by the word *apostasy* in Acts
21:21. There, apostasy was regarded as a departure from accepted
doctrine: "forsaking Moses."

On the basis of what follows, it is clear that Paul had already
taught them about the "apostasy." It seems best to assume that this
"falling away" which must precede the Day of the Lord is to be both
religious and political. It will involve not only a rebellion against
God but against government and civil order as well.

The second phrase introduces *"the man of sin,"* who is also *"the son
of perdition."* The word translated *"sin"* is *anomias,* literally "lawless."
This person is thus characterized as being opposed to God's law and
therefore destined to *"perdition"* which is destruction. The fact that
he is to be *"revealed"* (from *apokalupsē*) places him in contrast to Christ,
who will also be "revealed." While the idea of the Antichrist is not
specifically articulated until later in the New Testament period (1
John 2:18), the Antichrist is certainly latent in this figure of "the

man of sin." (For an excellent discussion of the Antichrist, see F. F. Bruce's commentary on 1 and 2 Thessalonians, *Word Biblical Commentary,* vol. 45, pp. 179–88).

Verse 4 gives us a fuller characterization of this diabolic person who sets himself up as God. Again, we would do better in interpreting the "apostasy" and *"the man of sin"* if we knew what Paul had taught them previously. One example of our difficulties with this passage lies in the portrayal of the man of sin sitting *"as God in the temple of God."* Does this mean the literal temple in Jerusalem (later destroyed by the Romans under Nero)? Or is this a metaphor, meaning that he usurps the very authority of God? The latter seems to be preferable.

The most significant aspect of this section is the seeming contradiction between what is taught here and what Paul taught in 1 Thessalonians 5:1–11. There he emphasized the fact that the time of the *parousia* could not be known. It would come "like a thief in the night." Here, Paul is saying that the Day of the Lord cannot come until certain things, yet in the future, take place. In one, he teaches that it can happen at any time. In the other, that it cannot happen until some other things occur.

The dispensationalists get the edge here, for by separating the Rapture from the Second Coming, they see the Rapture as able or likely to happen at any moment, while the apostasy and the man of sin follow after the Rapture.

But to those not making that distinction, the problem remains. It seems to me that Paul is in a situation in which every teacher often finds himself. What is taught is shaped to some degree by the error being confronted. For example, when Paul wrote to the Colossians and the Galatians, he was confronting situations in which they had become very legalistic and rule-oriented in their approach to Christian discipleship. He appealed to freedom, grace, and liberty. When he wrote to the Corinthians, however, he addressed an entirely different situation. They were pushing freedom and grace to the point of doing whatever they pleased. To them, the appeal was for restraint and responsibility.

Perhaps we have a similar situation here. In the first letter, he addresses those who were claiming to know that Christ's return was imminent, quitting their jobs to wait for it. To them, he uses the "thief in the night" picture to call them to desist from speculation and predictions.

In the second letter, however, he is addressing an entirely different situation. Now there are those who say that the Day is already present in some form. To them, he states that this can't be, because the apostasy and the man of sin, about which he had already taught them, had not yet become a reality.

But far from this being an indefinite postponement of the Day of the Lord, it's possible that there was good reason to believe that the then-current Emperor, Claudius, could well have been the man of sin. There's no evidence that Paul taught that, but it's not illogical to believe that they could have come to that conclusion.

To me, his teaching is not contradictory, granted that there was a body of teaching that we do not have, and that he was writing essentially to confront errors in the application of the original teaching.

THE RESTRAINER

6 And now you know what is restraining, that he may be revealed in his own time.

7 For the mystery of lawlessness is already at work; only He who now restrains will do so until He is taken out of the way.

2 Thess. 2:6–7

As if the passage were not difficult enough, we now meet the "restrainer," further adding to our complexities. Again, we point out that they knew what he was talking about, and we don't. What further confuses us in verse 6 is the use of both the neuter and the masculine in referring to the restrainer. In the first part of the verse, it is *"what"* is restraining. In the second part, *"he"* is going to be revealed.

In the long and complex history of the interpretations of this passage, every possible alternative to the identification of this restraining force or person has been suggested. I'm sure that one would be safe in offering a cash reward to anyone who could offer an option not yet suggested.

Our translation suggests that the "restrainer" is God Himself, thus capitalizing the pronouns in verse 7. But even our translation recognizes the difficulty by suggesting the footnoted uncapitalized "he." Other suggestions range from interpreting the restrainer as the Emperor Claudius who was holding back the appearance of Nero; or, emphasizing the neuter, as the Roman Empire itself, which Paul generally regarded as being a positive help in the spread of the Gospel. The neuter could also mean the personification of Roman law or even of Jewish law, or the Jewish state itself.

Perhaps the most honest and frank view of this passage about the "restrainer" was put forth by St. Augustine in the fifth century (*City of God,* chap. 20): "I admit that the meaning of this completely escapes me." Three cheers for Augustine!

The Coming and Triumph of Christ

8 And then the lawless one will be revealed, whom the Lord will consume with the breath of His mouth and destroy with the brightness of His coming.

9 The coming of the lawless one is according to the working of Satan with all power, signs, and lying wonders,

10 and with all deception of unrighteousness in those who perish, because they did not receive the love of the truth, that they might be saved.

11 And for this reason God will send them strong delusion, that they should believe the lie,

12 that they all might be condemned who did not believe the truth but had pleasure in unrighteousness.

2 Thess. 2:8–12

We may wish that Paul would have pandered to our desires to know more about the apostasy, the man of sin, and the restrainer. But he moves quickly to a description of the future, that Day when God's final word shall be spoken in the coming of Jesus Christ.

In every way, the lawless one, the man of sin and son of perdition, is portrayed as a counterfeit Christ. He professes to be God. He works *"with all power, signs, and lying wonders"* (v. 9). He will be *"revealed"* even as Christ will be revealed.

But he will be defeated and destroyed by Christ Himself: *"whom the Lord will consume with the breath of His mouth and destroy with the brightness of His coming"* (v. 8). The last phrase is *tē epiphanēia tēs parousias:* the epiphany of His parousia. Epiphany means "shining forth" or "brightness." While it is a word that figures prominently in the church calendar as the season following Christmas in which we proclaim the "shining forth" of Christ into the world, it occurs only six times in the New Testament, the other five in the epistles to Timothy and Titus. In 2 Timothy 1:10, it refers to Christ's first advent. In all the others (1 Tim. 6:14; 2 Tim. 4:1, 8; Titus 2:13), to His second advent. Thus, it has the same sense as *parousia* and here is used in conjunction with it. The coming of Christ is seen as a radiant, shining event.

Verses 10–12 portray the pathetic progression of sin and evil within the human heart. First is the rejection of the love of truth which comes from giving in to the deception of unrighteousness. And how deceptive and appealing unrighteousness can be. The ancient story of the temptation in Genesis rings so true! The serpent is attractive. The appeals are enticing because they offer wisdom, goodness, and life. The tempter is not so stupid as to try to lure us with offers of ignorance, evil, and death. The appeal of sin is that it promises so many wonderful things.

The rejection of the love of truth progresses readily to delusion and believing *"the lie."* How easily we get to believing that evil is good, that darkness is light, that might makes right, that hate is love. At one point a few years ago, we heard an army officer testify to the belief that we were helping the Vietnamese by burning their villages and killing them. And if we're not careful, we're likely to believe that we will save the world by nuclear destruction. Believing the lie is the final stage of the triumph of evil.

The condemnation of God is seen as a just consequence of our choice to reject the truth and to find pleasure in unrighteousness. We're back again to the reality that our choices and behavior do have lasting significance. In the deepest sense, this life is the arena in which we decide whether we want to choose the way of God or the way of the Lawless One. And the choice is not always that clear. Sometimes not to choose is to choose. Sometimes the way of compromise or procrastination is indeed a rejection of the truth.

A Personal Postscript

I have always found this one of the most difficult passages in all of Paul's letters. Writing about it has been challenging to say the least. I feel the need to conclude this chapter with a personal witness to my own feelings about the Second Coming of Christ.

The first teaching in eschatology that I received as a relatively new Christian came from the late Dr. Wilbur Smith, my professor of English Bible in seminary. He was a dispensationalist, and under his teaching I came to understand the dispensationalist interpretation of Christ's Second Coming. During my time with him as a student, I developed a great appreciation for Dr. Smith. He was a faithful student and teacher with a contagious love for his Lord.

But as I continued to study the Scriptures across the years, I became aware that the dispensationalist view was not the only option. I'm deeply indebted to those who encouraged me to interpret every particular Scripture in the light of all Scripture, and to study each passage in the light of the history of its interpretation by diverse Christian scholars across the centuries. I do not pretend to have done this thoroughly for all of Scripture, for such cannot be accomplished in a single lifetime.

But as I have tried to be faithful to these principles in my studies of the Old and New Testaments relating to "the last things," I have been impressed by at least four realities that, to me, are essential.

1. *Diversity.* There is probably more diversity in interpretations of different aspects of Christ's return than in any other area of biblical studies. From the insistence by Calvin and the Reformers of the sixteenth and seventeenth centuries that the pope was the Antichrist, to the current insistence of the dispensationalists that we live in "the terminal generation," serious biblical scholars have disagreed enormously on these matters. The principles by which one reads and interprets the Books of Daniel and Revelation have never come close to universal agreement.

Because of this long history of conflict and diversity, I appeal strongly not to divide and split the Christian community over these issues. To make a particular eschatological viewpoint a basis for acceptance and orthodoxy is, I believe, a denial of God's grace. Sincere Christians have always disagreed in these matters. We always will. But such disagreement never abrogates the mandate to love one another.

2. *The Day of the Lord.* But the foregoing is not to say that there is not uncompromising conviction explicit and implicit throughout the Scriptures that history will be consummated in the Day of the Lord, the Second Advent of Christ. The ultimate truth in the Scriptures, which simply cannot be ignored or eliminated, is Christ's return. It is beyond possibility to take Jesus and the Bible seriously without this. To view history as being without meaning, ending either in a

whimper or a bang, is contradictory to the Scriptures. And it is also contradictory to view history as gradually progressing through human effort to universal and enduring peace and love. The biblical view of history always points to the Day of the Lord.

3. *The Time of His Coming.* In the light of the clear teaching of Jesus that we cannot know the time of His coming, I continue to be amazed at the insistence that persists in forecasts and speculation. To use the Scriptures to try to predict the time of His coming, whether in terms of a specific date or of a generation, is to disobey the admonitions of Jesus and Paul. Again and again, these speculations and predictions are sources of division and tension within the churches and thus counterproductive to the building up of the Body of Christ. The history of such speculation, century after century, provides a word of caution and wisdom to us all.

4. *Comfort and Strength.* Consistently, Paul concludes his teaching sections on this subject with an admonition to use the doctrine to comfort one another, to edify and build up the church, and to strengthen our resolve to be faithful in our service to Christ and in our love to one another. To be sure, the Second Coming of Christ may well strike fear into the hearts of unbelievers, but it is always to be a source of comfort and strength for us in Him. We are called to fidelity, not forecasting—to steady perseverance as we bear witness to our unswerving faith in the hope of His coming. Rather than trying to convince each other of the rightness of our particular views regarding His coming, we are called to comfort and strengthen one another in the light of His coming, even though we may disagree on the details.

These are the convictions to which I have come, and by which I intend to live.

CHAPTER THREE

Strength for Today

2 Thessalonians 2:13—3:5

We can't miss the breath of fresh air that comes with the transition from the themes of judgment, punishment, the apostasy, and the man of sin to a warm thanksgiving and admonition.

It is helpful to read 2:13 as a reprise of 1:3. We have a similar pattern in 1 Thessalonians 1:2 and 2:13. In the first prayer in this letter (1:3), Paul's thanksgiving to God, is grounded in the growth of faith and love in and among the believers in Thessalonica. In this prayer, the gratitude is grounded in the Gospel itself, especially in the initiation of our salvation by God Himself.

In the initial five verses of this section, we really have a brilliant, concise summary of the theology of the New Testament, from God's eternal election to our glorification in Christ.

THE GOSPEL IN SUMMARY

13 But we are bound to give thanks to God always for you, brethren beloved by the Lord, because God has from the beginning chosen you for salvation through sanctification by the Spirit and belief in the truth,

14 to which He called you by our gospel, for the obtaining of the glory of our Lord Jesus Christ.

15 Therefore, brethren, stand fast and hold the traditions which you have been taught, whether by word or our epistle.

16 Now may our Lord Jesus Christ Himself, and our God and Father, who has loved us and given us everlasting consolation and good hope by grace,

17 comfort your hearts and establish you in every
good word and work.

2 Thess. 2:13–17

There are three movements in this delightful summary of the gospel: (1) our election by God (vv. 13–14), (2) our response to God
(v. 15), and (3) our support by God (vv. 16–17).

Our election by God. Paul's thanksgiving begins where the Gospel
begins—we are *"beloved by the Lord."* More and more, this has become
a treasured phrase to me. To be loved by the Lord! Pause. Reflect.
Bring this thought to the surface many times each day until it becomes
a regular part of your thinking and living. We are loved by the Lord!

Every discussion of divine election must begin with the reality
of being loved by the Lord. Otherwise it too readily gets bogged
down in philosophical speculation. If we make God's love for us
the starting point of election, we immediately confront the seeming
difficulty of God's election of us *"from the beginning."* While interpreters
of this passage differ as to whether *"from the beginning"* here refers
to the beginning of creation or the beginning of the Gospel in Thessalonica, there is no ambiguity about Paul's view of this in Ephesians
1:4, "He has chosen us in Him before the foundation of the world."

While the thought of God's choosing us before the world was
even created transcends our capacity to understand, we still have
to raise the question as to when God's love for us begins. Does it
begin for us at birth? At the point of our coming to faith in Christ?
At some other point in time? Paul places God's love for us in cosmic
dimensions. What a remarkable thought! God's love for us is not
limited by any human or temporal factor. Do you dare to try this
on—"God loves me, even if I had never been born"? This is to say
that God's love is unlike any other love. His love transcends all of
our categories. It is infinite and eternal.

It's important to link God's love with His election of us. Of some
interest is the fact that the word translated chosen in this verse is
used only here in the New Testament. It is a verb meaning simply
God's choosing of His own people. Certainly it is used here with
the same meaning as the compound word Paul uses in 1 Thessalonians
1:4 which means "to call out."

God is always portrayed in the Bible as taking the initiative in
choosing people to serve Him. He chooses Abraham and his descendants. But the choosing was not merely conveying privilege—it was

127

always a call to responsibility. Abraham and his descendants were given the weighty assignment of being the channels through which God would make Himself known to the rest of humankind. If we keep this sense of God's "choosing" in focus, we avoid the implication that God's choice of some means that all the rest are damned. Quite the contrary! God has chosen (and, we might add, specially blessed) some in order that all might come to know His love and salvation.

This thought is amplified in the word translated *"from the beginning"* in verse 13. A preferred translation could be, "God has chosen you as first fruits for salvation." The decision hangs on whether the text reads *ap archais* (from the beginning), or *aparchēn* (first fruits). The manuscript evidence is slightly stronger for the latter. And it is the idea of the first fruits that best expresses the concept of the divine election of some to bring His blessing to all. Those who are chosen are the first fruits. And the first fruits are always seen as the guarantee that a rich and full harvest will follow.

I feel strongly that we must emphasize our election as a specific call of God, not just to our salvation, but to the salvation of the world through our witness and our service. And seeing our election as "first fruits" at least keeps us moving in the right direction.

The believers in Thessalonica had indeed responded to God's choosing as first fruits. And whenever the church is faithful to the choice and calling of God, we are the promise of the harvest to come.

We are the first fruits of salvation *"through sanctification by the Spirit and belief in the truth"* (v. 13). To sanctify means to set apart for special use. In the Old Testament, things were set apart for special service to God. The Book of Leviticus has all kinds of instructions and regulations for the setting apart of such objects for the worship of God. As things were set apart, so people are sanctified—set apart for the service of God. It is the Holy Spirit, God present and active, who is the means by which we are set apart for the communication of God's love to all. A part of that sanctification is belief in the truth to which we have been called by God.

And this election culminates in *"the obtaining of the glory of our Lord Jesus Christ"* (v. 14). I take this to mean our final glorification with Christ in His *parousia*.

This, then, is our election by God. It is the expression of His love for us of His own initiative. It is eternal and unconditional. It is a call to be His agents of love and reconciliation in the world. To respond to His choosing of us makes us first fruits of a great harvest of love and grace. And as the harvest continues, we look toward our future glory in and with Christ.

Our response to God. The divine initiative seeks and awaits human response. Thus, Paul's magnificent statements of the Gospel regularly conclude with a *"therefore,"* followed by an appeal to commitment and obedience. Here the response called for is to *"stand fast,"* and to *"hold the traditions."*

A boyhood memory shapes my image of standing fast. Near the elementary school I attended was a grove of stately California eucalyptus trees. One of the ways some of us chose to demonstrate our budding manhood to each other (and, I suspect, to the girls in our class) was to ride our bikes full speed through the trees. Since the trees were not in straight rows, a great deal of dexterity and derring-do was required. One day, what I can now see as the inevitable happened. Right in the middle of my all-out slalom, my front wheel caught on a fallen branch, and I took on the next tree directly. It was, indeed, the immovable object. Unfortunately, I was not the irresistible force. It stood fast.

When we are faithful to be the first fruits of salvation, we will be impacted by rejection and even opposition. We are to stand fast, like that sturdy eucalyptus that probably still stands in the same grove. It may have received some scars on its trunk—and even some carved hearts and initials on it—but it stood fast. And we, too, are called to stand fast with the Gospel of Jesus Christ.

We are also called to hold the traditions which we have been taught. To the Thessalonians, Paul sees the tradition as both oral and written. What he had taught and preached in his short time there was the tradition. And now what he wrote in these letters took its place as a part of the tradition.

There is great power in being part of a tradition. A football player at a school like Notre Dame or USC is inspired by the traditions of such institutions. The "big games" between rival schools produce surprising and remarkable plays and results because of the motivating power of great traditions.

In the struggle to endure incredible persecution by the Russians, Tevye, the father in *Fiddler on the Roof,* witnesses to the power of tradition.

And so it is with us in Christ. If anything, tradition should be a more powerful force for us than it could have been for the Thessalonians because we have 1900 more years of it. The saints, the martyrs, and millions of common folks like us have shaped the traditons by which we now live.

This does not mean that all tradition is to be revered. Tradition is not a sacred cow, never to be challenged. The question of tradition was a critical issue between the Pharisees and Jesus. They chided Him for breaking with some of their cherished traditions regarding the Sabbath (Luke 6:1–11) and rituals associated with eating (Mark 7:1–16). Jesus made a sharp delineation between "the traditions of men" and "the commandments of God."

Here we can draw the line between two views of tradition. Tradition can be regarded as what we have always done before. Or it can be regarded as the accumulation of wisdom. Tradition based upon "we've always done it that way" needs to be challenged again and again. Only when tradition is clearly the product of the wisdom of previous generations is it worth holding. Such is the wisdom that is ours in Christ.

The Word of God Incarnate and the Word of God written are the standards against which our traditions must always be weighed and measured. But the power of tradition must always be treasured and maintained.

Our support by God. It would appear that Paul concludes this letter with a benediction in verses 16 and 17. But there are two additional benediction prayers to follow (3:5 and 3:16). It seems to me that there is a pattern in the Thessalonian letters with which every preacher can identify. Assuming that Paul dictated these letters orally, we can understand how he can come to what he intends to be the conclusion of the letter and then think of something else he still wants to say.

In the first letter, for instance, he gives a beautiful benediction in 3:11–13. Then he begins another thought with the words, "Finally then . . . " After some added appeals about the quality of their lives, he then deals with the questions that were troubling them about the return of Christ. He includes some additional practical admonitions and then comes to his final benediction in 5:23, one of the most beautiful in the New Testament.

In this letter, this benediction could well bring the letter to a strong conclusion. But he continues again with "Finally, brethren, pray for us," concluding with a short benediction (3:5). Not through yet, he addresses a troubling question among them, coming to his final benediction in 3:16.

The next time you hear a preacher say, "and in closing," don't be totally surprised if one or two more things follow. I don't advocate this with my students in preaching classes, but I have to admit that I do it occasionally—and I'm glad I'm in good company.

I see this benediction as a magnificent affirmation of God's support of us as we respond in faith and obedience to His election of us to be the first fruits of salvation. It is perhaps significant that in the benediction in 1 Thessalonians 5:11, the order is, "our God and Father Himself, and our Lord Jesus Christ." Here, the order is reversed to, "our Lord Jesus Christ Himself, and our God and Father." Such a casual reversal would seem to indicate that in Paul's mind, God and Christ are so much the same that the order is of no consequence.

God is affirmed as supporting us in three ways in verse 16: (1) He has loved us. (2) He has given us everlasting consolation. (3) He has given us good hope by grace.

Again, God's love for us is crucial to life itself. The force of the Greek tense points to an action completed in a point of time. Thus, God's love is here regarded as the manifestation of His love in Jesus Himself. Jesus is the full expression of God's love, once and for all. We are supported, day in and day out, by God's love.

The same tense is used in the next phrase, *given us everlasting consolation.* Consolation is a misleading translation of the word *paraklēsin.* This is the Greek word used to denote the Holy Spirit in John 14:16, 26, and Jesus Himself as our advocate in 1 John 2:1. This word was used of one's counsel in a lawsuit, and carried the idea of one called alongside to strengthen, encourage, and support. Thus, God, in Christ, has acted once and for all to give us His strength and support. The adjective *"everlasting"* further underscores the fact that God's support of us cannot ever be weakened or withdrawn through any circumstances.

The third element of God's support of us is *"good hope by grace."* In an age of growing despair, how powerful hope is. Good hope. That good hope is grounded in God's grace. And He will never disappoint us or let us down.

Out of these three components of God's support there are two continuing products: (1) comfort (in) our hearts, (2) establishment in every good word and work.

Again, *"comfort"* is a translation of the verb *parakaleō,* in which the idea of strengthening and supporting is basic. *"Establish"* is also a word of strengthening, from the word used for a column in a building.

It never occurred to Paul to separate words and works, doctrine and practice.

What a powerful thought through this benediction! Not only does God choose us and call us to stand fast and hold the traditions; God supports us and strengthens us. The great God and Creator of the universe is actually at work, not only in the cosmic dimensions of His creation, but in the daily events of our lives.

A REQUEST FOR PRAYER

1 Finally, brethren, pray for us, that the word of
the Lord may have free course and be glorified, just
as with you,
2 and that we may be delivered from unreasonable
and wicked men; for not all have faith.

2 Thess. 3:1–2

Though he may have intended to close this letter with the preceding benediction, he could not close without asking for their prayers for him. Here is the strong and able apostle, expressing his need for their support. How good to know that Paul felt that need so strongly!

The prayer he requests has nothing to do with his own personal well-being as an end in itself. It is in order that his ministry for Christ might continue and expand. There are at least five other times in his letters where Paul asks for prayer. In Romans 15:30–32, he asks for prayer for continuing and extended ministry as well as for fellowship with them. In 2 Corinthians 1:9–11, he sees their prayers as a part of his continuing ministry. In Ephesians 6:17–21, he seeks their prayers that he might speak boldly for Christ. In Philippians 1:15–20, he affirms their prayers as a source of strength in his witness in and through his imprisonment in Rome. In Colossians 4:3–4, he solicits their prayers for an open door for his preaching.

Paul could not separate his ministry and preaching from the prayers of his brothers and sisters in Christ. Blessed, indeed, is the pastor who seeks and who receives the continuing prayers of the people. Blessed, too, is every man and woman who is seeking to make all of life a ministry for Christ and has the regular prayer support of caring friends.

Specifically here, Paul asks for their prayers in order that *"the word of the Lord may have free course."* The verb literally pictures the Word of the Lord as running in a race. Here, the Word is pictured as strong and active, an idea expressed in a different metaphor by Paul: "The sword of the Spirit, which is the word of God" (Eph. 6:17). A vivid and similar expression was given us by the writer of Hebrews: "For the word of God is living and powerful, and sharper than any two-edged sword . . ." (Heb. 4:12).

How transforming for those of us who preach and teach the Word of God! We are to think not merely of communicating words and ideas, but of releasing and transmitting this all-powerful, active, and dynamic Word into the lives of others. I have a growing conviction that what is needed desperately in our time is a growing conviction in the power, not of our words, but of the Word of God.

This Word, running its course, will be *"glorified."* Another translation could be "received with honor." What could be more gratifying and rewarding than to know that because we have taught and proclaimed the Word of God, it has been received by some with honor?

The second part of Paul's prayer request has to do with a specific situation from which he sought some release. The use of the article (not translated) with *"unreasonable and wicked men,"* along with the verb tense implies a definite group of people. As he writes from Corinth, there must have been some who were going to great lengths to oppose and hinder the progress of the Word of God there. The word translated *"unreasonable"* really means "out of place." It is usually used of things, and this is the only place in the New Testament where it denotes persons. Here, then, were people, totally out of line, and actively wicked in opposition to the Gospel. Paul's desire to be delivered from them had nothing to do with his own comfort or safety—he was concerned, rather, for those who did not yet *"have faith."*

GREAT IS THY FAITHFULNESS

Even as Paul solicits their prayers for his troubles with opposition in Corinth, he recalls that the Christians in Thessalonica are also under attack. And so comes a word of strong, affirming encouragement.

3 But the Lord is faithful, who will establish you and guard you from the evil one.

4 And we have confidence in the Lord concerning
you, both that you do and will do the things we
command you.
5 And may the Lord direct your hearts into the
love of God and into the patience of Christ.

2 Thess. 3:3–5

There appears to be a play on words at the beginning of this sentence. The last word of verse 2 was *pistis,* faith. The first word of verse 3 is *pistos,* which can mean "believing" or "faithful" in the sense of trustworthy. It is obvious that Paul here affirms the faithfulness of God. And what a contrast between this and the unbelief of men and women! Especially stark is the contrast between the unfaithfulness of the "out of place and wicked men" and the faithfulness of God. It is at the point of discouragement with people who oppose us or let us down that the faithfulness of God needs to be recalled.

God in His faithfulness is both the source of our strength (*"who will establish you"*), and the One who guards and protects us. While *"evil"* here can be either neuter or masculine, most scholars prefer the masculine "the evil one" for two reasons. First, it seems as though the contrast between the Lord and the evil one makes the sentence more consistent. In addition, there is the same ambiguity here as in the version of the Lord's Prayer in Matthew 6:13, where the masculine is the preferred reading. God is thus seen as strengthening and guarding us, not just from evil in principle, but from one who is evil personified.

This is certainly consistent with Paul's view of evil expressed in Ephesians 6:12—"For we do not wrestle against flesh and blood, but against principalities, against powers, against the rulers of the darkness of this age, against spiritual hosts of wickedness in the heavenly places." Martin Luther is quoted as saying, "If you don't believe in the devil, it's because you've never resisted him." If we are not to some degree aware of our need for God's strength and protection, it may well be that we have capitulated to the enemy.

Some commentators feel that *"the Lord is faithful"* may have been a phrase used in the synagogue worship as we might use "Amen" or as a response to the reading of the lesson from the prophets. If so, some recovery of this reassuring phrase could be a welcome addition to our liturgy.

Paul affirms his continuing confidence in them in verse 4 in a way characteristic of him. He really twists their arms in a not-so-subtle way. He expresses faith in the Lord that they will do the things he had commanded them. In the vernacular, we might respond, "Don't lay your trip on me!" We can't deny that Paul is using his confidence in the Lord to put pressure on them. If Paul was misreading God's will for them, he was, indeed, being quite manipulative here. But if Paul was rightly delivering the Word of God to them, he had every right to put it to them as directly as he did.

Paul concludes this section with the second benediction in verse 5. And again we have one of those beautiful and priceless gems of simple profundity. He prays that the Lord will direct their hearts into the love of God and into the patience of Christ.

The language is unclear as to whether *"the love of God"* means His love for us or our love for Him. Paul's most common usage suggests God's love for us. But in the deepest sense, the two always go together. It is God's love for us that generates our love for Him.

The *"patience of Christ"* puts us in touch with our good friend *hupomonē* that we met in 1 Thessalonians 1:3. This is no passive word of endurance in order to survive. It is active and unswerving fidelity in the midst of any and all adversity, that then uses the adversity creatively and constructively. Jesus Himself is the definition of *hupomonē,* for He took the rejection and the shame of the cross and used it for the redemption of all humankind.

As I have pondered this powerful section of Paul's letter, I've found myself humming and singing one of my favorite Christian songs, "Great Is Thy Faithfulness":

> Great is Thy faithfulness, O God my Father,
> There is no shadow of turning with Thee;
> Thou changest not,
> Thy compassions, they fail not;
> As Thou hast been Thou forever wilt be.
> Great is Thy faithfulness!
> Great is Thy faithfulness!
> Morning by morning new mercies I see;
> All I have needed Thy hand hath provided,
> Great is Thy faithfulness, Lord, unto me!*

---

* Copyright 1923. Renewal 1951 by Hope Publishing Company, Carol Stream, Illinois.

CHAPTER FOUR

The Dignity of Work

2 Thessalonians 3:6–15

The letter could have ended very well with the beautiful benediction in 2:16–17. Or it could have concluded very nicely with the second benediction in 3:5. But before Paul brings this epistle to its final benediction, he must deal with a problem that is crucial among the believers in Thessalonica. The fact that this section is second in length only to that on the return of Christ indicates its importance.

It seems fair to assume that some of the Thessalonians had quit their jobs, ostensibly because of their belief in the Lord's imminent return. As time went by, they refused to work and became dependent upon the generosity of others for their support. This problem appears to have been addressed mildly and somewhat indirectly in 1 Thessalonians 4:11–12 and 5:14, in the latter case with the assumption that some of these folks had become "unruly." If this was the case, things must have gotten worse since writing the first letter, bad enough for Paul to tackle it head on.

THE TOUGH QUESTION OF CHURCH DISCIPLINE

6 Now we command you, brethren, in the name of our Lord Jesus Christ, that you withdraw from every brother who walks disorderly and not according to the tradition which he received from us.

14 And if anyone does not obey our word in this epistle, note that person and do not keep company with him, that he may be ashamed.

15 Yet do not count him as an enemy, but admonish him as a brother.

(2 Thess. 3:6, 14–15)

I choose to treat verses 14 and 15 with verse 6 because they provide together the purpose of this section. And to those of us who have emphasized unconditional love as the basis of genuine Christian community, this is a tough section to accept and apply. Unconditional love is often expressed as "I love you, no matter what." But Paul calls them to withdrawal and separation. Love, then, cannot mean infinite toleration of any kind of behavior.

The passage conveys an authoritative mood. The opening word is the language of a general commanding his troops. Even more dramatic is the call to authority *"in the name of the Lord Jesus Christ."* Paul had no stronger language. This is obviously a very serious issue. It is being confronted with intense feelings.

And who were the problem people? Three things are said of them in verses 6 and 14: (1) They walk "disorderly" (also v. 11). (2) They walk contrary to the "tradition." (3) They do not obey the word in this epistle. This is all we really know of their behavior. If we add 1 Thessalonians 4:11–12, 5:14, and 2 Thess. 3:11, we gain a little more insight into the problem: (4) They were not leading "quiet" lives. (5) They were butting into other people's affairs. (6) They were choosing not to work. (7) They were "unruly."

These are the pieces of the puzzle that we must fit together to describe more specifically the behavior of those who were threatening the peace, unity, and purity of the church there. One assumption can be that their erroneous views of the Second Coming of Christ were related to their behavior. It's not too difficult to reconstruct a scenario in which people had become so convinced that Christ was just about to return—or in some way had already returned—that they refused to work. Why work to earn a living when you are certain there is no tomorrow on this earth? It's a small step from that position to begin to tell everyone else how to run their lives. Minding everyone else's business is regarded with the sense of divine calling. From that point, conflict is inevitable and there soon follows the noisy disruption of community.

A key word used twice by Paul to describe the problem people was *ataktōs*. It is translated "unruly" in 1 Thessalonians 5:14, and *"disorderly"* here in v. 6. This is a military term used to describe a soldier who steps out of the ranks. It is used to refer to anyone or anything out of place. The word ultimately portrays intentional idleness or what we would call "loafing" or "goofing off." Thus, the disorderly and unruly are to be seen as loafers. Their idleness was a matter of their own choice, not of being unemployed or unemployable. And what made the whole thing so destructive was that this refusal to work was very likely defended on theological grounds.

Such behavior was *"not according to the tradition"* which had come to them through Paul's teaching and writing (2 Thess. 2:15). Again, the importance of tradition as accumulated wisdom is held as crucial to the life of the Christian community. And such behavior was from this point on contrary to *"our word in this epistle."* This certainly establishes this letter, in Paul's intention, as a part of the tradition.

Now come the tough questions about the response to the problem people. Paul calls the Thessalonians to: (1) withdraw from each of them, (2) *"note"* each of them, and (3) not to keep company with them.

Thus there is a point in the Christian community where lines must be drawn. This introduces the question of church discipline. Every denominational tradition I know has some provisions for discipline in the church. These usually range from basic requirements by which "good standing" in the church is maintained to the more dramatic situations requiring censure or exclusion from membership. Rarely is church discipline exercised.

When I was a pastor in western New York I used a few snowbound hours to browse through the minutes of our church's congregational Sessions from the 1890s. I was astounded by the frequency of disciplinary matters! Again and again, some member of the church had been called before the Session and confronted with evidence of immoral behavior—adultery, drunkenness, wife and child abuse, and even financial matters—with repentance and restitution demanded as a condition for continuing fellowship in the church.

Now I'm not about to suggest that our elders make nightly bed checks or require copies of our tax returns. But perhaps our quests for church renewal are going to have to raise some tough questions about standards and discipline. The church is called to be different from the world around it. That's why Paul was so concerned about this issue among the Thessalonians. There were undoubtedly plenty of loafers and busybodies in Thessalonica. But as far as Paul was concerned, there was no place for them in the church. From such, the believers in the church were to withdraw.

But the withdrawal, the "noting" of the person, and the avoidance of company, were not the same as rejection. We really don't know how the person was to be "noted" or "marked out." But while such a person was to be avoided within the fellowship, the believers are instructed to relate to the problem person not *"as an enemy"* but *"as a brother."*

There seems to be a more severe level of discipline as indicated in 1 Corinthians 5:9–11, the only other place in the New Testament where the Greek verb meaning *"do not keep company with"* is used. There the issue revolves around those who openly profess the faith, but who is "a fornicator, or covetous, or an idolater, or a reviler, or a drunkard, or an extortioner." The Corinthian Christians were commanded, not only to avoid keeping company with such, but "not even to eat with such a person" (1 Cor. 5:11). This passage indicates situations in which people are to be excluded from any level of relationship in the fellowship. By the way, isn't it interesting that covetousness is placed right alongside fornication?

In 2 Thessalonians, a less severe approach is indicated. The discipline has a redemptive goal. Its essential goal is *"that he may be ashamed."* It is to bring a person to a proper sense of guilt. I've heard it said that we should never try to get people to change by creating guilt. The fallacy with that statement is twofold. First, guilt is not always negative. It can be a source of positive and creative change. Second, guilt is not created by the one who confronts the guilty person. The admission of guilt is the response that can lead to forgiveness and wholeness. The denial of guilt is the unhealthy response. There is such a thing as real sin and real guilt. To help one in the fellowship own up to the reality of sin and guilt is an act of love. The primary reason for church discipline must always be to redeem—to bring the person to a genuine sense of guilt so that forgiveness may be sought and given.

Paul further amplifies the redemptive nature of this kind of discipline in verse 15. It is intended to keep the person in the fellowship as a brother, not to exclude him as an enemy. In the Corinthian church, the situation was regarded as irredeemable, and exclusion was called for.

How we discipline in the church must vary in different times and places. But the issues must be addressed if the church is to be the church. Church growth and renewal cannot ignore the fact that we are called to be different from the world system around us. The church that lives by the same standards of covetous greed and consumerism may well be successful in gaining adherents to its undemanding membership standards, but it may fail miserably in developing serious disciples of Christ. What are the things that make our congregations truly different from the social and service organizations in our town that do not claim to be directly related to Jesus Christ?

THE EXAMPLE OF THE APOSTLES

7 For you yourselves know how you ought to follow us, for we were not disorderly among you;

8 nor did we eat anyone's bread free of charge, but worked with labor and toil night and day, that we might not be a burden to any of you,

9 not because we do not have authority, but to make ourselves an example of how you should follow us.

2 Thess. 3:7–9

There's an old saying, "What you do speaks so loudly, I can't hear what you say." This could not be said of Paul, Silas, and Timothy. They lived by what they taught. They practiced what they preached. So when they addressed the question of the loafers and the busybodies, they were not reticent to point to their own example. They had also pointed to their own conduct in 1 Thessalonians 2:9–10. While in Thessalonica, they made it clear that they (1) were not loafers, (2) did not receive gifts, and (3) were self-supporting.

This section begins and ends with the statement that *"you ought to follow us."* In the situation in which the apostolic party brought the Gospel for the very first time to a key place like Thessaslonica, they were very sensitive to the power of their example. They had a pressing concern that they not be written off merely as some sharpies who were making a living and profiting by the Gospel, as he stated forcefully to the Corinthians: "For we are not, as so many, peddling the word of God" (1 Cor. 2:17). Paul was thoroughly circumspect and beyond reproach in all financial matters. The history of his followers in the clergy is terribly clouded.

He chose to follow the "tentmaking pattern" of ministry. He made his own living by plying his own trade as a tentmaker, as he made clear here: *"but worked with labor and toil night and day, that we might not be a burden to any of you."* This was not required of the apostolic vocation. Quite the contrary! Jesus had established the principle, in sending out the twelve, that "a worker is worthy of his food" (Matt. 10:10). In the accepted tradition of the itinerant rabbis, the twelve were to be received and cared for by the people to whom they were sent. Thus, they were not to take money, nor extra clothing, nor food with them.

Paul and his companions, however, chose to follow a different pattern in order not to be misunderstood or accused of being profiteers. In a lengthy discussion of this matter, he explained his rationale to the Corinthians (1 Cor. 9:3–15). He never denied anyone the right to earn his sustenance by preaching the Gospel. He did not require others to follow his chosen pattern. He declined his rights in order to establish his own example. And in this case, his position over against the idlers and the busybodies was certainly much stronger.

There is a strong word in this section to all of us who have chosen to exercise our rights to "live from the gospel" (2 Cor. 9:14). While the professional ministry is authenticated by Jesus Himself, there's a great gulf between living by the Gospel and becoming rich by the Gospel.

There's something incongruous about affluent clergy folks. To be sure, the wide divergence of costs of living and costs of raising and educating families makes affluence relative, but certain questions need to be kept in mind. While most congregations will not create problems of affluence for most pastors, there are still many ways for clergy to pursue wealth and comfort to the point of being far removed from the simplicity of lifestyle and the priorities of the Kingdom of God to which Jesus calls us (Matt. 6:19–34).

The issue is not how much one makes. It is, rather, what is done with what is received. Genuine stewardship is the recognition that everything belongs to God. The issue is how much we spend on ourselves as over against how much we give away.

Clergy whose lifestyles parallel the affluent in our society can hardly be said to belong to the company of these apostles who forsook their rights to much more. In doing so, they certainly kept in fellowship with the One who accumulated nothing, who lived simply, and who didn't even own a place to lay His head.

THE COMMAND OF THE APOSTLES

10 For even when we were with you, we
commanded you this: If anyone will not work, neither
shall he eat.
11 For we hear that there are some who walk among

you in a disorderly manner, not working at all, but
are busybodies.

12 Now those who are such we command and
exhort by our Lord Jesus Christ that with quietness
they work and eat their own bread.

13 But you, brethren, do not grow weary in doing
good.

2 Thess. 3:10–13

"If anyone will not work, neither shall he eat." This proverbial saying is
of unknown origin and may have been original with Paul. Some
trace its roots back to Genesis 3:19: "In the sweat of your face you
shall eat bread till you return to the ground, for out of it you were
taken; for dust you are, and to dust you shall return." Others see
it as a Jewish proverb, though it is not found in the Old Testament.
Still others see it as a Greek saying. Some even try to trace it to
Jesus through His own labor in the carpenter shop (Matt. 6:3).

Whatever its origin, it may well be one of the most misquoted
sayings of Scripture, second only to "You have the poor with you
always" (Matt. 26:11). Such statements, taken out of context, can
be used to support uncaring and harsh treatment of the needy.

We have already seen the context of this proverb. The reference
is clearly to a small group of people within the church at Thessalonica
who were refusing to work, perhaps because of their erroneous eschatological beliefs, and who were becoming a burden to the others
and a stumbling block to the witness of the church in the community.

Wherever the Gospel of Christ has truly taken hold of the lives
of people, difficult questions arise with regard to the poor and needy.
The initial impetus of the Bible, New and Old Testaments alike, is
the responsibility of the better-off to help and care for those in need.
But having said that, the questions must still be raised as to why
they are in need. Sometimes it is a matter of tough luck, sometimes
a matter of circumstances, sometimes a matter of physical or mental
limitations, sometimes a matter of geography and/or politics. The
reasons are many and often complex.

Here, the only people to whom the proverb was applicable were
those who were quite capable of working and for whom work was
available, but who persisted in their refusal to work. Not only were
they refusing to work, but they had become busybodies as well,
minding everyone's business but their own. Such loafers and meddlers
are strongly mandated *"through our Lord Jesus Christ that they work in
quietness and eat their own bread"* (v. 12).

When I hear this saying being used to justify our lack of care for the poor, I must rise to protest such flagrant misuse of the Bible. Unless we have a local situation closely akin to the Thessalonian problem, caution is in order in using this proverb. It certainly has no application other than to believers within the church who flatly refuse to work when work is available.

There's a widespread assumption among the relatively affluent that no one in America need be poor if they are willing to work. Poverty is assumed to be a product of laziness or ignorance. But such is not always the case. That some folks are poor because they won't learn or work is true. But the vast majority of today's unemployed would welcome the opportunity to be regularly and gainfully employed. In recent months, I've taken the time to talk with people who are trying to help them. I'm absolutely convinced that the assumptions that tie their plight to laziness need to be challenged, exposed, and rejected.

Rather than being quick to quote this text to defend our callousness, it may be time to quote James: "If a brother or sister is naked and destitute of daily food, and one of you says to them, 'Depart in peace, be warmed and filled,' but you do not give them the things which are needed for the body, what does it profit? Thus also faith by itself, if it does not have works, is dead" (James 2:15–17). Or Jesus: "Give to him who asks you, and from him who wants to borrow from you do not turn away" (Matt. 5:42). And we do well to remember Jesus' portrayal of the final judgment, when God judged the nations by whether they fed the hungry, gave drink to the thirsty, hosted the stranger, clothed the naked, and visited the sick and the prisoners (Matt. 25:31–46).

We are on shaky ground whenever we try to use Scripture to justify our right to accumulate wealth and to live in relative affluence while surrounded with people who are poor and needy. We may be touching another point here pertaining to church renewal. It's not likely that a church turned in upon its own success and security is going to experience genuine spiritual renewal. We may succeed in building larger and larger churches and attracting more and more customers but until we get serious about the hungry, the thirsty, the refugees, the sick, and the captives, we simply are not the church of Jesus Christ.

It is on a tender note that Paul concludes this section. *"Do not grow weary in doing good."* Doing good, especially in the nitty-gritty of obedience to the Lord's mandate to feed the hungry and care for

143

the poor, has a way of becoming downright exhausting, physically and emotionally. None of us, individually or collectively, has the resources to solve all of the problems. Yet tackle them we must. In this sense, we are called upon to fight losing battles, though our ultimate victory in Christ is assured.

We live in a time when many people have taken up causes that are rightly the business of the church, without claiming any motivation rooted in Christ. I celebrate this and am happy to work with anyone who cares to join us in feeding the hungry, caring for the homeless, or working for peace and justice. But I find many cause-oriented people lacking in staying power. This, I'm convinced, is one of the differences in work motivated by our commitment to Christ. Far from being those who flit from cause to cause on the basis of the possibilty of success, we are those who *"do not grow weary in doing good,"* because we know that God calls us to be faithful whether or not we succeed.

I doubt that we will ever succeed in eliminating poverty or hunger on a national, much less a global scale. But we are called to hang in there, no matter what.

I'll never forget the day I spent in a large, sprawling hospital in Soroti, Uganda. I visited two men who had been shot and beaten by bandits the night before. I talked with middle-aged people who were dying of causes treated routinely in our hospitals. I visited a heavily populated measles ward and witnessed the deaths of three children that morning.

As I walked across the grounds with a Ugandan nurse, a committed Christian, I asked her, "Don't you ever get discouraged? This situation is so beyond hope. Don't you just want to give up sometimes?" Tears streamed down her beautiful black cheeks. "Yes, every day I want to give up. But, I'd rather do what little I can—than do nothing."

And ever since that day, those words have been ringing in my heart. We won't solve all of the problems of human need—we may not solve any. *But*. . . I'd rather do what little I can, than do nothing!

CHAPTER FIVE

The Final Benediction

2 Thessalonians 3:16–18

We have already noted that this is the third benediction in this letter. And with this, the Apostle closes the epistle.

> 16 Now may the Lord of peace Himself give you peace always in every way. The Lord be with you all.
> 17 The salutation of Paul with my own hand, which is a sign in every epistle; so I write.
> 18 The grace of our Lord Jesus Christ be with you all. Amen.
>
> *2 Thess. 3:16–18*

Peace is the ultimate blessing of God. Here is the divine shalom active in our lives. It is a gift given by God. We really can't achieve it. It is not the absence of conflict or storm. It is an inner confidence and hope in the midst of stress and strain. Christ is our peace.

"The Lord be with you all" could well have been a phrase often used to close a service of worship, as was probably the case with the call for the grace of Christ to be with us.

The personal signature of Paul in verse 17 was an attestation of the letter's integrity. He has pointed out that already other letters were being circulated, purporting to be from him (2 Thess. 2:2). His way of exposing such forgeries was to affix his signature. This also seems to indicate that the letter was dictated by Paul, along with Silas and Timothy, and would have been transmitted in the writing of the scribe.

No words could better bring this or any other letter to a close than the prayer, *"The grace of our Lord Jesus Christ be with you all."* From start to finish, everything that we are and have is all by His grace.

Introduction to 1 Timothy

We begin our studies of the letters to Timothy and Titus with the awareness that, with the exception of Philemon, they are the only ones written to individuals rather than churches. In the history of their interpretation, they have always been treated as a unit. They were first named "The Pastoral Epistles" by D. N. Berdot in 1703, and that has become their common name ever since.

The term *pastoral Epistles* can be misleading. It would seem to indicate that we have a manual intended to give comprehensive guidance in the structure and governance of churches. Such is not the case. Pastors then, and even more so now, need to know and do much more than the few things covered in these letters. It has been observed that some 10 percent of the material in the pastoral Epistles deals with church organization and program. 1 Timothy 3:1–13, 5:3–22, and Titus 1:5–9 are the passages in this category, and obviously do not give us a comprehensive manual of pastoral practice.

To refer to these letters as pastorals is accurate, however, as long as we regard the title as describing the fact that they stand alone among the letters of the New Testament as having been written to two men who were pastors. While all of the other letters (except Philemon) were obviously written to churches and intended to be read to a general audience, these letters were written to Timothy and Titus personally. Whether it was ever the author's intention to have them read publicly remains unknown to us. Timothy and Titus shared them with others, and they have thus been handed on to us.

This leads to the assumption that these letters may well have been only three of a much larger number that Paul wrote to his friends and colleagues. There's every reason to believe that Paul was a prolific letter writer. If so, he must have written letters to people like Barnabas, Silas, Luke, and others. The fact that these are the only three personal letters that either survived or were considered worthy of inclusion in the New Testament canon makes them stand in a class all by themselves.

Authorship and Authenticity

We cannot engage in a study of the pastoral Epistles without recognizing the complexity of the scholarship surrounding these letters, especially as to their authorship and authenticity. While it is not the purpose of this commentary to deal with such technical questions, let alone resolve them, we cannot ignore them.

Until 1807, the traditional view of the Pauline authorship of these letters was virtually unquestioned. The first scholar to insist that Paul could not have written them was Friedrich Schleiermacher, primarily on the grounds that they contain so many words used nowhere else in the letters of Paul. Beyond the vocabulary itself, Schleiermacher also insisted that there were concepts in the letters that were contradictory to Paul's theology as set forth in other epistles.

Not only did schools of thought develop around these linguistic and grammatical reasons for holding Paul's authorship to be improbable or impossible, but historical and ecclesiastical questions came to be raised as well. The argument was put forth that the letters reflect a structure of church order with bishops and elders and traditions which could not have existed until the second century, perhaps not before A.D. 150. Since Paul was martyred prior to A.D. 70, the conclusion from such an assumption was obvious.

There developed yet another line of reasoning leading to a second century date for the letters. This was the theological line. A case was made that the heresies that Paul was attacking were those of an advanced gnosticism that did not develop until long after Paul's death. Gnosticism was a complex, philosophical-theological view of God and the world which held, among many other things, that God stands away from and over against the world, not *in* the world as with our theology grounded in the Incarnation. The idea of God in human flesh was utterly alien to the Gnostics. If, indeed, the pastorals are dealing with heresies that did not exist in Paul's lifetime, the conclusion that he did not write them is undebatable.

What has always been impressive to me in the vast amount of scholarship on this subject over the last 175 years is the number of genuine heavyweights on both sides of the issue. And it's not just a matter of the conservatives on one side versus the liberals on the other. Many who deny Paul's authorship of these letters take them very seriously as Scripture and give them all the weight accorded them by those who defend the traditional view.

In a recent conversation with a world-class New Testament scholar, I asked for his view of the authorship of the pastorals. "This is about as close to a tossup as anything in New Testament scholarship," he replied. He then went on to share some of his reasons for believing in the Pauline authorship. I think it best that we study these letters with an awareness that the debate is likely to remain unresolved.

I'm satisfied that one can affirm Paul's authorship of these letters on good grounds, just as there are good grounds for placing them in the second century. I choose the former.

If the linguistic and grammatical arguments are applied rigidly and consistently to a collection of anyone's writings over a period of years, there are likely to be significant differences. I'm sure that my preaching and writing today have some nuances in vocabulary and style different from twenty years ago. At least I hope so!

Likewise, theological emphases change from time to time and from place to place. As always, with Paul's letters, we are hearing only one end of the conversation. Frequently, the actual issues being addressed could have been known for sure only by the immediate recipients of the letters. To hold that a highly developed gnosticism was being confronted in these letters is, at best, a matter of speculation. The same or similar problems were addressed in Colossians, widely accepted as a letter from Paul.

As to the ecclesiastical questions, we shall see in our studies that the terms for bishop and elder need not reflect the office of bishop that eventually emerged in the hierarchical establishment. From its earliest times, a basic form of leadership by deacons and elders was found in the church.

Let us move into the letters—with all respect for those who differ—with the assumption that Paul wrote 1 Timothy, Titus, and 2 Timothy, in that order, with 2 Timothy having been written just prior to his martyrdom by the executioner's axe.

For an excellent discussion of the questions surrounding the authorship and authenticity of the pastoral epistles, see Donald Guthrie, *The Pastoral Epistles,* Tyndale Bible Commentary, pp. 11–53 and 212–28 (Grand Rapids: Eerdmans, 1957).

An Outline of 1 Timothy

CHAPTER ONE

Maintaining the Glow

1 Timothy 1:1–20

"Wait 'til the honeymoon is over!"

One of the most destructive myths about marriage assumes that the glow of a lifelong relationship is but a brief prelude to what must become a comparatively dull and lackluster routine. If this premise is accepted, it easily becomes a self-fulfilling prophecy, attested by ever so many "normal" marriages.

The same assumption has a way of taking its toll on careers as well. I think of doctors who began medical school with a passionate commitment to become helpers and healers, but years later go about their rounds as a necessary routine to support their desired lifestyle. I think of pastors who knelt for their ordination with tears of gratitude and breathless wonder with God's gracious call, but four churches later have merely settled for ecclesiastical games and accruing pension credits. How sad!

The first chapter of this letter, written after three decades of apostolic ministry, strikes the deathblow to the "honeymoon-is-over" approach to life or career. If one knows one's calling, one's Gospel, one's self, and one's mission, all of life and ministry can be lived with love, joy, and peace.

KNOW YOUR CALLING

1 Paul, an apostle of Jesus Christ, by the commandment of God our Savior and the Lord Jesus Christ, our hope,

2 To Timothy, my true son in the faith:

> Grace, mercy, and peace from God our Father
> and Jesus Christ our Lord.
>
> *1 Tim. 1:1–2*

The old pro has been involved in his ministry for Christ for a long time. But his opening greeting breathes all of the joy and commitment that he felt years before on the road to Damascus. His sense of vocation never became old hat. In the opening greetings of his letter, he often affirmed his pride in being an apostle. And his pride was not in an ecclesiastical title or office, but in a mission and a service. For *apostle* means "one who is sent" on a mission for another. And Paul had been sent on his lifelong mission by the command of God. Paul never forgot for a single moment that he was a man under orders.

How proud Paul is with this identity! With every letter, he begins by shouting to the housetops his joy and gratitude in being an apostle and a servant of Jesus Christ. Would that we could all keep the glow alive! That glow that we felt in our conversion, in special moments of renewal, in our ordination or baptism. And the glow is sustained, not by contrived techniques, but by keeping in touch with one's sense of being loved and called by God. There's no need for our sense of awe and wonder to disappear.

And nothing comes off with less appeal than the ministry or witness of one who no longer exudes a sense of gratitude and pride in being an ambassador for Christ.

Our Savior and our hope. The two phrases used by Paul provide a clue as to his very reason for being: *"God our Savior"* and *"The Lord Jesus Christ, our hope."*

While it is unusual for Paul to speak of God as our Savior, the idea is deeply rooted in the Old Testament. The psalmist celebrates the righteousness that comes from "the God of his salvation" (Ps. 24:5). In the Magnificat, Mary sings, "My soul magnifies the Lord, and my spirit has rejoiced in God my Savior" (Luke 1:46–47). We do well to keep a strong emphasis upon this thought. Trinitarian thought has a way of slipping into tri-theism. For example, it's possible to think of Christ as our Savior in the sense that He was appeasing a wrathful God. His death could come to be regarded as a sacrificial act on our behalf to placate an angry God. Trinitarian theology is an affirmation that "God was in Christ reconciling the world to Himself" (2 Cor. 5:19). It is good to be reminded that God—Father, Son, Spirit—is our Savior.

And it is the Lord Jesus Christ who is our hope. Our translation changes both the order and the language of the Greek text, presumably to be consistent with common usage. The title "Lord" is not in the original, and the order that Paul used both times in verse 1 was Christ Jesus. It was not uncommon for Paul to call Him both Jesus Christ and Christ Jesus. As we saw in 1 Thessalonians 1:1, Jesus was His name and Christ was the messianic title. To say Christ Jesus, therefore, places the emphasis upon His messianic work and power.

Hope, in the New Testament, is never merely wishing for something. Paul's affirmation to the Colossians captures the essence of this theme: "Christ in you, the hope of glory" (Col. 1:27). It is Christ in us who is the basis of our confidence. Hope is the opposite of despair. In our weakness and failure, we need not despair. Christ is our hope! In the worst of times and circumstances, we need not despair. Christ is our hope! In the final moment of death, we need not despair. Christ is our hope!

Life, ministry, witness can never degenerate into dull routine or monotonous tedium for those of us who maintain our conscious awareness of God as our Savior and Christ Jesus as our hope.

"Timothy, my true son." The most intimate of all Paul's relationships was probably with Timothy. And one thing that makes their friendship all the more intriguing was their differences. There was the difference of age. When Paul first visited the little town of Lystra, it's possible that he stayed in Timothy's home (Acts 14:3–21). If so, Timothy was probably a young lad, and one can imagine the impression that the remarkable guest would have made upon him.

On Paul's second visit to Lystra (Acts 16:1–3), Timothy's life took an entirely new direction. Even as a youth, Timothy had become one of the bright lights in the congregation there, so much so that Paul invited him to be his special traveling companion. Imagine young Timothy's elation with such an invitation! From then on, Timothy had a relationship with Paul closer than anyone else. He became Paul's most trusted companion and helper. Their differences in age resulted in a father-son relationship, but always with a sense of partnership and parity in Christ.

There was also a remarkable difference in their temperaments. Paul comes across as bold and daring—Timothy, as shy and reserved. Paul

was ever the innovator and adventurer. Timothy the helper and sup-
porter. It was their emotional and functional differences that created
and nurtured their constant need for each other.

Over the years, my life has been enriched through relationships
with all kinds of people. But in recent years, one relationship has
come to have very special meaning to me. And it's with a person
who is, functionally and temperamentally, about as different from
me as could be. Bill Cunningham and I have been associate pastors
for more than eight years. I have never worked with anyone whom
I trust, respect, and need more. I shared in a small group exercise
not long ago in which we were asked to list three persons we would
want to have with us if we knew we were dying of a terminal illness.
Bill was one of those three. And I'm convinced that the depth
of my love and need for him is because of, not in spite of, our essential differences. I feel a Paul–Timothy relationship with him, not in
the sense of father–son or greater–lesser, but in the sense of partnership and friendship. Such relationships are the very essence of life
itself.

"Grace, mercy, and peace." The final words of the salutation are unique
to the pastoral letters. In all of Paul's other letters, the greeting ends
with grace and peace. In the pastorals, *"mercy"* is added. You can
make as much or little of this as you wish, but I feel that the addition
of *"mercy"* in the last of Paul's letters simply reflects an insight that
matured in Paul with the passage of time.

The more you live with the powerful realities of grace and peace,
the more mercy comes to be appreciated. Grace is the ever-present
thread in the fabric of the Gospel. It is God's free and unconditional
offer of His forgiveness and His love. Peace is the natural flow of
grace. It is that inner sense of well-being that is grounded in the
certitude of God's grace. It is calm in the midst of the storm, coolness
in the heat of battle, poise in the midst of conflict.

"Mercy" grows out of an Old Testament word used again and again
in the Psalms and translated "lovingkindness." *"Mercy"* is the word
assuring us that God is actively at work for good in our lives. To
ask for God's mercy is to ask for God's gracious goodness. Indeed,
the longer we live with grace and peace, the more we appreciate
God's continual mercy.

Paul's opening salutation lays the groundwork for what is to follow
on true and false teachers and teaching. The first mark of the true
teacher is his or her calling. And blessed is the teacher whose sense

of divine commissioning never fades and for whom the honeymoon is never over!

Not only must one have a continuing sense of one's calling by God, but there must also be a profound commitment to the Gospel itself. And this requires constant review in order to maintain the proper priorities.

KNOW YOUR GOSPEL

3 As I urged you when I went into Macedonia—
remain in Ephesus that you may charge some that they
teach no other doctrine,

4 nor give heed to fables and endless genealogies,
which cause disputes rather than godly edification
which is in faith.

5 Now the purpose of the commandment is love
from a pure heart, from a good conscience, and from
unfeigned faith,

6 from which some, having strayed, have turned
aside to idle talk,

7 desiring to be teachers of the law, understanding
neither what they say nor the things which they affirm.

8 But we know that the law is good if one uses
it lawfully,

9 knowing this: that the law is not made for a
righteous person, but for the lawless and
insubordinate, for the ungodly and for sinners, for the
unholy and profane, for murderers of fathers and
murderers of mothers, for manslayers,

10 for fornicators, for sodomites, for kidnappers, for
liars, for perjurers, and if there is any other thing that
is contrary to sound doctrine,

11 according to the glorious gospel of the blessed
God which was committed to my trust.

1 Tim. 1:3–11

In this section, we have another of Paul's many definitions of the Gospel. From the opening sentence (which he never really completed) to the closing phrase, *"the glorious gospel of the blessed God,"* Paul is reviewing with Timothy what the Gospel really is. The strength of this section is in its smooth blending of doctrine and behavior. The Gospel is not only a way of thinking. It is a way of living. And it always involves both doctrine and practice.

Timothy may well have been struggling with the question, known well by most pastors, of whether to continue his ministry in Ephesus. How can he know when it's time to move to another place or type of service? He was fortunate to have the counsel of an intimate and older friend. And Paul was not only giving advice; he also appealed to Timothy to remain in Ephesus. Whether the word Paul used had the force of "urging" is questionable, but he is certainly encouraging Timothy to stay. Paul's reason for this is the need for a strong confrontation with some false teachers who were troubling the church in Ephesus. And Timothy is being called to dig in and stand up to them.

The false teachers were not only deviating from the Gospel as it had been taught by Paul, but they were adding some things referred to as *"fables and endless genealogies."* We cannot be certain what these false teachings really were. To insist that they comprised a well-developed gnosticism, not evident until the second century, is possible but not necessary. They were certainly akin to the Colossian heresies to which Paul has already written. The ultimate problem with the false teaching was that it engendered disputes rather than godly edification. To edify is to build up, and it should be a test of doctrine. How many needless arguments would be avoided if the discussion began with the question, "Does this really build up?"

Too often, doctrinal debate only ends up setting Christians against each other instead of building each other up for our work and witness in the world.

Part of the problem is our insatiable appetite for the new and different. I was asked the other day about a new teaching based upon some system of giving all of the Greek letters a number value and then studying the sums of each word. I couldn't comment on the system, since I had no knowledge of it. But I have to confess a total lack of interest in that kind of thing. There's always a following out there for teachers who develop clever variations of the Gospel, but the bottom line is godly edification, not getting a following.

Christian doctrine can never afford the luxury of *"fables and endless genealogies."* All of the theological debate in the world is never a substitute for the quality of life that flows from doctrine.

With verse 5, Paul spells out more clearly the marks of true teaching. *"Commandment"* probably means more than the law of Moses. More likely, Paul had the whole area of Christian ethics and moral responsibility in mind. Here, the true teacher who really knows and communicates the Gospel will produce love: *"from a pure heart," "from a good conscience," "from sincere faith."*

Here is another magnificent trilogy. Nowhere else does Paul describe the wellsprings of love so vividly. As the Gospel is linked to edification in contrast to speculation, the end product is love. To love God with all of one's heart, soul, and mind, and to love one's neighbor as oneself is always the essence of Christianity.

"A pure heart." The love of which we are speaking flows from a pure heart. Purity of heart has to do basically with motives. Kierkegaard gave us the classic definition: "Purity of heart is to will one thing." The one thing to be willed is the love of God, and the love of God always involves the love of people. Purity of heart may also be equated with hungering and thirsting for righteousness. It is longing, above all else, to do what is pleasing to God, and thus helpful to others.

I'm reading from one well-known commentary that "a pure heart is a heart whose motives are absolutely pure and absolutely unmixed." Then follows a description of one who is prompted only by "love of truth and love of men" so that all behavior is totally like Christ's. When I read such counsels to perfection, I want to run for the nearest exit. I'm enough in touch with myself to know that some of my noblest actions are done from mixed motives. Leading in public prayer gets clouded with my desires to impress others with my ability with words. Even writing this commentary is motivated by some needs less honorable than pure love for God. How do we achieve purity of heart? We don't! At least not in the sense of some perfect state of pure and unselfish motives. But we can know that purity of heart in which the struggle to seek God's will above all else is paramount, even in the midst of our failures and detours, which always cast us back on the grace and mercy of God.

"A good conscience." Again, I feel strongly that we must avoid creating guilt by unrealistic standards of perfection. From the same commentary: "To have a good conscience is to be able to look the knowledge which one shares with no one but oneself in the face, and not to be ashamed of anything in it." Who could possibly claim to be able to do that? Jesus is the only one I know who could make such a claim. A part of a good conscience is to be in touch with our failures—our inability to live up to the best that we know. Since the Gospel

of God's grace has everything to do with forgiveness, we need not pretend that we have no sin. The good conscience comes not from being perfect, but from having nothing hidden from God. Our consciences can rest in God's forgiveness in and through Jesus Christ.

"Sincere faith." A sincere faith is a faith that goes beyond concern for outward appearances. How easy it is for faith to take the form of outward profession. Such a faith is more concerned with being accepted in particular groups than it is with demonstrating a quality of life shaped by Christ. Again, this is not a counsel to perfection. As Paul said in 1 Corinthians 13, even our knowledge and faith is incomplete until that future time when we shall be with Him.

While purity of heart, good conscience, and sincere faith cannot be ours perfectly, to stray or turn aside from them leads to a religion of *"idle talk"* and false teaching. Such teachers are noted for their ability to say things that sound very profound but are not even understood by the teachers themselves. This is the subtle temptation for all of us who engage in scholarly pursuits. The preacher and teacher of the Word of God must ever be mindful that the task of the true teacher is to communicate the Gospel in terms that can be clearly understood.

I recall years ago expressing my frustration after listening to a lecture by an eminent theologian. I said to a learned friend, "I really didn't understand what he was saying." "You're not supposed to," came the reply. "That's what makes him a great theologian!" I disagree. To me, a great theologian is one who can take complex ideas and communicate them in meaningful ways to simple folks. All of us who preach or teach should be required to speak to children on a regular basis. During the Sundays of Advent, I am asked to give a brief message to the children who share in the early part of our worship services. Nothing is more challenging to me than trying to communicate the meaning of Christ to little children. And I've been amazed at how much the adults tell me they've learned from the children's sermons!

As Paul disparages these *"teachers of the law"* for their falsity, he makes it quite clear that he is not devaluing the law which they misrepresent. This is a fine but important point. It is often because of the false teachers that the Word of God is ignored or rejected. The baby gets thrown out with the bath water. With all of his disdain for the false teachers of the law, Paul affirms his high regard for the law itself. By the law, he probably means not only the Ten Commandments, but the whole ethical system which grows out of them as well.

Paul's statement of the value of the law in verse 8 is perfectly consistent with his view of salvation by grace alone through faith in Jesus Christ. To use the law *"lawfully"* is the key to the Gospel. This Greek adverb is used only here and in 2 Timothy 2:5 in the New Testament. It is a way of saying that the law has its place, though a limited one. What follows is another way of saying what Paul said to the Romans: "By the deeds of the law no flesh will be justified in His sight" (Rom. 3:20). The law provides no means to *make* people righteous. The kinds of people listed in verses 9 and 10 are only some examples of the behaviors that stand condemned by the law. This is certainly not an exhaustive list, as indicated by the catch-all phrase with which it ends. Its point is that while such people are clearly declared guilty before God by the law, that's all that the law can do. The law is like a yardstick by which we are measured. It does not have within it the power to change us.

Thus, *"the law is not made for a righteous person,"* is another way of saying that righteous people need no law. Translated into the context of the Gospel, this means that since God declares and makes us righteous through faith in Jesus Christ, we behave according to the law, not out of the fear of being caught or punished, but out of love for God and one another. Our goodness proceeds from the love of God in our hearts, in and through Christ. Our fear is not that of judgment, but only that we might disappoint the One who loves us so.

There is a fine line between keeping the law and legalism in the Gospel of grace. Legalism is intent on keeping the law in order to achieve goodness. It regards morality as an achievement and pursues righteousness as a prize to be won. Inevitably it produces pride and a judgmental spirit toward nonachievers. Keeping the law, however, is a flow of life issuing from God's acceptance of us in Christ. It's as natural for a man or woman in Christ to keep the law as it is for an orange tree to produce oranges. And a right understanding of Christ as the source of our goodness eliminates all grounds of pride and boasting. Pride is replaced with gratitude.

In this remarkable section of the letter, Paul makes it unmistakably clear that the true teacher really knows the Gospel and steadfastly refuses to tamper with it. The essence of the Gospel never changes. It is God's free and gracious gift in Jesus Christ of forgiveness and salvation. It is *"the glorious gospel of the blessed God,"* as committed to Paul's trust (v. 11). To stay with this Gospel, year in and year out, is to be assured that the honeymoon of serving Christ will never be over!

Paul not only models the sustaining power of a strong sense of calling and of a deep commitment to the essentials of the Gospel, but he also demonstrates the power of having come to terms with himself.

KNOW YOURSELF

12 And I thank Christ Jesus our Lord who has enabled me, because He counted me faithful, putting me into the ministry,
13 although I was formerly a blasphemer, a persecutor, and an insolent man; but I obtained mercy because I did it ignorantly in unbelief.
14 And the grace of our Lord was exceedingly abundant, with faith and love which are in Christ Jesus.
15 This is a faithful saying and worthy of all acceptance, that Christ Jesus came into the world to save sinners, of whom I am chief.
16 However, for this reason I obtained mercy, that in me first Jesus Christ might show all longsuffering, as a pattern to those who are going to believe on Him for everlasting life.
17 Now to the King eternal, immortal, invisible, to God who alone is wise, be honor and glory forever and ever. Amen.

1 Tim. 1:12–17

Here is another of Paul's testimonies. D. T. Niles of Ceylon was fond of describing evangelism as "one beggar telling another beggar where he had found bread." No sooner has Paul finished wrestling again with the essence of "the glorious gospel" than he literally explodes into a joyous celebration of his own personal relationship with Christ. Though many years had passed, Paul never got too far away from his conversion experience. And the message that comes through his story is the assurance that if Christ could indeed change him, He can change anyone else.

As the essence of the Gospel is Jesus Himself, so the essence of Christian witness is telling how the story of Jesus has shaped our own stories. Here is part of Paul's story. A blasphemer, a persecutor of the followers of Jesus, and a man of insolent violence who enjoyed inflicting pain upon others, he had been singled out by Jesus Himself for special service in the Kingdom of God.

Dealing with the past. For a long time, the phrase *"But I obtained mercy because I did it ignorantly in unbelief"* was a real enigma to me. It seems to imply that God's mercy was granted to Paul, not solely by grace through faith in Jesus Christ, but on the basis of Paul's ignorance in unbelief. I'm not satisfied that the Greek words hold any hidden meaning that fully resolves this problem. I can only suggest that this was not intended as a theological statement—for it would clearly contradict Paul's understanding of the Gospel. I think rather, that it was a brilliant statement designed as a corrective to a common error in giving testimonies.

Many times I have heard testimonies in which past sins were virtually glorified. Often, the person most sought after on the testimony circuit is the one who has the wildest stories of raunchy behavior to tell. I'll never forget the woeful comment of an outstanding girl in our youth group after we had featured the witness of a former pimp and drug addict: "I guess the only way I could possibly be anybody in Christian witness would be to become a junkie and a prostitute, and *then* get converted!" She had a point because of the way the testimony had glamorized past wickedness.

There's a difference between testifying to God's power to change a person's life and intentionally, or unintentionally, glorifying sin. I choose to read this difficult statement of Paul as pointing to that difference. Having described his past behavior, I hear him saying that there was nothing chic or glamorous about what he had done. As a matter of fact, it was grounded in his unbelief and thus utterly stupid. There's nothing smart or glamorous about sin, whatever form it may take. And let's be careful in our testimonies that we don't make sin appear to be anything other than it is. It is always the product of unbelief—the conscious refusal to trust and obey the loving God. It is always the mark of ignorance, and Paul does not equate ignorance with innocence. Notice that Paul did not go into gory details about his past behavior. He was much more interested in getting to the point of the grace and salvation of Christ. We do well to be on constant guard against glorifying past sins through dwelling on them, pandering to the curiosity of vicarious thrill-seekers.

But the other side needs to be stated. There is nothing in our past that needs to be hidden. Paul has nothing to hide because God has forgiven everything in his past. This doesn't mean that he started every testimony or every conversation with the rehearsal of past sins. But it does mean that he exercised his freedom to share them whenever he felt it appropriate and helpful to his witness.

Exceedingly abundant grace. The only reason for Paul's brief recitation of his past was to show dramatically the unlimited scope of the grace of God in Jesus Christ. Verses 14–17 comprise a staccato hymn of praise and joy. It is good to stay close enough to past sins and failures that we never take for granted God's grace and mercy. Even the word *"abundant"* wasn't big enough to express Paul's gratitude for grace. He added a big adverb to expand it.

Already in the early church, some sayings had developed to express the Gospel in brief and memorable ways. We often call such sayings "clichés." I've heard it said that we should avoid all clichés in communicating the Gospel. While clichés can be trite and objectionable, they can also be powerful instruments that pack a wallop. And sometimes a cliché that works at one time loses its effectiveness later on or in a different setting. The cliché I just used (packs a wallop) may or may not communicate to you what it does to me. I like it, so I used it. Every time we use a cliché, we take a risk. And no one bats 1.000, not even in the Big Leagues.

I think we do best by recognizing Paul's *"saying"* in verse 15 as a cliché. To him, and most likely to Timothy, it was a powerful way of expressing a world of theology in ten words or less. "Christ Jesus" expresses precisely what the Gospel is all about. Christianity is Jesus Himself. And reference to Christianity which is not explicitly or implicitly tied to Jesus simply is not Christian.

"Came into the world" is a concise statement of incarnational theology. If Paul was confronting some type of gnosticism, this indeed was the ultimate rebuttal. Any understanding of God that separates Him from the world is not Christian. Some of the earliest Christian heresies were grounded in the denial that Jesus was truly human. The Gospel is grounded in the inexplicable mystery of Emmanuel: God with us, among us, for us, and in us.

"To save sinners" is Paul's succinct way of stating the bottom line of the Gospel. Jesus did not come into the world to develop new theological or ethical systems. He did not come into the world to make good people better. He did not come into the world to found

a new religious establishment. Nor did He come into the world to create a new social order. Some or all of these things, of necessity, have been shaped and formed because of His coming.

But He came into the world to save sinners. Period!

"Of whom I am chief" was Paul's way of declaring, not that he had committed all or the worst of sins, but that he was as needy of God's salvation as the worst or the best person by any standard. In that sense, all of us are fellow-chiefs with Paul.

Here it is for all time—a faithful saying, a powerful cliché. Like all sayings, it can suffer from overuse or misuse. And it can be abused by casual or trivial use. But, to me, it's a cliché that's worth keeping— dare I say?—on the front burner!

Paul cites the grace of Jesus Christ operating in his life as a *"pattern"* to those yet to come to faith in Christ. The word that he uses is the word that we would use for a prototype model. A few years ago, a friend of mine in aircraft design showed me a model of the Lockheed L-1011. On a recent flight, I sat in seat 20-7 (economy class) of an L-1011 enroute from New York to Los Angeles. I never board this type of airplane without remembering that model, which was the pattern upon which all of the aircraft of this type were built.

Paul saw the grace of God in salvation for him as the prototype for every human being. I think we have every right to take this a step farther and say that every man and woman in Christ becomes yet another prototype for someone else. If God can redeem Paul from his guilty past, He can save me. If God can save me from my broken and futile past, He can redeem you. Our churches and groups are the design studios where the models are being developed for people around us to see what God can do to create order out of chaos, beauty out of ugliness, and love out of indifference in these sinful lives of ours.

As is a pattern with Paul, he gives us a benediction with no intention of concluding the letter. I can't read this one without bursting into song:

> Immortal, invisible, God only wise,
> In light inaccessible hid from our eyes,
> Most blessed, most glorious, the Ancient of Days,
> Almighty, victorious, Thy great name we praise.
> Walter Chalmers Smith

This apostle certainly hasn't lost the glow after all these years of ministry. For him the honeymoon is far from over because he kept in touch with himself—past, present, and future.

The glow was perpetual with Paul because he knew his calling, he knew his Gospel, and he knew himself. And he never lost sight of his mission in life. In the closing words of this great chapter, Paul calls Timothy to the same sense of mission that had been his own for all of those years since his encounter with the risen Lord on the Damascus road.

KNOW YOUR MISSION

18 This charge I commit to you, son Timothy, according to the prophecies previously made concerning you, that by them you may wage the good warfare,

19 holding faith and a good conscience, which some having rejected, concerning the faith have suffered shipwreck,

20 of whom are Hymenaeus and Alexander, whom I have delivered to Satan that they may learn not to blaspheme.

1 Tim. 1:18–20

The commissioning. We'll probably never know exactly what Paul meant by *"the prophecies previously made concerning you."* It's likely that there had been some formal act of commissioning or ordaining with the laying on of hands, setting Timothy apart for his particular ministry. I like to think that this happened in his home church in Lystra as he accepted Paul's invitation to the missionary partnership. Prophecy was regarded as a gift of the Holy Spirit in which a person was given a word for the community or for an individual. Like all things of value, it was subject to counterfeits and misuse, but it was ranked by Paul second only to love (1 Cor. 13–14). It appears that in his ordaining or commissioning, some of those who were present had been given prophecies for Timothy.

We must not think of prophecy here primarily as a prediction. Though we tend to use the word in that sense, prophecy was more commonly an exhortation or an encouragement, which would have certain consequences for obedience or rejection. To some degree, then, prophecy was predictive. Do this, and you will live. Do that, and you will suffer. But to prophesy was not a matter of forecasting the future, certainly not with regard to the return of Christ.

The prophecies that had been given to Timothy were affirmed by Paul as a source of strength. Probably the closest thing that we have to this comes in the charge to the candidate in our service of ordination. I recall vividly and specifically some of the exhortations given to me by Dr. Charles Fuller in my ordination service. To me, they were words of prophecy, and I have drawn on them for strength and renewal many times.

I wish we could incorporate this beautiful concept of commissioning and the prophetic word much more widely into our life in the churches. To limit this kind of experience only to those who are ordained as ministers of the Word is much too exclusive. Many of us also include this in the ordination of elders and deacons, but even this ignores the fact that every person in Christ is called to a life of ministry.

Some of our churches rightly affirm baptism and reception into church membership as a commissioning to ministry. Sadly, however, these moments are observed so routinely, and with such a lack of expectation, that they rarely ignite any fires. Why not a service of commissioning for our Sunday school teachers and youth leaders? Why not a service of commissioning for men and women who truly want their lives to be a ministry for Christ at work and in their neighborhoods? Why not a service of commissioning for those going out to make evangelism calls or stewardship visitations? Why not a service of commissioning for those who sing in the choir? And why not the laying on of hands and prophecies in every commissioning?

Recently, I had the privilege of returning to East Africa for what has become an annual visit to lead in pastors' conferences in Uganda, Kenya, and Tanzania. In our staff meeting two days before my departure, my colleagues initiated a time of prayer and commissioning for this mission. As I knelt in their midst, they laid their hands upon me with their prayers. As I write these words, I am in Nairobi, having completed three conferences and about to begin another. The power of that commissioning is felt each day and is a constant source of renewal.

There is strength to be found in such living traditions!

The command. In a military metaphor, Paul's command is given to his young lieutenant. No glorification of militarism need be drawn from this command, but the simple fact is that those who choose to take Christ seriously in the common rounds and relationships of daily life will readily discover that there is an enemy, and there is a battle. No less than ten times in recent years I've returned to *The Screwtape Letters* by C. S. Lewis. This is a contemporary Christian classic and should be required reading for every believer. To wage good warfare requires a realistic appraisal of the nature of the battle and the strategy of the enemy. While preoccupation with the enemy can lead to despair, to ignore the enemy is to invite disaster.

And how is the battle waged? Not with physical might, but with *"faith and a good conscience."* Had Paul not previously written Ephesians 6:10–20, he probably would have inscribed it here. Ours is a spiritual battle and the weapons are spiritual. We go forth with faith in God. Faith in His grace, His goodness, His redemptive love for the world. Living by that faith sets us free from the guilt of a cluttered conscience, for by His grace we are forgiven, and nothing need be hidden.

The caution. Even in the exhilaration of the commissioning and the command, a word of caution is in order. We don't know who Hymenaeus and Alexander were, and we have no knowledge of the details of their shipwrecked faith. Whatever they did must have been terribly upsetting to Paul to warrant his action toward them, "whom I delivered to Satan." Again, care must be taken for we really don't know what he meant by this. Many explanations have been suggested, but all have to go beyond what we can know from the text.

The most important thing to note is that the delivering to Satan was redemptive in its intent. Though some separation from active fellowship in the life of the church seems to be implied, there is still the hope that they will be restored as they *"learn not to blaspheme."*

The whole question of church discipline is raised with this statement, as it is in other parts of Paul's letters. Generally speaking, discipline is almost nonexistent in most of our churches, except in cases of extreme, usually sexual, immorality. And it is more likely to be exercised upon the clergy than upon the membership of the church. A church that does not exercise some discipline of its members and leaders loses strength and vitality. When the church consists of people who can pretty much come and go as they please, give of themselves as much or as little as they wish, and do virtually whatever they want to do, we can hardly call it the family of God, much less an army of the Lord.

On the other hand, when church discipline becomes harsh and

punitive, losing its goal of reconciliation and restoration, it can have devastating results. The reasons effective church discipline has come to ebbtide in most of our churches are rooted in previous abuses. Frequently, in the 1800s and early 1900s, church discipline was applied judgmentally and legalistically with little concern for redemption. Situations not unlike that of the woman taken in adultery (John 8:1–11) were enacted again and again. Harsh treatment of people with alcohol problems before the nature of alcoholism was understood was not uncommon. Our aversion to discipline in maintaining some level of standards for church membership is, partially at least, a reaction against unfeeling misuse of discipline in our past.

But this is no basis for dispensing with discipline altogether. The time has come to reexamine this whole matter of church discipline. Hopefully, with our understanding of the church as a caring, redemptive, healing fellowship of fellow-sinners, we can recover the positive values of church discipline without returning to the horrendous and heartless practices of the past.

Let this chapter from Paul be our constant and continuing affirmation that the honeymoon of Christian discipleship and service need never end. By knowing our calling, our Gospel, ourselves, and our mission, we can live day by day in a growing and joyous marriage with Christ and one another.

Let the honeymoon continue!

CHAPTER TWO

The Life and Worship of the Church

1 Timothy 2:1—3:13

"Let all things be done decently and in order" (1 Cor. 14:40). So Paul ended his instructions to the Corinthians, where worship services had become sources of confusion and conflict rather than renewal and unity. One of my friends is fond of saying, "People sure have a way of lousing things up!" And the church is not exempt. From the beginning, dealing with conflict and tension has been a part of being involved in a church. Even something seemingly as simple as worshiping God together can become a battleground.

We only make matters worse if we project our wish-dreams for our ideal human society onto the church. I began my Christian journey in the fellowship of folks who idealized New Testament Christianity. The "New Testament Church" was our way of referring to a church that was pure in its motives, programs, and relationships. As time passed, I discovered that the quest for this pure church was like hunting for grunion in the High Sierras. I abandoned my search for the perfect church when I accepted the fact that the New Testament Church itself was far from perfect. Even that first church of the twelve, in the presence of Jesus Himself, couldn't get it all together.

The fact that Paul had to appeal for things to be done decently and in order obviously meant that things were being done indecently and out of order. We might expect that in a wild place like the seaport town of Corinth. But in Ephesus? If there was one church in which Paul invested more of himself than any other, it was in Ephesus. He had lived and taught there for two years (Acts 19:10). He had sent his most trusted associate, Timothy, to be their pastor. And yet there were problems in their life and worship—problems relating to prayer, to the behavior of some women in the church, and to the standards and conduct of bishops and deacons. It is because

Paul dealt with those practical matters of congregational life that this letter is rightly called a "pastoral Epistle."

CAN PRAYER CHANGE THE WORLD?

1 Therefore I exhort first of all that supplications, prayers, intercessions, and giving of thanks be made for all men,
2 for kings and all who are in authority, that we may lead a quiet and peaceable life in all godliness and reverence.
3 For this is good and acceptable in the sight of God our Savior,
4 who desires all men to be saved and to come to the knowledge of the truth.
5 For there is one God and one Mediator between God and men, the Man Christ Jesus,
6 who gave Himself a ransom for all, to be testified in due time,
7 for which I was appointed a preacher and an apostle—I am speaking the truth in Christ and not lying—a teacher of the Gentiles in faith and truth.
8 Therefore I desire that the men pray everywhere, lifting up holy hands, without wrath and doubting;

1 Tim. 2:1–8

Since Paul had digressed from the main thought of his charge to Timothy in 1:19 and 20, he uses a *"therefore"* to tie what follows to his continuing concern for the quality of Timothy's pastoral leadership in Ephesus.

It's best to begin by observing that the central theological thrust of the paragraph is not so much on prayer as on the universality of the Gospel. The phrase *"first of all"* is to be read in the sense of "as of primary importance." In other words, of all the pastoral advice that is to follow, this is the most important. And what is important is not just to pray in corporate worship, but to pray for *"all men."* The emphasis is unmistakable—*"all men"* (v. 1), *"all men"* (v. 4), *"for all"* (v. 6).

The close connection that Paul makes between the universality of the Gospel and prayer in public worship is far-reaching in its implications. The all-too-typical pastoral prayer in corporate worship can hardly be said to be of first importance. And it certainly can't be regarded as a vital force in changing the world. Paul is reaching for something much deeper than mere liturgy. He is calling us to radical change in life and worship.

The kind of prayer to which Paul is calling us can indeed change the world. But it's going to have to be something radically different from just saying eloquent prayers in public worship.

Paul's logic is at its best. If we are really to pray for all people, we must believe that God loves them all without distinction and that Christ's sacrifice on the cross was indeed on behalf of all. It's difficult for us to appreciate the struggle that those early Jewish followers of Jesus had with this. Imagine being raised in the tradition in which the world was divided into two camps, Jew and Gentile, the children of light and the children of darkness, and then, through faith in Christ, learning that God loves all people and that the old distinctions are invalid. It took a lot of doing to work out this new reality in which Jew and Gentile, slave and free, male and female, educated and uneducated are called to live together in a fellowship that seeks and accepts all people alike.

As a matter of fact, we haven't worked it out yet. The churches in America, for the most part, merely reflect the social, ethnic, and cultural distinctions of the world around us. It's obvious that the world has shaped the church more than the church has impacted the world. This is not to accuse the churches of creating or of consciously perpetuating ethnic, cultural, and economic segregation. That's just the way things are.

As I've come to know the pastors and people of hundreds of churches in East Africa, I have come to appreciate the complexities of their struggles with the divisive forces of ancient tribalism. Even in the Church of Uganda, where the Holy Spirit has been mightily at work through the Revival, a renewal movement which began in 1936, tribal divisions continue to be a source of tension. Baganda, Munyoro, Muganda, Bahororo, Karamajong all have great difficulty overcoming centuries of ill feelings and strained relationships. The great witness of the Church of Uganda is in those places where the power of Christ to create unity and love across tribal divisions is clearly demonstrated.

Now, I've never met anyone who professed a belief that God only desired the salvation of the rich, the educated, the whites, or the males. I've never heard anyone preach that Christ gave Himself as a ransom only for a particular group or tribe of people. Not even in South Africa. In a recent visit there, I was privileged to have lunch with a member of Parliament who was a staunch advocate of the official state doctrine of apartheid, the enforced separation of the races. An elder in his church, and a student of church history, he held strongly that salvation is for all, black and white alike, and we had no theological disagreement at that point. I think we've all pretty well covered that ground and agree that salvation in Christ is offered to all men and women without distinction.

But how long can we go on saying one thing and doing another? Whether it's in South Africa, Sri Lanka, South Korea, or Southern California, the church rarely looks any different from the community center or country club nearby. Can we really pray and give thanks for all people if we're not actively seeking to enter into active relationships with them? Can we really proclaim that God desires all people to be saved as long as they stay in their own places as determined by race, sex, or money? Can we offer the Gospel of Christ's redemption to all without offering ourselves? Absolutely not!

It is evident that churches have allowed the world around them to control their agendas. The "homogeneous unit" principle of church growth is a fact. Churches that slant their appeal to their own kind are the churches that most often grow in numbers. Churches in America that reflect the culture of affluence and success are more likely to be successful. Churches like the one I serve would not tolerate any thought of a Gospel exclusively for well-educated, successful whites. But if someone from another planet were to visit us on a Sunday morning, they would have to get the impression that we are rather exclusive.

So what can we do? First, we can admit to the reality of our own indifference. We can stop ignoring the problem. As long as we defend our segregated churches on the grounds that there are no ethnics in our neighborhood or no poor people in our community, we simply perpetuate our own unwritten code of apartheid. There can be no forgiveness, healing, or change without the admission that we have a problem. We call this confession.

The step that follows confession is repentance, and that means a conscious change of direction. There is built-in resistance to change in all human behavior patterns. If you don't believe it, try to correct the slice in your golf swing. I am troubled that the church I serve doesn't really want to change in this area. It seems that we really don't want to be an all-inclusive church. If we did, our people probably wouldn't have moved to our suburban community in the first place. We prefer to be with our own kind. We are uncomfortable around folks who don't think, talk, and look like us. We really have to decide whether we want to change. So far, I don't see any dramatic changes in the offing. But certainly no change will ever occur until we begin with genuine confession and repentance. And I don't see how we can go on affirming the universality of the Gospel without trying to demonstrate it in actual relationships. To accept things the way they are is to continue to allow the world around us to write our agenda.

And how do we apply the universality of the Gospel to the incredibly complex problems of nationalism, militarism, and warfare? To return to Paul's logic: if we are really to pray for all people, we must believe that God loves them all without distinction, and that Christ's sacrifice on the cross was indeed on behalf of all.

Can we sincerely pray for the salvation of people at the same time that we are arming to kill them? The basic problem that I feel in addressing this question is the confusion that exists in our categories. It's as though we were trying to play basketball by the rules of football. The technology of warfare has moved rapidly in a short time. Our thinking has not caught up with the realities.

The ultimate example of this is talking about winning or surviving a nuclear war. The press recently carried reports of an evacuation plan for Southern California in the event of a nuclear attack. In the first place, anyone who drives the freeways at rush hour will attest to the impossibility of such a mass evacuation of more than five million people on what would most likely be less than thirty minutes' notice! One of our officials even said that one could survive by digging a hole and covering it with a wooden door and a lot of dirt! Our thinking has not caught up with technology. The old categories of shields to ward off spears, steel helmets to deflect bullets, and thick walls to resist cannonballs are no longer applicable.

It seems to me that's where our theories of deterrence break down. The fact is that technology has advanced beyond the point of capable defenses. This is true with the new breed of conventional weapons as well as with nuclear weapons. Official estimates are that a conventional war, involving Russia and the United States, if fought in western Europe would produce 500,000 military casualties in the first sixty days. To the United States, this would mean more casualties than we suffered in World War II and Vietnam combined. Remember, this is in just two months, without the use of nuclear weapons. And I haven't even mentioned the diabolical potentials, not so openly discussed, already developed for chemical and biological warfare. If you confront these realities openly and honestly, you may need more than a glass of warm milk to go to sleep tonight.

The maintenance of military strength with some equivalence among the superpowers is a fact of life in a sinful world. But the world arms race, in which each superpower has the capability of destroying the other thirty times over, is a stark symptom of technology out of control and far beyond our thinking. And perhaps the greatest danger to the world will come from a small country with nuclear capability and a dictator accountable to no responsible political process.

There can be no question in my mind that we as Christians must address these questions of nationalism, militarism, and warfare, not only because of their urgency and complexity, but also because of our beliefs as set forth in this passage. We are to pray for all people, especially political authorities *"that we may lead a quiet and peaceable life in all godliness and reverence."* And the reason that this is of first importance is that God desires the salvation of all people, and Christ gave Himself as a ransom for all people.

It is this universality of God's love and Christ's death for all people that calls us to a new way of thinking and a newer way of living. Where will the initiative arise for a new ideology if not from the Gospel? And where will the message of God's love for all people without distinction be heard, if not from the church? The old competitive nationalisms, with their seeds of the destruction of humankind, must be challenged by Christians in every country. The insane pursuit of military expansion and adventurism must be exposed by the prophetic voice of the churches in every land. The disobedience to the Word of God entailed in the squandering of our resources on weapons of war while millions of the people whom God loves are starving places us clearly under God's inescapable judgment.

To be silent or complacent in an hour such as this is to part company with Isaiah, Jeremiah, Amos, and all of the prophets, and also with Jesus. To allow any nationalism to control the agenda of the church is too tragic a failure to even contemplate. I see no way to talk about the universality of the Gospel, as Paul does here, without speaking out against the thought of sending millions of people into an eternity without Christ at the push of a button or the spray of a nozzle.

Can prayer change the world? I believe that it can. But not just by saying eloquent prayers in public. Paul closes our paragraph with the key in verse 8. He calls the men to *"pray everywhere, lifting up holy hands, without wrath and doubting."* Most commentaries break the paragraphs between verses 7 and 8. I feel strongly that verse 8 is the conclusion of the previous paragraph.

The picture of lifting holy hands not only harks back to the ancient Jewish traditions; it is also a picture of coming before God with clean hands and a pure heart. How can we lift holy hands to God if we are not actively seeking to relate to all men and women, whom He loves without distinction? How can we lift holy hands to God if we are not speaking and working for the reduction and elimination of the forces and weapons poised to destroy the very people God loves and for whom Christ died? To raise holy hands, without wrath and doubting, is clearly of first importance in our worship agenda. Such is the prayer and the worship that could change the world.

When I reflect upon the prophets of the Old Testament, I often raise the question, why did God choose a particular nation, as He did Israel, to be His chosen people? They preferred to think of their election as a privilege, but the prophets saw it as a responsibility. The divine call and love, while indeed a privilege, must always be regarded as an awesome responsibility.

And why does God work through a particular people such as Israel then, and the new Israel, the church, now? I believe He does this in order to show to everyone else, through those chosen people, what His design for life, His love for all people, really is.

When Israel allowed the world around it to write its agenda, it failed to show the world God's agenda. When we allow the world around us to control our agenda to fit its prejudices, its nationalisms, and its militarisms, we have failed to show our world that God desires all to be saved and that Christ gave Himself a ransom for all.

Saying prayers in public worship becomes an object of God's scorn where those prayers are not expressions of the universality of the Gospel in word and deed. How shocked were the people and priests when Amos presented God as saying:

> "I hate, I despise your feasts,
>   and I take no delight in your solemn assemblies.

Even though you offer me your burnt offerings
and cereal offerings,
I will not accept them,
and the peace offerings of your fatted beasts
I will not look upon.
Take away from Me the noise of your
songs;
to the melody of your harps I will not listen.
But let justice run down like waters,
and righteousness like an everflowing stream."

Amos 5:21–24 (RSV)

Prayer can change the world, but it's going to have to be a way of praying different from merely saying prayers.

TROUBLING QUESTIONS ABOUT WOMEN IN THE CHURCH

I've been around long enough to remember reading this passage without batting an eyebrow. More than any other time in Christian history, this passage, along with others like 1 Corinthians 11:2–16; 14:34–35; and 1 Peter 3:1–6 cannot be read without causing many temperatures to rise.

9 in like manner also, that the women adorn
themselves in modest apparel, with propriety and
moderation, not with braided hair or gold or pearls
or costly clothing,
10 but, which is proper for women professing
godliness, with good works.
11 Let a woman learn in silence with all submission.
12 And I do not permit a woman to teach or to
have authority over a man, but to be in silence.
13 For Adam was formed first, then Eve.
14 And Adam was not deceived, but the woman
being deceived, fell into transgression.
15 Nevertheless she will be saved in childbearing
if they continue in faith, love, and holiness, with self-
control.

1 Tim. 2:9–15

Before we examine the text itself, it's important to establish some ground rules on how we will read it. Let me suggest three:

1. We must read the passage in the light of all other Scripture. It is not the purpose of this commentary to present a thorough technical study, but the serious student may begin with Genesis 1:26–28, 2:18–25, 3:1–24 and work through numerous passages, all pertaining to our understanding of male and female. Simplistic generalizations barring women from public ministry have no place, for instance, when Priscilla is called by Paul "a fellow worker in Christ Jesus" (Rom. 16:3), and when Euodia and Syntyche are referred to as "these women who labored with me in the gospel, with Clement also, and the rest of my fellow workers" (Phil. 4:3). The whole of Scripture must be considered in the interpretation of any given passage.

2. We must distinguish between passages that describe events or practices at the time, and those that clearly teach principles designed for universal and timeless application. This ground rule is extremely important, for example, in the Gospels and in the Book of Acts. It's one thing to read that Jesus turned water into wine, but that is no indication that we are called to do the same in the continuing life of the church. Similarly, just because certain things happened as described in the Book of Acts, does not necessarily mean that they are to be regular patterns in the church. It may not be easy to decide whether a given passage was intended primarily as narrative or teaching or both. But the question must be considered.

3. We must read the passage within its cultural, social, and historical setting. It shouldn't startle anyone to be told that the Bible was written by real people, struggling with real problems, in real places and times. To read it with first century eyeglasses and hear it through twentieth century headsets is not always easy. But that is our task and privilege.

With these ground rules established, let's play ball. As stated before, I choose to relate verse 8 to the previous paragraph, but verse 9 clearly contains a continuity of thought. Remember, the original text did not have sentence or paragraph divisions. I see the *"in like manner"* saying in effect that as the men are to lead in public prayer, not just by the words that are spoken, but with "holy hands" by the quality of their lives, so the women are to show their faith both by their outward dress and by their good works. The paragraph deals with three themes: clothing and Christian witness (9–10), leadership in the church (11–12), and the Fall revisited (13–15).

Clothing and Christian witness (vv. 9–10). In Paul's mind, which was steeped in the Scriptures, any description of a virtuous woman had to reflect Proverbs 31:10–31. No passage in the Bible, or perhaps in all ancient literature, exalts a woman with higher praise. The woman of that passage is no shrinking violet, blending into the wallpaper. Of her it was said, "strength and honor are her clothing; . . . Charm is deceitful and beauty is vain, but a woman who fears the Lord, she shall be praised" (Prov. 31:25, 30).

The issue before us is that of values: what makes a person valuable, and what should a person hold valuable? Paul addresses the issue specifically for women. This could well indicate that Paul was confronting a problem that had arisen on the local scene. Perhaps some of the women in the church in Ephesus had begun to use their new freedom in Christ wrongly. This reality of their new freedom must not be overlooked.

Here is where an understanding of the social and cultural background of the New Testament period is essential. Christians in Ephesus were from both Jewish and Greek backgrounds. In the Jewish tradition, a woman was regarded more as a piece of property than as a person. She was without rights or power. In spite of the honor given to her in such a passage as Proverbs 31, in actual practice outside of the home, she was not regarded as a person. There was a Jewish prayer in which the man thanked God that he was not a Gentile, a slave, or a woman. One could have lovely daughters, but a marriage without a male heir was considered a disaster.

Women were also held to be nonpersons on the Greek side of the ledger. The life of the Greek woman was confined mostly to the home. And even at home, she was her husband's property. She lived in her own quarters and did not appear in public alone. She was rarely involved in community meetings or activities. Though there were some women in business, such as Lydia in Philippi (Acts 16:14), they were the exceptions and not the rule.

I first experienced this view of women in a visit to Afghanistan in 1970. For the most part, the streets and bazaars were filled with men. I never saw a woman alone in public, and most of the women wore traditional long tentlike dresses and veils. In a dinner in an Afghan home, only the men gathered around the table and we were served by the young men of the household, though I assumed the mother and daughters were in the kitchen preparing the meal. As we left the home, the wife was brought to the door to greet us— and she was veiled. To be sure, those traditions are changing throughout the world, largely due to Western influence, but they can still be found in many countries, especially in Muslim culture.

One group of women in the New Testament period who did appear outside of the home were the sacred prostitutes. In Corinth, the Temple of Aphrodite boasted a thousand of them, and their activities were not confined to the Temple. It may have been difficult to walk the streets of Corinth without being confronted by some of them. In Ephesus, the Temple of Diana had hundreds of sacred prostitutes. Prostitution was regarded as a form of worship to some of the gods.

What we must realize is that when a woman became a Christian, she was, for the very first time in her life, regarded fully as a human being. The way in which Paul singled out women and preached to them (Acts 16:13) was a radical departure from Jewish and Greek culture. Treating a slave girl as a human being landed Paul in prison (Acts 16:16–24). From the very beginning, women were sought and accepted in the fellowship. When Mark underscored the fact that there were a number of women who traveled with Jesus, he was pointing to something very different and significant about the ministry of Jesus. And, of course, Paul summed up this radical difference that the Gospel made: "There is neither male nor female; for you are all one in Christ Jesus" (Gal. 3:28). Does this obliterate all distinctions between male and female and make the Christian community unisex? Of course not! But it does make a clean break with all cultural mores based upon some assumed inherent superiority of male over female.

What does all of this have to do with clothing and Christian witness? A great deal. As women received their liberation in Christ from the old Hebrew and Greek suppressions, we have to believe that some of them went beyond the boundaries of common sense in expressing their new-found freedom and power. And one of the ways they announced their new-found status could well have been in the way they dressed and fixed their hair. That's still a way that women work off some of their frustrations. Going out to buy a new outfit and stopping at the hairdresser on the way home is sometimes good therapy. But if a woman, or a man for that matter, starts measuring personal worth by the clothing worn and the outward appearance, it becomes a case of misplaced values.

The old cliché "Clothes make the man" applies to women as well. But, all it can really mean within the bounds of healthy values is that clothing is often the first statement we make about who we are to those who do not know us. If I wear my painting clothes to the first day of a new class that I teach at the seminary, I will be thought of quite differently than if I wear a jacket and tie. When I arrive to begin a conference with pastors in Uganda, I don't wear shorts and a T-shirt. As people get to know me, what I wear might not make a great deal of difference in their opinion of me. But I cannot separate my clothing from what I want to say about myself.

Because clothing says something about the person wearing it, it is related to Christian witness. If the newly liberated women in the church at Ephesus were coming to the meetings in all kinds of finery and lavish accessories, they were making a statement as to what this new Christian community believes about values. Extravagance and ostentation are always to be avoided, partly as our witness to our belief that our money should be used, not for selfish consumption, but for the Kingdom of God.

And let's be willing to struggle with all of the ambiguities that this matter presents. Customs and fashions vary from time to time and place to place. On a tour group in Israel, one of our women was a good representative of accepted clothing styles in Southern California. Her sundresses and halter tops would raise no questions at one of our weekday Bible study groups. But in Israel? She was not allowed to enter the shrines and holy places. I overheard a comment from a local, "She looks like a prostitute!" No one would say that of her at home. But in another culture, her clothing made a different statement.

It may well have been that the Christian women in Ephesus were looking more like prostitutes than like newly redeemed children of God. Could it be that in many of our churches on Sunday mornings we look more like commercials for the American image of success than like people concerned with the hungry and naked of the world?

Paul's admonition to the women at Ephesus needs to be heard by us all. Our culture drives us to place all too much value on outward appearance. We need to be reminded that God looks upon the heart. We are each of infinite value, not on the basis of what we wear or own, but on the basis of God's love for us. We should thus hold valuable, not the things on which price tags are so readily placed, but those things which are eternal. To adorn ourselves with good works is the best fashion advice ever given.

Leadership in the church (vv. 11–12). It's my guess that these two verses will continue to be a source of disagreement among Christians for a long time to come. Our convictions and traditions in the matter of women in leadership in the church are often deeply imbedded and strongly felt. I have some Christian friends who will have nothing to do with a church that ordains women to leadership positions. I have other Christian friends who would have nothing to do with a church that doesn't. I find myself praying that we'll find a way to love one another across this battleline and stop fighting each other for the sake of our common mission to the world.

However, I have to express my conviction that if we read this passage and its companion in 1 Corinthians 14:34–35 in the light of our three ground rules, we will be able to come to some reasonable conclusions.

As is true in all of his letters, Paul is addressing specific people and specific situations. Rarely do we have access to the actual problems. But is it not safe to assume that some of these newly liberated women in Christ had become overly aggressive in the meetings of the congregation? The Jewish woman had never been allowed to read the Scriptures in the synagogue or to teach in a school. In the temple at Jerusalem, she could only go as far as the outer court. (To this day, she is confined to a smaller section of the Western Wall in Jerusalem.) The Greek woman had rarely had an opportunity to be heard by anyone outside of her home.

It would be difficult for me to believe that some of the women in this new and exhilarating climate of the Gospel wouldn't get carried away. It doesn't take much imagination to visualize a scene in which a few women seized power and were dominating the leadership and worship of the church in Corinth and in Ephesus. There's no indication that such problems existed in places such as Thessalonica, Philippi, or Rome. In fact, as we have already seen, Paul referred to women in Rome and Philippi as "fellow workers."

What the interpreter must decide, then, is the scope of application. Were these only local situations that needed the drastic remedy that Paul prescribed, or was Paul setting forth a universal rule to be applied in all churches, in all places? I prefer the former. This preference seems to be supported by Paul's use of the first person singular in verse 12. Paul is clearly referring to his personal practice. It seems to me that this practice is to be limited rather than universal in the church.

And, by the way, the admonition to the women to learn in silence isn't bad pedagogical advice for men either. How else does most learning take place? I get the feeling that Paul was addressing some women who had lost the art of listening. Coming out of the deprivations that had long been imposed upon them, they had a lot to learn, a lot of catching up to do. They needed to do a lot of listening, and thus the appeal to *"learn in silence with all submission"* may not have sounded to them the way it sounds to us. I prefer to hear it as good pedagogical advice in that particular setting, a corrective to some local abuses which could occur anywhere, anytime.

Before we leave this subject, I need to express a conviction and a hope. My conviction is that we have no basis for relegating women to subservient roles in the church on the basis of the whole of Scripture. Functional roles are not clearly established by the New Testament. The long history of the emergence of different structures and officers in the churches certainly attests to the fact that no single pattern is set forth in the Scriptures. To take the Bible seriously must mean that we begin with the creation of male and female, *both* in the image of God. It must also mean that we honor the gifts of the Holy Spirit given to all believers. To restrict the recognition of such gifts on the basis of sexuality is hardly consistent with Paul's classic statement: "There is neither male nor female; for you are one in Christ Jesus" (Gal. 3:28).

My hope is that we will grow in our ability to love and respect one another in our differences. I want to grow in my willingness to accept those who insist on a universal application of what I consider to be a local and historical matter. At the same time, I pray that those who differ will recognize that we take the Scripture no less seriously in departing from the traditional views of all-male leadership in the church. To make this matter a test of orthodoxy can only be detrimental to the Body of Christ.

The Fall revisited (vv. 13–15). The third, and by far the most complex, issue raised in this paragraph is Paul's view of woman in relationship to the Fall. Even as I say "Paul's view," I recognize the fairness of pointing out that the statements in verses 13 and 14 were probably representative of the prevailing view of the rabbis at that time. The same idea is expressed in 1 Corinthians 11:8–9, in which the fact that man was created first, and that woman was created from the man, is said to establish man's priority and superiority over the woman. The rabbis also added that though woman was second in creation, she was the first to sin.

It need not be surprising that Paul reflected the view of the Fall which prevailed in his time. To make this a case for the inherent inferiority of women is neither necessary nor good. This is not the only passage by Paul which presents us with difficulty. His allegorical treatment of Sarah and Hagar, with Hagar corresponding to Mount Sinai and the earthly Jerusalem in contrast to the heavenly Jerusalem (Sarah) (Gal. 4:21–31), is not as clear as we might wish. Likewise, his argument in Romans 11 and the statement that "all Israel will be saved" (11:26) is a source of continuing difficulty, and interpreters have been unable to agree upon a universally acceptable solution.

Rather than make a case for a rigid view of the inferiority and subservience of women, why not place this passage in the category of those remarkably few statements of Paul which best be admitted to be beyond our grasp? There's no question in my mind that it reflects a debatable view. To argue that the sequence of the creation narrative teaches the superiority of the man certainly goes beyond anything said in Genesis.

Two classic statements in Matthew Henry's eighteenth century commentary are worth recalling: "Eve's being made after Adam, and out of him, puts an honor upon that sex, as the glory of man, (1 Cor. 11:7). If man is the head, she is the crown. . . . The man was dust refined, but the woman was dust double-refined, one remove further from the earth." The second has been more widely quoted: ". . . not made out of his head to rule over him, nor out of his feet to be trampled upon by him, but out of his side to be equal with him, under his arm to be protected, and near his heart to be beloved."

While the traditional view didn't leave much hope for the woman, we can be grateful to Paul for daring to go beyond that view in verse 15. Unfortunately, scholars still can't agree on what he meant. The exhortation to women to continue in *"faith, love, and holiness, with self-control"* applies to men as well and expresses the norm for Christian living. What is perhaps the most difficult phrase in the pastorals, however, is *"she will be saved in childbearing"* (v. 15). A number of interpretations have been suggested.

Some of them have to do with the meaning of the word for *"saved"* used here. To make childbirth a means or requirement for being saved is clearly inconsistent with Paul's view of salvation "by grace through faith in Jesus Christ" (Eph. 2:8–9). But the Greek word for *"saved"* is not used in the New Testament exclusively in the sense of spiritual salvation. It is also used to mean "health or wholeness." It is used in the Gospels in connection with Jesus' healings. But even if it is taken in that sense here, we still have the implication that women can find true wholeness only through bearing children. Many single women would testify otherwise.

A more ancient interpretation emphasizes the presence of the definite article in the Greek text before *"childbearing."* Here, the reading is *"the childbearing,"* meaning the birth of Jesus by Mary. If Paul wanted to say that the salvation of women would come by the birth of Jesus, this was an awkward and obscure way of saying it.

Others tie the statement to Genesis 3:15, in which, after the Fall, it is said that the seed of the woman would crush the serpent's head. This, again, is a variation of the messianic theme above.

Yet another approach is to regard motherhood in general as a very wholesome and health-giving experience, reinforcing the traditional view of the Hebrew and Greek cultures that woman's basic value was in giving birth to children and raising them.

I'm convinced that the meaning of these verses will never be resolved and that we do well to accept our limitations in interpreting them.

As Paul has begun these practical instructions for the life and worship of the church, it is certainly clear that he did not intend to deliver a comprehensive manual of polity and worship. He is only addressing some specific needs in that particular situation, out of which comes helpful guidance for the churches in all times.

He will now turn to questions about officers and leaders in the church.

THE OFFICE OF BISHOP

1 This is a true saying: If a man desires the position of a bishop, he desires a good work.

2 A bishop then must be blameless, the husband of one wife, temperate, sober-minded, of good behavior, hospitable, able to teach;

3 not given to wine, not violent, not greedy for money, but gentle, not quarrelsome, not covetous;

4 one who rules his own house well, having his children in submission with all reverence

5 (for if a man does not know how to rule his own house, how will he take care of the church of God?);

6 not a novice, lest being puffed up with pride
he fall into the same condemnation as the devil.
7 Moreover he must have a good testimony among
those who are outsiders, lest he fall into reproach and
the snare of the devil.

1 Tim. 3:1–7

Paul begins this paragraph on bishops by quoting what was apparently a well-known saying about the work of a bishop. It is *"a good work."* Whether or not it had yet taken on the vocational aspect of what we now know as the clergy is open to question. But obviously, by this time, some offices of leadership had emerged within the church.

"Bishop" is a misleading translation of the word *episkopos* because of the formal nature the office of bishop has become in ecclesiastical tradition. There certainly was no New Testament equivalent of the present office of bishop as we now have, for example, in the Anglican and Roman Catholic traditions. An order of professional clergy with designated rank did not emerge until much later than Paul.

Again, it's important here to decide whether or not Paul was writing a comprehensive manual on church government. I'm convinced that church organization was quite simple at this stage. But, even in its simplest form, some kind of overview was needed. This was provided by these *episkopoi* who, very likely, earned their living in other pursuits. The best translation of their title is probably "overseer," preferred by most contemporary translations.

Most of the scholarship on the term *episkopos* focuses on its relationship to the word *presbuteros,* commonly translated "elder." Elders were central to the life of Israel from time immemorial. Every synagogue had elders who guided and directed, taught and led in the worship, and were regarded as the leaders of the community. Thus, it was natural for the early church to appoint elders (*presbuteroi*) as their leaders. Paul and Barnabas appointed them in every church (Acts 14:23). Titus was told by Paul to appoint elders in every city in Crete (Titus 1:5).

The question surrounding the history of the interpretation of this passage is whether *episkopos* and *presbuteros* refer to the same or to different leaders in the church. Contemporary scholarship predominantly holds that the two titles were used interchangeably to describe one and the same office. Among every group of elders, it was necessary

184

that someone should be an overseer, and it could well be that while every overseer was an elder, not every elder became an overseer. But there seems to be no basis at this early point in church history for a formal office of bishop as we have come to know it. There is an interesting use of *episkopos* and *presbuteros* in Acts 20. Paul calls the Ephesian *presbuteroi* together (v. 17), and in his address to them, reminds them that they were the *episkopoi* of the church (v. 28). The terms appear to be interchangeable here.

This does not mean to me that present forms of church government that have bishops are "unbiblical." The fact is that there is no single "biblical" form of church government, if we recognize the structure reflected in the pastorals as being local and suited for their times and places. No matter what, some form of structure and government must be developed for any continuing fellowship, and any claim by a church that their structure is the only form set forth in the New Testament is unwarranted.

The practice of the churches in East Africa is a living example of a different structure than we take for granted in the States. While we struggle with the problems of declining membership and an overabundance of clergy, they struggle with rapid growth and a severe shortage of clergy. Other than in a few metropolitan areas, most pastors in Presbyterian, Methodist, and Anglican churches have the oversight of ten to twenty congregations! I know one who has twenty-six. To regard them as pastors in our American and European sense of the word is impossible. In reality, they are overseers of their churches. (And women are being ordained in growing numbers in all these denominations.)

With clarity and precision, Paul lists the qualities essential in an overseer. It is a well-documented fact that similar lists of qualifications were common in Greek circles for occupations as diverse as generals and midwives. It has also been observed that the need to single out such negative standards as "not given to wine" and "not violent" suggests that the general run of candidates was not of the highest caliber. But this is also an indication of the fact that the first generation of Gentile Christians had come from a background devoid of high moral ideals or standards.

Rather than doing a detailed analysis of the sixteen standards set forth for the overseers, I prefer to raise the question often discussed among today's seminarians and clergy. Is it fair to demand higher standards of conduct for some than others? I have sensed a rebellion against the double standard by many of my clergy colleagues. If we believe that everyone in the Body of Christ is called to ministry, why should one group have to live by higher standards?

I'm of the old school here, for I believe that the demand for high standards is legitimate and necessary for the leadership of the church. This is not to say that the same standards should not be held as the ideal for every believer. But leadership must always have its special demands, for at least two reasons.

First, leadership in the church is voluntary. The church does not draft its leaders. An individual may be urged and encouraged to seek ordination to a leadership position, but he or she can never be required to do so. And, the ordination vows of every church I know involves a commitment, in some form or another, to live an exemplary life. Everyone who accepts a role of leadership in the church voluntarily accepts the standards attached to that office. The outspoken United States president, Harry Truman, used to say of his office, "If you can't stand the heat, stay out of the kitchen!" Any reservation about double standards should be faced before taking vows as pastors, elders, deacons, bishops, superintendents, or whatever.

The second reason has to do with organizational dynamics. Every organization must have some people who are willing to make extra efforts and special sacrifices for the good of the whole. It would be magnificent if everyone in a given church were to accept the highest standards and live by them. But the reality is that a small percentage of the people carry the bulk of the load. And the fact that those few take the vows and hold the banner high, provides hope and direction for the many. A vital church must have leaders who are willing to accept the highest standards, and, by the grace of God, strive to live by them.

Now, there's always the danger of spiritual pride. How tragic when leaders start thinking of themselves as better than others. In Christ, we are what we are by God's grace and mercy, and pride has no place. Paul's admonition must ever be before us: "Let us not become conceited, provoking one another, envying one another" (Gal. 5:26).

The one qualification of the sixteen most difficult to interpret is *"the husband of one wife."* This could either be a prohibition against polygamy, as practiced by some in the surrounding culture; or the elimination of the more-than-once-married, whether by reason of divorce or death. There are problems with either view, especially if it is insisted that these are universal rules for all time.

To read this as prohibiting polygamy only among the overseers ignores the fact that polygamy was never accepted as a Christian norm. How the early church handled polygamous converts never received attention in the New Testament writings. This has made the problem a difficult one in the history of Christian missions in polygamous cultures. In the end, the Christian Gospel always exalts and produces monogamous fidelity. Thus, to read this passage as requiring monogamy only of the overseers doesn't seem to fit all of the facts.

To read this as a prohibition of second marriages seems to be the better reading. And this would have to include previous marriages ended by death as well as by divorce. This also requires that the overseers all be married. There must have been some compelling reasons to require that the overseers be married, and married only once. What those reasons were, and whether or not they were applied to all of the churches, we simply do not know. And each church will have to decide whether or not to take this as a universal rule.

THE OFFICE OF DEACON

8 Likewise the deacons must be reverent, not double-tongued, not given to much wine, not greedy for money,
9 holding the mystery of the faith with a pure conscience.
10 And let these also first be proved; then let them serve as deacons, being found blameless.
11 Likewise their wives must be reverent, not slanderers, temperate, faithful in all things.
12 Let deacons be the husbands of one wife, ruling their children and their own houses well.
13 For those who have served well as deacons obtain for themselves a good standing and great boldness in the faith which is in Christ Jesus.

1 Tim. 3:8–13

The office of deacon is unique to the Christian church. Its genesis is recorded in Acts 6:1–7, and the essence of the office was service. Stephen, the first recorded Christian martyr, was the first-named of the original seven deacons. The word *diakonos* means "servant," and the deacon has always been a servant order in the church.

To me, the deacons are the unsung heroes of our congregation. How blessed we are to have fifty-four deacons actively seeking out the needs of our people and serving, serving, serving. What a joy it is to make a hospital call and hear that a deacon has already been there. Not long ago, I received a call midafternoon that one of our men had just died of a heart attack in his front yard. When I got to the home, a deacon, a widow herself, was already there. In the weeks and months following, that deacon maintained continuing contact and support with the widow. Frequently, as I look out on our congregation at worship, I see the two of them sitting together.

The deacons are clearly regarded by Paul as special leaders of the church. The special qualifications and high standards required of them are quite similar to those for the overseers.

As with the overseers, a time of testing, training, and maturing is required. This is an important principle in leadership development. I shall never forget a situation in a previous congregation I served in which a man was given a great deal of leadership responsibility shortly after accepting Christ in an evangelistic meeting. He was a bright, gifted, talented person, obviously leadership material. But when everything didn't go his way he blew up and burned out. I wondered then, and I wonder now, if the story wouldn't have been different if we had taken Paul's counsel seriously. How much better it would have been to have worked him more gradually into leadership responsibilities, giving him a chance to grow into a deeper understanding of the realities both of the faith and the church. Just as we require candidates for the ordained ministry of the Word to undergo a period of training and testing, so a similar approach to the development of church officers and leaders is important.

Verse 11 raises the question as to whether the reference is to the wives of deacons, as in our translation, or to a separate order of deaconesses. Strong arguments can be made for either view, and the wording of the Greek can go either way for it simply says "the women." If that reference is to the wives of deacons, the implication is that the work of the male deacon would best be shared by his wife. If a separate order of deaconesses is being introduced, the requirements are similar to those of the deacons, and their ministries were likewise of a servant nature.

For the deacons who serve well, two things are promised: *"a good standing"* for themselves and *"great boldness in the faith."* Genuine servanthood has its rewards. I take *"a good standing"* to mean respect within

the Christian community. Such respect is a natural response to the
one who serves with integrity and sincerity. And with growing respect
comes increasing confidence in the faith. While study and reflection
is one of the paths to growing boldness in one's faith, active service
to others is also essential.

Far from being a comprehensive manual on church organization,
Paul has dealt only with some of the more pressing problems in
the church at Ephesus. To what extent we are to apply Paul's words
to Timothy to our own situations will have to be determined conscien-
tiously and prayerfully in our congregations and fellowships. But
there can be no question that we have here timeless wisdom from
Paul as to the life and worship of the church.

CHAPTER THREE

Wise Counsel for a Young Pastor

1 Timothy 3:14—4:16

If you're not an ordained pastor, you might think this chapter isn't for you. But let me urge you to study it with me because it has some great truths for all of us, pastor and people together. Here is the old pro at his best. Paul was hoping very much to return to Ephesus for a visit with his young protégé, Timothy. His departure, perhaps, had been somewhat hasty, and a lot of things had been left unsaid. But pressures were mounting on Paul, and any certainty of his getting to Ephesus was fading. Fortunately for us, Paul wrote the letter to his young pastor friend—just in case.

THE MYSTERY OF GODLINESS

14 These things I write to you, hoping to come to you shortly,
15 but if I am delayed, that you may know how you ought to conduct yourself in the house of God, which is the church of the living God, the pillar and ground of the truth.
16 And without controversy great is the mystery of godliness:

God was manifested in the flesh,
Justified in the Spirit,
Seen by angels,
Preached among the Gentiles,
Believed on in the world,
Received up in glory.

1 Tim. 3:14–16

190

Timothy's mentor bore a constant concern for him. How important it was to Paul—so great was his love for Timothy—that his young friend conduct himself well in his leadership in the church at Ephesus. And that kind of love and caring is a source of great strength to a younger pastor. Until his death, I always got that kind of encouragement from my father-in-law, a retired pastor. I called him "Coach." And I'll always treasure the courage and strength I got from him, just knowing he really wanted me to do well.

How normal it was for Paul to write to Timothy on *"how you ought to conduct yourself in the house of God."* The urgency of the matter is heightened by the nature of the task entrusted to Timothy—and to everyone called to leadership in the church. For it is the *"church of the living God."* Thus, the house of God is no mere building. It is a gathering of people called together by God Himself. Paul employs a metaphor used only here, *"the pillar and ground of the truth."* There is a difficulty in this phrase in that it could possibly be read as giving the church primacy over the truth. But in the Greek there are no articles with either *"pillar"* or *"ground,"* and this certainly allows for the metaphor to be read in general terms. Can we not view every church, every congregation, as such a pillar and ground? The smallest and most remote congregation is a pillar and a base upon which the truth of the Gospel is held aloft. What a thought for every congregation, small and large!

Before Paul goes on with his practical counsel for young Timothy, he bursts forth into a great hymn. So majestic is the verse, Paul introduces it with a phrase which occurs nowhere else in the Bible: *"great is the mystery of godliness."* What a magnificent way to herald the encapsulation of the Gospel that follows. The lyric quality of the Greek is lost in English translation, but we must try in our imagination to put it to music.

In our translation, the verse of the song begins with *"God was manifested in the flesh."* But virtually all contemporary translators use "Who" or "He," because the word "God" is not in most manuscripts. The "Who" or "He" obviously refers to Christ, and it is most likely that Paul is quoting only a part of the stanza in which Christ has already been mentioned.

The six great lines that we have are only a part of the *"mystery of godliness."* Read and ponder each line separately. While there is no reference to Christ's death and resurrection, it is in every way implied and assumed. Even as we sing the hymn and proclaim that the mystery of godliness has been revealed in Christ, it is still a profound mystery, beyond our ability to explain or define. But why bother with definitions or explanations when we can worship and sing His praises!

THE APPROACHING APOSTASY

Though the final outcome of Christ's struggle has been secured through His victory over sin and death, guerrilla warfare continues until He shall come in glory. Resistance to His love continues. And some will even depart from the faith—an act known as apostasy.

> 1 Now the Spirit expressly says that in latter times some will depart from the faith, giving heed to deceiving spirits and doctrines of demons,
> 2 speaking lies in hypocrisy, having their own conscience seared with a hot iron,
> 3 forbidding to marry, and commanding to abstain from foods which God has created to be received with thanksgiving by those who believe and know the truth.
> 4 For every creature of God is good, and nothing is to be refused if it is received with thanksgiving;
> 5 for it is sanctified by the word of God and prayer.
>
> *1 Tim. 4:1–5*

By using the phrase *"in latter times,"* Paul is referring to a more specific time than in his phrase "in the last days" in 2 Timothy 3:1. Here, he seems to be thinking of a time that Timothy will clearly face in which some will depart from the faith. The language of *"deceiving spirits"* and *"doctrines of demons"* is a reminder that "we do not wrestle against flesh and blood, but against principalities, against powers, against the rulers of the darkness of this age, against spiritual hosts of wickedness in the heavenly places" (Eph. 6:12). We do well to be constantly aware that there is a spiritual warfare always going on. To underestimate the power of the enemy is to invite capture.

The fact that people can come to a point when they can speak lies in hypocrisy and have no sense of wrongdoing is hard for most of us to identify with. In my pastoral experience, I have seen this only rarely. I think of a former pastor colleague whom I see from time to time. When I first knew him, we were truly brothers in the ministry. Sharing in common concerns, working together in many endeavors. Along the way he apostasized. He denied any validity to the Gospel and even insisted that he had never really meant anything he had said or done in the ministry along the way. I'm convinced that he levels with me when he insists that he has no qualms or feelings of guilt in his departure from the faith. I consider him to be a prisoner of war, held captive and brainwashed by the enemy. And I pray for his liberation.

While most commentators tie the two marks of departing from the faith in verse 3 with the two in verse 2, I choose to separate them. I can't equate hypocritical liars with seared consciences (v. 2), with an asceticism which forbids marriage and develops scruples about certain foods (v. 3). It seems to me that we have before us two different directions that apostasy can take. The first direction of lying and seared consciences is obvious. But the second is rarely considered a departure from the faith. In fact, when it comes to demanding abstention from certain foods (or drinks), some consider these marks of a superChristian.

In what sense can such rules and regulations become a departure from the faith? When they become substitutes for salvation by grace through faith. It is in his letters to the Colossians and Galatians that Paul delivers the deathblow to Christian asceticism. We are dependent on Christ and Christ alone, grace and grace alone, and any rules and regulations that get between Christ and us are antithetical to the Gospel. To begin with Christ and end up with such rules is a contradiction.

A good God created a good creation. Such was the rhythmic cadence of the creation story in Genesis 1 and 2. "And God saw that it was good. . . . and God saw that it was good. . . . indeed it was very good. . . . and God rested." To "throw away" (the literal meaning of *"refused"* in verse 4) anything in God's creation is to deny God's goodness. How consistently Paul stressed this, and how consistently we distort this truth.

It is not the Christian's assignment to ferret out everything that is evil in God's creation. Such would be to assign evil to God. It is rather our task to use everything in God's creation wisely and well. To forbid to marry suggests that there is something evil in sex or marriage or both. But God created us as sexual beings. Therefore, both are good when properly used. The challenge ever before us is to discover how to use everything in God's creation for the well-being of all of God's children.

The stark tragedy of modern technology is all too apparent at this point. The potential for goodness for humankind within the nucleus of the atom is without limits. But we have perverted that potential into weapons of mass destruction. It seems to me that our understanding of the difficult phrase in verse 5 comes into play here. To say that anything in God's creation can be received with thanksgiving when it is *"sanctified by the word of God and prayer"* is a sad commentary on modern technology.

Instead of laying our discoveries one by one on the altar of God to be used for His love and goodness in the world, we have chosen to use them as though they were ours, and we have brought God's good creation to the brink of destruction. It may be that we have just about completed the new Tower of Babel—only to discover that it doesn't reach God after all.

Such is the inevitable product of apostasy, at whatever level it occurs. It is time for a new reformation. It is time for Christians to recover the goodness of all God's creation.

The Power of Godly Living

6 If you instruct the brethren in these things, you will be a good minister of Jesus Christ, nourished in the words of faith and of the good doctrine which you have carefully followed.

7 But reject profane and old wives' fables, and exercise yourself rather to godliness.

8 For bodily exercise profits a little, but godliness is profitable for all things, having promise of the life that now is and of that which is to come.

9 This is a faithful saying and worthy of all acceptance.

10 For to this end we both labor and suffer reproach, because we trust in the living God, who is the Savior of all men, especially of those who believe.

1 Tim. 4:6–10

It's good to remember that the underlying reason for this entire letter was the need for Timothy to confront and correct some false teachers in Ephesus. The closest that we get to the nature of the false teaching has been in the preceding section. Paul does not linger long on the content of the errors to be confronted. He prefers again and again to major on positive teaching and exemplary living. His letter to Colossians is an excellent example of this. And so here he now exhorts Timothy—not to develop elaborate arguments disproving the false doctrines—but to a way of teaching and living which will point clearly to Jesus Himself.

The *"these things"* of verse 6 grows out of the previous sentence of verses 4 and 5. The best way to confront the errors of those who had departed from the faith was to continue solid teaching, with the emphasis upon the goodness of everything in God's creation when it is received with thanksgiving through the Word of God and prayer.

Nourishment. The good minister of Jesus Christ majors on positive teaching. Such a minister will be engaged in a continual process of spiritual nourishment. The *"words of faith"* and *"good doctrine"* become the staples in the daily diet of the one who would be a true servant of Jesus Christ. This is why daily study of the Scriptures, with periods for reflection and meditation, are such an integral part of the life of the Christian. A day without intentional reflection on the Word of God is like a day without nourishment. Down through the centuries, believers attest to this universally. There simply is no substitute for the daily nourishment that we need from God.

And the fast-food outlet approach is inadequate. Believe me, I've tried it! The greater the pressure and the more rapid the pace, the more I need to take significant blocks of time regularly for study and reflection upon the Bible and the great truths of the faith. A quick bite here and there, Jack-in-the-Box style, just doesn't do it.

Exercise. As Paul uses the parallel of physical and spiritual nourishment, there comes to mind the similarity of physical and spiritual exercise. The call to *"reject profane and old wives' fables,"* has a touch of humor. When you are convinced that some teaching is false, don't take it too seriously. Such teaching is empty and foolish and doesn't deserve a great deal of our energy and time. Rather, we are to exert ourselves by conditioning ourselves in godliness.

I find it difficult to think of Paul as a jogger or a regular visitor to the local health club. But he did give a tip of the hat to *"a little"* value in physical exercise. Our present emphasis in America and Europe on running and fitness is a necessary corrective to our working and eating styles. In Paul's time, and for most people in the world in our time, exercise was and is a necessary part of one's daily routine. For the vast majority of people living today, walking or bicycling is the primary means of transportation. Not long ago, I preached in the Cathedral of the Diocese of Kigezi in Kabale, Uganda, where Bishop Festo Kivengere resides. There were three thousand people in the service, a normal Sunday's attendance. The church has no parking lot, and there were not more than ten cars to be seen. I did not invite them to become joggers.

It is our sedentary lifestyle and our overabundance of high-calorie food and drink that has made exercise programs a must in our part of the world. I'm absolutely convinced that a program of regular exercise and weight control is not only in my own best interests, but also a part of my stewardship of the body that God has given me. Since there's no way to return to a world without automobiles, at least where I live, I'll have to replace the exercise lost with intentional exercise.

But like so many things, in some circles physical exercise has been made into a virtual religion, with its priests, temples, and liturgies. We now spend millions of dollars on diets and exercising to offset the effects of the millions of dollars we spend on rich foods and automobiles. Hopefully, God has a sense of humor. But in the meantime, millions of people are starving and suffering because of our sorry stewardship.

The issue is one of priorities and proportion. Bodily exercise does profit a little. The necessity for it in our time and place is well established. But it must not be allowed to place inordinate demands upon the stewardship of our time and money. I have a friend who spends two hours a day running, thirty minutes (plus showering and dressing time) three times a week in a health club at substantial cost, and three hours or more per week playing racquetball. In addition, he belongs to the local tennis club and plays there once or twice a week. He appears to be in excellent physical condition.

He asked me to lunch not long ago because he wanted to talk personally. The all-too-common story was shared of a lack of joy in his work and family in particular, and a growing sense of boredom and frustration with life in general. I asked him if he was willing to take an honest inventory of himself. He was. He discovered that the time and energy spent on the physical compared to the spiritual was one hundred to one! His conclusion: "I'm physically fit, but spiritually flabby." That may become the epitaph on too many of our headstones.

We may well be in need of regular physical exercise, and we should not ignore our physical fitness. But our spiritual fitness is of much greater importance. It has to do not only with the quality of this life, but *"of that which is to come."* Paul's point is clear. Physical exercise profits in this life, but *only* in this life. Spiritual exercise profits in this life *and* in the life to come. The clear priority must be on spiritual fitness. A rule of thumb of two hours of spiritual exercise for every hour of physical exercise, with regularity, will produce some very healthy Christians!

Hard work. Only those who are in good condition engage in strenuous labor. And Paul ends this section on that note in verses 9 and 10. Scholars debate as to whether verse 9 points to verse 8 or verse 10 as *"a faithful saying."* Either could well be a popular adage, but in the light of Paul's customary usage, it seems likely that the *"saying"* is in verse 10.

I prefer the translation "labor and strive" rather than our version's *"labor and suffer reproach."* "Strive" (*agōnizometha*) has greater manuscript support than "suffer reproach" (*oneidizometha*). It also is more in keeping with the context. The picture is of one engaged in demanding and fatiguing toil. To be genuinely engaged in Christian service and ministry requires total fitness, physical and spiritual. The needs are overwhelming. The demands are constant. Only those who are in top condition can do the work required.

The reason given for persevering in such arduous toil is our *"trust in the living God."* The word used here for *"trust"* (*ēlpikamen*), is in a tense that makes it mean a continuing state of hope. I would paraphrase this, "because we have anchored our hope in the living God." I recall one of my summer jobs during my seminary years, working for a construction company in Los Angeles. My job, day after day, was to remove wallpaper with a steamer from some old buildings that were being renovated. Working with that steam machine on smoggy days in ninety-five degree temperatures qualified as exhausting and strenuous toil! They paid us at the end of each day. I can tell you that the only thing that kept me going through those dogdays was the hope centered on that pay check!

How much more we can endure fatigue and frustration in the service of Christ with our hope anchored in the living God. He will not disappoint us or forsake us. And in the end, we will be glorified with Him. What a payday that will be! For He is *the Savior of all men, especially of those who believe.*" It is probably best to take the word *"Savior"* in this colloquial saying in the common sense of "preserver." This is consistent with the context. God's mercy and sustenance embrace all people, and those who believe will become the full recipients of His grace and salvation.

In this delightful section, Paul calls each of us, along with Timothy, to a life of godliness in a way that we can never forget. As we must exercise and be nourished to be fit for physical labor, so must we be conditioned and nurtured for our work for God. And we pursue His work in confident hope in His full salvation.

The power of verses 11–16 lies in the intensity of personal concern with which it is written. Paul now zeroes in on his young friend in a most personal way, and the years of intimacy between them come to fruition.

AN URGENT APPEAL

11 These things command and teach.
12 Let no one despise your youth, but be an example to the believers in word, in conduct, in love, in spirit, in faith, in purity.
13 Till I come, give attention to reading, to exhortation, to doctrine.
14 Do not neglect the gift that is in you, which was given to you by prophecy with the laying on of the hands of the presbytery.
15 Meditate on these things; give yourself entirely to them, that your progress may be evident to all.
16 Take heed to yourself and to the doctrine. Continue in them, for in doing this you will save both yourself and those who hear you.

1 Tim. 4:11–16

Many believe that Timothy was a timid and shy person. If so, confronting false teachers was not his cup of tea, and there was all the more reason for Paul's continuing admonitions to him to be strong, to take charge, and to lead. Here, Paul speaks as warmly and personally as possible with his young friend and colleague. Timothy is to assert authority, as the word *"command"* indicates. His authority is delegated to him, not only by Paul, but also by Christ Himself. But that authority can only be exercised through his own integrity and example.

Immediately, Paul separates authority from seniority. Authority has nothing to do with Timothy's age or experience. By now, Timothy is no longer a mere youth, and the word *"youth"* in this setting (*neotētos*) may refer to anyone up to age forty! In this sense, youth is always relative. My father-in-law always called me "kid" even when I was in my fifties—but he was then in his eighties. Recently, I enjoyed a reunion with the "kids" I had in my youth group at the University Presbyterian Church in Seattle in the early 1950s. My kids were remarkably middle-aged, but they are still youth to me. So it would ever be between Paul and Timothy—authority does not depend on age.

Timothy's authority is to be grounded, rather, in his example in at least five areas. The words *"in spirit"* have little support in the early manuscripts and must have been inserted much later. The idea of leading by example has been much debated among the current generation of younger clergy. My students in seminary sometimes express their unwillingness to accept a double standard. "Why should more be expected of us than others?" I've already stated my feelings about this in conjunction with 1 Timothy 3:1–7. In our ordination vows, we promise to live exemplary lives. Such voluntary commitment to be examples is of the essence of Christian leadership.

"Word" and *"conduct"* have to do with his outward life, *"faith"* and *"purity"* focus on the inner life, and *"love"* is the bridge that holds them together. The word and the conduct must always go together. What we do speaks every bit as loudly as what we say. In fact, what we do can drown out virtually everything we say. I think of a Christian leader who became involved in a series of scandals, buttressed by denials, only to finally admit guilt. After he had been removed from his leadership position, he was remembered only for that behavior. People quickly forgot the many good things he had said and done.

As we have said before, this does not mean that we only have authority to lead if our word and conduct are perfect. There is no such thing as perfection in Christian conduct, except in Jesus Himself. But we are to strive for the kind of integrity and quality in life and relationships that bears witness to the love and presence of Christ.

Faith and purity, for the most part, are inner attitudes and beliefs. The reference is not to moral and sexual purity as such, but to that purity of heart and mind which is set upon seeking and doing the will of God. Thus faith and purity are closely linked and have a great deal to do with the setting of one's mind and will on God.

Love stands in the middle of this pentad, for it is the bond that ties the outer and inner life together. Love always involves the whole of life. Outward expressions of love that are not rooted in inner love quickly wither and die as insincerities. Inner love that is not expressed by open giving and caring turns to self-adulation and decay. The love of Christ is intensely personal. It is also intensely public. It simply does not exist one way without the other.

The three activities in which Timothy is to engage have to do with leadership in public worship. These three components have long been established as central to gatherings of Christian believers. The reading of Scripture is essential to Christian worship. The exhortation is rightly based upon the Scripture that is read. And the doctrine is the teaching that grows out of the Scripture.

I'm often amazed at the casualness, and even downright sloppiness, with which the Scriptures are read in public worship. Sometimes this is regarded as a nice little thing for lay people to do—implying that no harm can be done by a poor reading of Scripture. It doesn't matter who reads the Scripture, but let us *"give attention"* to reading it. This admonition of Paul suggests preparation. Let the reader prepare in advance to read the Word of God with the conviction that it *is* the Word of God. If the Scriptures are read in a dull and sing-song manner, mostly emphasizing the punctuation marks, harm is done to a worship service. I'm more and more convinced that the reading of Scripture is a channel through which God speaks directly to us. It deserves genuine attention and emphasis.

Paul urges six more things upon Timothy in verses 14–16: (1) *"Do not neglect the gift that is in you."* (2) *"Meditate on these things."* (3) *"Give yourself entirely to them."* (4) *"Take heed to yourself."* (5) *"Take heed . . . to the doctrine."* (6) *"Continue in them."*

These six are important to each of us as well. It was at his ordination where, through a prophetic word and the laying on of hands by the presbytery, Timothy received a special gift for his ministry, not named specifically here. We err if we make spiritual gifts individualistic. Gifts are given by the Holy Spirit for the building up of the entire body. They are not achieved by individuals for their own sake. It is thus the body, here the presbytery—the gathering of the *presbuteriou*—that recognizes and affirms the gifts of the Holy Spirit. The rampant individualism that too often characterizes our emphasis upon the gifts of the Spirit needs this constant corrective of the place of *"the presbytery"* in the transmission of these gifts.

Progress is set forth as a product of meditation and commitment. There are many current fads surrounding techniques of meditation. Meditation has some place in all religious traditions, and many of the exotic techniques of meditation coming to the West grow out of or represent Eastern religions such as Hinduism and Buddhism. It's a well-concealed fact that meditation is an integral part of our Christian faith, though it is not presented to us in the New Testament replete with gurus and esoteric techniques. It's a very simple and natural thing. It is being quiet before the Lord. It is withdrawal and reflection. But the process Paul is talking about in verse 15 is more than this. It is only completed when we give ourselves *"entirely"* to the things we have meditated upon. Like love, meditation must be both an inward and an outward journey.

Finally, we are to *"take heed,"* both to ourselves and to the doctrine. This is to take oneself and to take doctrine seriously. It is to keep a strict eye on the self and on the teaching. How easy it is to become lax and to allow our eyes to wander.

As we continue in what we see by taking heed to ourselves and to doctrine, salvation comes both to us and to those who hear us. Here, we work out our salvation as in Philippians 2:12, but salvation can only be worked out because it has been placed within us by Jesus Himself. The role of our ministry to one another in the transmission of salvation must never be minimized.

There is a great danger of neglecting our own salvation in our commitment to the salvation of others. If we emphasize the aspect of salvation best known as wholeness, this is demonstrably evident. The stories abound of those who, intensely involved in serving others, burn out or destroy themselves. It need not be either/or, but we who serve must learn to say "no" enough to sustain our own wholeness.

I promised you at the beginning of this chapter that there would be some rich rewards in its study even if you're not an ordained pastor, especially since we are all called to be ministers of Jesus Christ. I hope you agree. And I hope you'll use this chapter again and again as wise counsel for you in your ministry.

CHAPTER FOUR

A Church That Cares

1 Timothy 5:1—6:2

For too long I've passed by this chapter in my reading of Timothy with little more than a tip of the hat. Fourteen of its twenty-five verses have to do with caring for widows in the church, and to tell you the truth, that's never been a major problem in our congregation. The only possible point of interest seemed to be verse 23, if one were seeking some justification for an occasional glass of wine.

But thanks to this assignment, I've discovered this chapter as a living word for the very first time. It is a beautiful word calling every congregation to be a church that cares. If we walk slowly enough through this chapter, we will learn a great deal as to what it means to be a caring community.

DIFFERENT STROKES FOR DIFFERENT FOLKS

1 Do not rebuke an older man, but exhort him
as a father, the younger men as brothers,
2 the older women as mothers, the younger as
sisters, with all purity.

1 Tim. 5:1–2

Every congregation is composed of all different types of people because every person is unique. The basic principle of a church that cares is *diversity*. Every congregation, small or large, must become a place where each person is treated and cared for as an individual. Yet many things in the life of the church work against this ideal.

Timothy is directed to treat older men differently from younger men, and older women differently from younger women. The word *"rebuke"* means a very severe censure. The older folks are to be spared such censure. The picture that comes to me is one in which older people are treated more tenderly, while younger folks sometimes need stronger confrontation. This is good, common sense. As I am, it seems more rapidly, becoming one of those older people, I'm very aware that I do not respond to *"rebuke"* the way I did when I was younger. The older we get, the less likely we are to change. With increasing years, I find that the gentler the confrontation, the more likely I am to consider change.

I'm not suggesting that younger people respond with instant change to severe censure. But I recall well that on many occasions, had the confrontation not been direct and sometimes severe, I probably wouldn't have heard it. I look back on some of the coaches and teachers I had. Those I remember most vividly as having the greatest influence upon me were those who were quite direct and forthright in their demands. They always made their expectations quite clear. I recall the story of the farmer who hit his mule on the rear three times with a board before giving it an order. When the severity of his approach was challenged by a visitor from the city, the farmer replied, "You've got to get his attention!" Younger folks often need more directness in order to get their attention.

This is neither to say that we should be less loving or caring for the younger nor that we should be patronizing to the older. But happy is the pastor or church leader who learns how to treat different folks with different strokes. A church that cares is a fellowship in which each person, young and old, male and female receives correction and guidance in ways that take their differences respectfully and seriously. This passage is more readily understood and accepted, I find, in East Africa where the tribal traditions hold the elders in great respect. It is in need of greater emphasis in our culture which generally ignores or rejects the elderly.

The Christian community treats its older men and women with firm and tender exhortation as fathers and mothers. It exhorts and trains its younger folks as brothers and sisters—and the pastor Timothy is reminded that the relationships with the younger sisters needed special precautions for obvious reasons.

Special Strokes for Special Folks

It is obvious that Paul is here setting forth specific guidelines for the treatment of widows in Ephesus. I find the passage to be of great value by expanding its principles to include any particular group of people with special needs. Try reading this passage to apply to all folks with special needs.

3 Honor widows who are really widows.

4 But if any widow has children or grandchildren, let them first learn to show piety at home and to repay their parents; for this is good and acceptable before God.

5 Now she who is really a widow, and left alone, trusts in God and continues in supplications and prayers night and day.

6 But she who lives in pleasure is dead while she lives.

7 And these things command, that they may be blameless.

8 But if anyone does not provide for his own, and especially for those of his household, he has denied the faith and is worse than an unbeliever.

9 Do not let a widow under sixty years old be taken into the number, and not unless she has been the wife of one man,

10 well reported for good works: if she has brought up children, if she has lodged strangers, if she has washed the saints' feet, if she has relieved the afflicted, if she has diligently followed every good work.

11 But refuse the younger widows; for when they have begun to grow wanton against Christ, they desire to marry,

12 having condemnation because they have cast off their first faith.

13 And besides they learn to be idle, wandering about from house to house, and not only idle but also gossips and busybodies, saying things which they ought not.

14 Therefore I desire that the younger widows marry, bear children, manage the house, give no opportunity to the adversary to speak reproachfully.

15 For some have already turned aside after Satan.

16 If any believing man or woman has widows, let them relieve them, and do not let the church be burdened, that it may relieve those who are really widows.

1 Tim. 5:3–16

Rather than studying this section verse by verse, I find it helpful to look at it under three headings and then to attempt some general applications beyond widows. Paul is speaking to and about three groups of people: the church, children and grandchildren, and widows.

The church and widows. The emphasis of the section, by virtue of its opening and closing words (vv. 3, 16), is that the church is to give special care to those who are *"really widows."* Everything in between deals with some of the questions that complicate the matter. But the central point must not be lost in the discussion. The church is to care for its widows with a special concern.

It's very difficult for us who have grown up in caring families, surrounded by a network of friendships and relationships, and covered by insurance, social security, and pension plans, to begin to identify with the plight of the widow in the times and places of the Bible. Her first problem was being a woman. She had no way of working to provide for herself outside of the home. If she had no children or grandchildren to provide for her, she was utterly without any source of help. There would be no source of income, no capital with which to work—only a roof over her head, if she were fortunate, with whatever might be in the house.

If the church did not care for her, no one else would. There were no community agencies or programs. The world was uncaring. The church had come to care. And so it was commanded, without qualifications, to *"honor"* and to *"relieve"* those who are *"really widows."*

I suggest that, for us, the widows of that day are representatives in our day of all who are without help, without resources, and without anyone to care. There are millions of them in our world, thousands of them in the United States. If the church doesn't care for them in special ways, who will? That governments and other agencies should and do provide some care, does not relieve the church of its mandate and responsibility.

We could wish that the task were simple. It never has been, and it never will be. As soon as Paul articulated the mandate, he had to deal with some of the complicating factors attending every effort to care for people with special needs.

The children and grandchildren of widows. The first responsibility for the care of the widow rested with her immediate family, the children and the grandchildren. Verses 4, 8, and 16 are quite clear on this. Such care is set forth as a matter of *"piety at home."* Paul ties piety to a very simple matter of repaying one's parents. The logic is inescapable. My parents brought me into the world. When I was helpless, they sacrificed to feed me, clothe me, shelter me, and nurture me. Now that my widowed mother is helpless, I can do no less for her. For the believer, one's love for God cannot be separated from loving and caring for one's parents. Piety—love for God—is shown through such caring, it is *"good and acceptable before God."*

Verse 8 states the negative side. Not to care for those of one's family and household is a denial of the faith. The close connection between the faith and such practical service is to be noted. The words of James come to mind: "What does it profit, my brethren, if someone says he has faith but does not have works? Can faith save him? If a brother or sister is naked and destitute of daily food, and one of you says to them, 'Depart in peace, be warmed and filled,' but you do not give them the things which are needed for the body, what does it profit? Thus also faith by itself, if it does not have works, is dead" (James 2:14–17).

The final reason for this mandate to the children and grandchildren to care for their widowed parent or grandparent is given in verse 16. It is not right for the burden to be cast upon the church. Even when the families take care of their own, the church will still be faced with plenty of people with special needs.

There is an underlying point in this section that we must not miss. Writers like Michael Novak and George Gilder underscore the virtue of accumulating wealth by the appealing logic that the rich care for the poor; the poor cannot care for the poor. This may sound like good theory, but it is not the way things work out in practice. While it is true that many rich people are generous benefactors, two facts need to be faced. First, if Internal Revenue statistics are reliable indicators, the vast majority of wealthy people in the United States give less than 1 percent of their net personal income to charitable causes. And many of them give nothing. If the facts were available, I suspect that it is a relatively few wealthy people, mostly Christians, who account for the bulk of such giving. Many people are wealthy partly because they have chosen to give little or nothing away, in spite of the encouragement of tax laws.

The second fact is that most of the benevolent giving by the wealthy appears to be channeled to higher education institutional and building programs. I don't question the need for buildings and endowments, but I'm aware that in the midst of our growth and success in capital funding, we can't find a way to improve faculty salaries, let alone do anything for the *"widows."*

In reality, the poor care for the poor to a much greater extent than the rich care for the poor. I see it again and again in my visits to the poorest of the poor in many parts of the world. I never cease to be amazed at the remarkable ways that poor people care for each other. I'm not exalting poverty, but the myth that if people get wealthier they will care for the poor needs to be abandoned. In this sinful world, the burden for the poor falls mostly on the backs of the poor, and we do not serve the Lord well by justifying our wealth on the grounds that someday we might get around to caring for the *"widows"* of this world.

The children and grandchildren to whom Paul mandated the care of their widowed mothers, were, for the most part, very poor people. Their poorness did not exempt them from their responsibility to their own families. This ought to pierce the conscience, and perhaps, radically change the lifestyles and stewardship of those of us who, by global standards, are wealthy.

The widows. Paul defines at least two categories of widows, possibly three. The widow who is *"really"* a widow is defined in verse 5. She is (1) left alone, or truly desolate with no one to help; (2) a genuine believer in God; (3) a woman in constant prayer. Such widows are to be cared for by the church, in contrast with some who apparently resorted to immoral living as a means of support, and who are characterized as "dead" though alive.

The question of whether there are two or three categories of widows has to do with the meaning of verses 9 and 10. Some regard this as an extension of the qualifications of those who are *"really widows,"* while others see this as a separate category of widows who were enrolled in a special order for service and ministry, referred to as *"the number."*

The seven qualifications set forth in verse 9 would certainly eliminate some widows who were worthy of the care of the church according to verse 5. This appears to be a very special group of women admirably qualified for caring ministries. What a beautiful way of helping such widows by calling them to a ministry of caring for others! And what a blessing to a congregation to have such a group of women.

It is the specification of the age of sixty that creates the difficulty with both views. It's hard to believe that an arbitrary age would be set before the caring community would offer help to a destitute widow, implying a special order. But the age of sixty, advanced in that culture, would restrict the order to a small number. Perhaps just a few of the older widows were specially designated as "the number."

The remaining instructions apply to younger widows. And they must have been creating some real problems in Ephesus. Paul advises that it is best that they marry again and raise a family (v. 14). The picture seems to be one in which the younger widows were taking some kind of vows, and then breaking them as the opportunity for marriage presented itself. We do best to recognize that we really can't know what the local situation was.

The church today. If we just limit the meaning of this passage to widows, its application to the church today is quite limited. I choose to read this passage as having significant meaning to us. I hear it as a call to be a church that really cares for all in need. We must not ignore those who are *"really widows,"* but we can't draw the line there. The Lord's mandate for us to feed the hungry and care for the poor is articulated here in terms of one particular group. But the circle must be expanded to embrace all who are destitute with no one to help.

Many Christians I know are asking the question, "What does it mean to be a world Christian?" And when you ponder this, the next question is, "What other kind of Christian is there?" When I'm with my own congregation, I'm aware of our tendency to think primarily of our own needs. Courses and sermons on family life have much greater appeal than those on the growing global refugee problem. When I'm in Kenya, I see the same tendencies.

To me, the most important question of our day—forced upon us by instant communications and our potential for massive nuclear destruction—is how to be a world Christian. Nationalisms and tribalisms have no place in the thinking and vocabulary of the Kingdom of God. So the question really is, "How do we live as citizens of the Kingdom of God?"

I feel strongly that we can begin to answer this question by expanding our list of widows to include all of the world's poor and needy. Idealistic? Grandiose? Exactly. Because "God so loved the *world."* The Gospel is idealistic. The Kingdom is grandiose. God is the great God of the universe. And He loves every single person in this global village of His. Can we do less?

But the problems are insurmountable. That's right. The issue is not whether we can solve all of the problems. It is whether we are working at them as our response to God's love.

Why do I plead to expand our widows' lists? A few days ago I stood with Bishop Festo Kivengere on a little hill in a makeshift village in southwest Uganda. There was no electricity, no running water, no sanitation facilities, no shops or schools—just row upon row of hastily built thatched huts. More than six thousand displaced Ugandans have gathered here during the last four months. They're part of more than thirty thousand such folks who have been attacked by fellow Ugandans, professedly because of their tribal roots in Rwanda. At this moment, neither the Rwandan or Ugandan governments will even recognize the problem. They are a tiny segment of the five million refugees on the continent of Africa, a number growing daily.

As we stood there, a crowd of more than one thousand quickly surrounded us. Bishop Festo nudged me, "Say something to them." I told them God loved them. That seemed so trite to me, but it wasn't to them, for most of them are Christians. I told them I loved them. I almost choked on my words—the return portion of my round-trip ticket was in my wallet, along with more money than some of the young men will make in a lifetime, even if they find a place to go. I was struggling for words, and all I could say was that I would pray for them and do what I could to tell their story and pray that some help would come from somewhere. And there were tears, mine and theirs, as we shared the recognition of our mutual helplessness.

I don't have the answers. But I have to raise the questions that world Christians have to ask. And if the church doesn't ask these questions of itself and of its governments, who will? Sometimes, lying awake in the night hours, I see those dear people. And I hear my words to them. And I ask myself—will we rich and comfortable Christians ever become a church that really cares? Will we ever expand our widows' lists to include more of the world's destitute?

The church that learns to care in special ways for its young and old, male and female, and those with special needs, must also be caring for its leaders.

THE CARE OF LEADERS

17 Let the elders who rule well be counted worthy
of double honor, especially those who labor in the
word and doctrine.
18 For the Scripture says, *"You shall not muzzle*

> *an ox while it treads out the grain,"* and, "The laborer
> is worthy of his wages."
> 19 Do not receive an accusation against an elder
> except from two or three witnesses.
> 20 Those who are sinning rebuke in the presence
> of all, that the rest also may fear.
>
> *1 Tim. 5:17–20*

Three things are said regarding elders (*presbuteroi*): they are to be
paid; they are to be protected from irresponsible accusations; they
are to be strictly disciplined.

In the United Presbyterian Church, we used to refer to ruling elders
and teaching elders. The ruling elders were the elders ordained to
serve on the Sessions and in the judicatories of the church. The teaching elders were those ordered to preach, teach, and administer the
sacraments. Presumably the term "ruling elder" had its roots in verse
17, but here it clearly applies to those *presbuteroi* who preach and
teach *"the word and doctrine."* The distinction between ruling and teaching elders was misleading, if not erroneous, and has been abandoned.
Both functions are included in *presbuteroi*.

It is generally agreed that *"double honor"* (v. 17) includes financial
remuneration in the light of verse 18. It is an honor to be called by
the church to *"labor in the word and doctrine."* It is thus a double honor
to get paid for the first honor. I often point out to my seminary
students that we ministers of the Word are most fortunate. We get
paid to study, preach, and teach the Scriptures. I've always been
grateful for such a privilege and honor. I would study and teach
the Scriptures in any event.

Verse 18 gets attention in the critical commentaries because of
Paul's use of *"Scripture."* The first citation is from Deuteronomy 25:4
and creates no problem. The second, however, is not found in the
Old Testament, but is paralleled in Luke 10:7 as a saying of Jesus.
If the traditional dating of Luke is correct (A.D. 80–85), then someone
other than Paul must have written this. But could not Paul have
had access to this saying of Jesus in some pre-Lukan form? In Acts
20:35, he quoted a saying of Jesus not recorded in any of the Gospels:
"It is more blessed to give than to receive." And Paul certainly considered the words of Jesus as having the same authority as Scripture.
Both citations establish Scriptural authority for the remuneration of
those who preach and teach.

Because of the public nature of the work of those who *"labor in the word and doctrine,"* accusations should not be accepted without two or three witnesses. Stories abound of leaders in the church whose ministries have been undercut or destroyed by malicious rumors originated by one person. The principle of multiple witnesses, along with the right of the accused to be faced by his or her accuser, is absolutely essential for the well-being of all concerned.

But the other side of the coin is that the church has the right to expect high standards of practice from its ordained leadership. Discipline of *"sinning,"* the failure or betrayal of those agreed-upon standards, is to be done openly *"in the presence of all."* In our day, many of us react to the idea of motivating by fear, as stated in verse 20. But in reality, this can be another way of reminding us that we must accept responsibility for our actions and behavior.

I can't leave this passage without adding my own feelings about the attitude of the church toward paying its leaders—and this has to include professors in Christian colleges and seminaries. I feel I have a right to speak to this, as I am among the minority of clergy who can be considered, by any reasonable standards, to be adequately compensated. The leader who receives *"double honor"* does not live his/her life on the edge of poverty or in a series of financial crises. Yet that is the sad, lifelong plight of all too many ministers of the Word. They're always in a bind, but it is considered "unspiritual" to talk about their need for more money. Why? I insist that it's "unspiritual"—and unScriptural here—not to give the laborer adequate wages. And what is adequate? Certainly something in the midrange of the community in which he or she must work and live.

A church or institution that operates on the unstated assumption that it will pay its people as little as the traffic will bear is long overdue for an overhaul. I'm not advocating a clergy union for collective bargaining, but I'm encouraging pastors and church workers everywhere to make their needs known to the people who accept the responsibility to treat them with *"double honor."*

TAKE CARE OF YOURSELF

21 I charge you before God and the Lord Jesus Christ
and the elect angels that you observe these things
without prejudice, doing nothing with partiality.
22 Do not lay hands on anyone hastily, nor share
in other people's sins; keep yourself pure.

23 No longer drink only water, but use a little wine
for your stomach's sake and your frequent infirmities.
24 Some men's sins are clearly evident, preceding
them to judgment, but those of some men follow later.
25 Likewise, also, the good works of some are clearly
evident, and those that are otherwise cannot be hidden.

1 Tim. 5:21–25

The opening words of verse 21 certainly were designed to get Timothy's attention! Charging someone in the name of *"God and the Lord
Jesus Christ and the elect angels"* certainly makes it a weighty charge.
Not only is it a heavy mandate; it is warmly personal. It is Paul's
way of saying, "Take good care of yourself!"

Sometimes, those who labor "in the word and doctrine" can become
so consumed with caring for others that they neglect themselves.
But if they do not adequately care for themselves, eventually they
will have nothing to give to others. This is not an admonition to
have self-pity or to pamper oneself. But we must take God seriously
enough to take care of ourselves. I am the only self He has given
me. Taking care of that self is a part of my stewardship to God.
Timothy is to take care of himself by treating others impartially (v.
21), by the careful choice of leaders (v. 22a), by not going along
with the crowd (vv. 22b, 24–25), and by attention to his physical
needs (v. 23).

Treating others impartially. To treat others impartially and without
prejudice is not normally regarded in the realm of self-care. But for
the Christian leader, the connection is clear. Credibility in pastoral
ministry is closely tied to unprejudiced and impartial leadership. It's
normal and natural to develop "favorites," folks with whom we work
easily and naturally. But effective leadership requires that we work
just as supportively with those we may not like as well.

There has always been a question as to whether a pastor should
develop close, personal friendships within the congregation. The older
school of thought answers in the negative. Many of us are finding
it otherwise. We can't very well be the Body of Christ and not have
some close relationships. I thank God that some of my closest friends
are members of our congregation. And some of them have served
terms on the Session. But having friends and playing favorites do
not necessarily go together.

To work impartially with all requires constant awareness and self-discipline. For most of us, it does not come naturally. But leaders who cater to or are controlled by "favorites" sow the seeds of division that ultimately destroy the effectiveness of any group. This could well be a motto on every pastor's desk: *No prejudice, no partiality!*

The choice of leaders. While verse 22 may at first sound like counsel not to grab people around the neck, such counsel should hardly be needed by Timothy or any other Christian leaders. I take the laying on of hands here to have something to do with ordaining or commissioning people to leadership. It is never to be done hastily.

Again, we do well to think of our choice and commissioning of leaders as good care of ourselves. This does not mean that the pastor must be personally involved in choosing and training all of the leaders. But a basic role of leadership, often neglected, is the careful development of leadership. The more attention we give to the cultivation and care of leaders, the better we will feel and function.

Merely getting people to do a job because no one else will do it is to act "hastily." Running around willy-nilly just to fill positions on boards and committees is *not* leadership. There is another motto here: *Choose your leaders carefully!*

Following the crowd. There's a certain loneliness to be expected in leadership—especially pastoral leadership. The theme of verse 22b is continued in verses 24 and 25. There are times when the Christian leader has to be different. Some of those times are self-evident; others are more difficult to determine. The reality and results of some sins are not visible until much later.

When or when not to share in the party, when or when not to go along with the majority—these are the never-ending decisions required of the Christian leader. And the decisions we make are a matter of self-care as well as personal and public witness.

Whether or not we like it, we have to live in the proverbial fishbowl. Our public and private behavior is observed and measured by many people, even when we're unaware. That we can't please everyone all the time, and that we need not be intimidated by other's hang-ups, goes without saying. But there is still the necessity of avoiding *"other people's sins"* and of *"keeping yourself pure."*

This need not be a call to asceticism or to an external pietism that delights in being holier-than-thou. It is a call to be aware of the power of our example and a reminder that there will be times when we will have to stand apart from the crowd. So, here is a third motto: *Dare to be different!*

Taking care of one's physical needs. That Paul was not calling Timothy to a stringent asceticism is made clear in verse 23. As I was writing this section, I was completing a ten-day stint in some of the rural areas of East Africa where I had been drinking a variety of local waters. Apparently my American antibiotics were not designed for African bugs, and I knew at that moment exactly what Timothy's problem was. Paul's advice to avoid the local water and try a little wine was thoughtful and humane.

However, a lot of things have happened regarding alcohol between their time and ours, and we do well to apply this instruction cautiously. For some people, we know now, advice to *"use a little wine"* could be disastrous. These are the folks called alcoholics. For reasons that we do not yet fully know, one drink of alcohol in any form sets off a chain reaction leading to excessive drinking. No matter how bad the local water, we cannot encourage alcoholics to drink wine. About one person in ten in America has this problem. We can hope that some day we'll know a lot more as to the whys of alcoholism, but for now, we know for sure that the alcoholic cannot and must not drink alcohol in any form.

That leaves nine out of ten for whom alcohol does not necessarily lead to problem drinking. And in our culture, moderate drinking has certainly gained wide acceptance in recent years, even among some Christians for whom this was an absolute taboo a few years ago. At the same time, many Christians feel that total abstinence should be stressed as the only possible style because of the growing casualness toward what has become destructive for many.

We obviously can't address or resolve this problem in a few paragraphs. But two things can be said here. First, to use this passage to buttress either side of the moderation versus total abstinence argument is not warranted. This was very personal advice to Timothy in a culture in which drinking wine did not have the same connotations as "social drinking" in our day. A literal and general application of this personal advice could be damaging and dangerous.

My second concern here is that we not divide the Body of Christ by making moderation or total abstinence a test of orthodoxy. There are and will continue to be strong feelings of difference among Christians on this subject. Excessive use of alcohol—or anything else for that matter—is always inconsistent with our profession of Christ.

I'm convinced that a church that really cares will avoid both a harsh judgmentalism of those who drink in moderation, and a demeaning put-down of those who choose total abstinence.

EVEN MASTERS NEED CARE

> 1 Let as many servants as are under the yoke count
> their own masters worthy of all honor, that the name
> of God and His doctrine not be blasphemed.
> 2 And those who have believing masters, let them
> not despise them because they are brethren, but rather
> serve them because those who are benefited are
> believers and beloved. Teach and exhort these things.
>
> *1 Tim. 6:1-2*

Our section on a caring church ends with what is a most unlikely appeal. It's a plea for the weak to take care of the strong. Our translation should read "slaves" rather than *"servants,"* for the *douloi* were literally slaves who were owned by their masters. As such they were powerless, and their masters had complete control of them.

Just as the Gospel elevated women to a new status (and created new problems), so it likewise brought slaves to a new level. Within the Christian community, there was "neither slave nor free" (Gal. 3:28). But while the slaves were accepted as equals within the church, they were still slaves to their masters in that economic system. The seeds of the Gospel would ultimately destroy the institution of slavery, but in the meantime, a difficult situation was created.

The two admonitions in verses 1 and 2 are directed just to the slaves. In verse 1, those who had unbelieving masters are counseled to continue honoring their masters so that *"the name of God and His doctrine may not be blasphemed."* There are those who would prefer that Paul would have called for the overthrow of the system, but he didn't.

In verse 2, the other situation is addressed in which the master of the Christian slave was a brother in Christ. The likelihood was that the slave would take advantage of this new-found fellowship in the congregation and demand special privileges at home and work. This could lead to sharp resentment if such special treatment was not granted. Paul insists that Christian slaves serve their Christian masters with the special motive that they are bringing service and joy to their brothers in Christ. The classic and expanded application in this situation is found in Paul's letter to Philemon.

There are great difficulties in the contemporary application of this passage. Why didn't Paul call for the overthrow of such a dehumanizing system? We'll never know. But in retrospect, it's easy to see that slavery and the Christian faith are incompatible. Eventually, the Gospel indeed broke the bonds of slavery—but not until someone, like an Abraham Lincoln or a Wilberforce, put his life on the line.

We certainly must not use this passage as a justification for supporting the status quo. The issues of when to speak out, when to take a stand, when to break with a system of injustice, are always complex, and we do not find easy answers in the Bible. That Paul and the early Christians had their reasons for not attacking the system, we will have to accept and respect. But to use them as defenses to justify our unwillingness to speak out and work for justice is, in my judgment, a flagrant misuse of Scripture.

In this section, we have seen a beautiful portrait of the church that really cares; a community shaped by Jesus Christ in which every person, young and old, male and female, needy and sufficient, weak and strong, follower and leader, is cared for, loved, and nurtured by one another—and thus by Jesus Himself.

CHAPTER FIVE

Sound Doctrine and Right Living

1 Timothy 6:3–21

This last section of the letter is fascinating, because while it appears to have no orderly structure, deeper reflection discovers a remarkable coherence in Paul's thoughts. He begins by warning Timothy about wasting his time and energy on the false teachers who enjoy nothing more than debates and arguments. Such teachers actually regard godliness as a means of getting wealthy. This thought leads to some profound insights about the dangers of pursuing wealth. Then Paul delivers a most stirring, personal challenge to Timothy, closing with a benediction. But Paul is not quite through, and adds two postscripts—one directed to the wealthy and one to Timothy—both as follow-ups to what had already been said.

AVOID THE FALSE TEACHERS

> 3 If anyone teaches otherwise and does not consent
> to wholesome words, even the words of our Lord Jesus
> Christ, and to the doctrine which is according to
> godliness,
> 4 he is proud, knowing nothing, but obsessed with
> disputes and arguments over words, from which come
> envy, strife, reviling, evil suspicions,
> 5 useless wranglings of men of corrupt minds and
> destitute of the truth, who suppose that godliness is
> a means of gain. From such withdraw yourself.
>
> *1 Tim. 6:3–5*

The first question that confronts the translator is whether to include the sentence "Teach and exhort these things" with verse 2, as in our translation, or with verse 3, as in the Revised Standard Version and others. It seems best to tie this phrase to what follows.

The very command to teach brings to mind the false teachers who were polluting the atmosphere of Ephesus. The picture is that of teachers who major on words and arguments that become smoke screens for godless and selfish living. The key to true teaching is articulated in verse 3. It is *"the words of our Lord Jesus Christ, and . . . the doctrine which is according to godliness."* This close linkage of doctrine and deportment, belief and behavior, is crucial.

If I were to repeat my years of youth and campus ministry, I would spend less time debating doctrine and more time confronting the issues of lifestyle. I think of one particular student with whom I met again and again over a long period of time. He was very adroit *"with disputes and arguments over words."* He used them effectively in avoiding the kind of commitment to Christ which would necessitate basic changes in the values by which he lived. As long as he could keep God at a distance by his argumentation, he justified his own lifestyle. Looking back, I might have helped him more by confronting the issue of obedience to God rather than trying to win the intellectual arguments.

Disputes, arguments over words, and wranglings can become mere excuses for avoiding the tough issue of the obedience and stewardship required of disciples of Christ. Doctrine detached from life leads to the final degradation in which godliness is regarded as *"a means of gain."* That the reference is to material and monetary gain is clear from what follows in verses 7–10.

Here we have to ask ourselves some troubling questions. To what extent are our appeals for others to accept Christ based upon selfish motives of gain? To what degree are our appeals for others to give based upon the promise that God will give them more in return for what is given? I've heard many television evangelists tell the story of a person formerly in dire personal and financial straits, who after receiving Christ, then became the recipient of more money and security than ever before. The evangelist then implies that if you will support his ministry, God will give you more money in return (stewardship as a sure-fire investment). A regular tool of the trade.

Such appeals to materialistic gain make a travesty of stewardship in that the person who responds to them ends up trying to use God for material gain. To try to use God for anything is a form of blasphemy—of using God's name in vain! The selfish use of God's name is a snare that threatens each of us relentlessly. In a culture saturated with materialistic greed, some people regard wealth as a sure sign of God's blessing. If wealth were always such a sign, wouldn't we then have to believe that pornographers and the bosses of organized crime must have a special relationship with God? The refusal to regard God as a means of gain might be costly to churches and movements whose ultimate goal is to attract more adherents and supporters, but hasn't the time come to question some of our practices? I think so!

And what is Timothy called to do? He is to withdraw himself from such practitioners. There comes a time when we cannot waste our time and energy in more debate and argument. Such folks are not worthy of any more attention. Withdrawal is not easy for most of us, for it can appear to be a surrender. And if you're like me, competitive at heart, you prefer to stay and win the battle. A strategic withdrawal, however, is sometimes in the best interests of one's continuing witness and ministry. And it's not always easy.

Before Paul continues his urgent and personal appeal to Timothy (vv. 11–16), he pauses for a moment on the theme of money. The very thought that some think they can use God as a means of gain leads Paul to reflect more deeply upon the meaning of money.

THE LOVE OF MONEY: A ROOT OF EVIL

6 But godliness with contentment is great gain.

7 For we brought nothing into this world, and it is certain we can carry nothing out.

8 And having food and clothing, with these we shall be content.

9 But those who desire to be rich fall into temptation and a snare, and into many foolish and harmful lusts which drown men in destruction and perdition.

10 For the love of money is a root of all kinds of evil, for which some have strayed from the faith in their greediness, and pierced themselves through with many sorrows.

1 Tim. 6:6–10

Growth in godliness does not guarantee material gain. The gain of godliness is godliness itself. And with it comes *"contentment."* The word translated *"contentment"* is used as a noun in the New Testament only here and in 2 Corinthians 9:8, where it is translated "sufficiency." The idea is that of a state or condition in life in which one needs no other help or support.

Among the many things I have learned from some of the Christians in Uganda is the truth of this powerful little sentence. The first time I was among them, I was feeling pity for them because they had so little, in terms of material things. But I experienced among them an incredible joy—the kind of *"contentment"* of which Paul speaks. I've come to learn that their godliness—their love, devotion, and commitment to Christ—is the source of their well-being.

How backwards and upside down we've gotten it! The idea that one can come to a place in life in which we are complete, without having enough money and goods, is foreign to us. We intellectually accept the fact that money in itself cannot bring us *"contentment,"* but we are still hooked on the premise that it is in some way essential. Our preoccupation with material security and economic abundance makes this quite clear. There's a great difference between seeking godliness as an end in itself or as a means of gain. The temptations here are many, especially to the person in Christian leadership.

The rest of this paragraph is a delightful blending of folksy proverbs, providing a profound basis for a healthy view of money. The first step in developing one's attitude toward money is to put it in perspective. *"We brought nothing into this world, and it is certain we can carry nothing out."* "You can't take it with you." "Shrouds have no pockets." Such proverbs are hardly debatable. I've never heard anyone argue to the contrary.

So why do we spend so much time and energy multiplying and accumulating wealth? The reason most often given is that we should "save for a rainy day." This makes a lot of sense, and it might well be irresponsible to fail to provide some hedge against future needs if one is able to do so. Multiplying and accumulating wealth so that one will not become a burden to others certainly seems prudent—from a human point of view.

But what warrant is there for this viewpoint if we take Jesus seriously? We readily quote Matthew 6:33, "But seek first the kingdom of God and His righteousness, and all these things will be added to you." But are we truly aware of the force of these words? The context of Matthew 6:25–34 determines their meaning:

"Therefore I say to you, do not worry about your life, what you will eat, or what you will drink; nor about your body, what you will put on. . . . Look at the birds of the air, for they neither sow nor reap nor gather into barns; yet your heavenly Father feeds them. Are you not of more value than they? . . . So why do you worry about clothing? Consider the lilies of the field . . . if God so clothes the grass of the field . . . will He not much more clothe you? . . . Therefore do not worry, saying, 'What shall we eat?' or, 'What shall we drink?' or, 'What shall we wear?' . . . For your heavenly Father knows that you need all these things. *But* seek first the kingdom of God and His righteousness, and all these things will be added to you. *Therefore,* do not worry about tomorrow."

I emphasize the "but" and the "therefore" because they tie the whole argument together. Jesus is insisting that God will take care of our basic needs. He speaks in the form that the philosophers have come to call the *ad hominem* argument: *If* this, *how much more* that. *If* God takes care of birds and lilies, *how much more* will He take care of us?

When seen in this light, the multiplication and accumulation of wealth can become a curse rather than a blessing. In two ways. It removes us from the place of being truly dependent upon God. And its management demands more and more of our time and energy.

We are bombarded constantly with the message that financial independence is the great goal of the good life. From life insurance to money market funds, pension funds to IRAs, investments to real estate. The great design is to achieve financial security and independence. As in so many things, half-truths have a way of dominating the whole. I'm not going to argue against wise planning that can keep one from being a burden to others. But I would like to raise some questions about the system so easily taken for granted.

If we can and do achieve the kind of financial security and independence so highly touted, at what real points in life do we have to trust God? Is our trust in God limited only to "spiritual" things, or is He the Lord of all of life? Does God really promise to provide for our necessities? What are necessities? At what point do we cease expanding our "needs" list? How much is enough?

It is past time for us American Christians to begin to wrestle with these questions. Consumerism is an infectious lifestyle, and most of us are more deeply infected than we realize or admit. How long can we justify our mad pursuit of accumulating and consuming wealth while millions of our brothers and sisters are in dire and desperate need?

A clear and simple principle of the Christian view of wealth is set forth for all time by Paul in 2 Corinthians 8:9–15. It begins with Jesus Himself: "For you know the grace of our Lord Jesus Christ, that though He was rich, yet for your sakes He became poor, that you through His poverty might become rich" (8:9). The principle is clear. The rich are to divest themselves for the sake of the poor. This is what Jesus did. It is what we are to do. Any sense of accumulating wealth in any form for personal security or comfort is simply foreign to Jesus. The well-known encounter of Jesus with the rich young ruler certainly establishes this point. Jesus left him no loopholes!

There was a memorable line in the movie *Oh, God!* John Denver is talking with "God" (in the form of George Burns) and raises the classic question, "If you're so loving and good, how come there are so many people starving in the world?" To which "God" replies: "Look, I gave you plenty to go around for everyone. As long as some of you insist on having more than you need, others will go hungry." And that's the way it is!

Paul sets forth a second principle in 2 Corinthians 8:13–14: "For I do not mean that others should be eased and you burdened; but by an equality, that now at this time your abundance may supply their lack, that their abundance also may supply your lack—that there may be equality." The shifting sands of economics create changing scenes of wealth and poverty. Wealthy nations become poor nations, and poor become wealthy—witness some of the oil-producing countries in the Middle East over the last fifty years. Wealthy individuals become poor, and vice versa—we're seeing a lot of changes presently in our own community. The principle of equality, set forth by Paul, puts life on the teeter-totter. When you're up, you help the one who is down—when you're down, you'll be helped. For underneath it all, God provides enough for all of us and holds us responsible for the distribution. It's hard to believe that it is responsible and faithful stewardship of God's good earth when 6 percent of us consume and control 50 percent of the world's resources.

Paul concludes his statement to Timothy by pointing out what the pursuit of wealth does to us. The desire to be rich causes us to *"fall into temptation and a snare, and into many foolish and harmful lusts."*

Note well that the issue is not having wealth, but *desiring* it. The very desire is the trap. The desire for wealth has a way of becoming all-consuming. As a pastor for nineteen years in an affluent suburb, I witness this daily. I see people all around me for whom the drive for wealth is nothing less than an obsession.

A good question to keep check on your own desires is: "How much of my time and energy today was spent in thinking about my finances?" The quest to gain increasing independence from the concern about money is essential to spiritual growth. Thus Jesus' counsel: "Do not lay up for yourselves treasures on earth. . . . But lay up for yourselves treasures in heaven. . . . For where your treasure is, there your heart will be also" (Matt. 6:19–21). And how do we change our mental orientation? By focusing our thoughts more and more upon "whatever things are true, whatever things are noble, whatever things are just, whatever things are pure, whatever things are lovely, whatever things are of good report" (Phil. 4:8). To break the pattern of the desire for money takes serious and concentrated mental effort.

Unchecked desire for money leads to the love of money. And the love of money is *"a root of all kinds of evil."* Two things are important here, for this is a much misquoted text. How often I've heard it said, "Money is the root of all evil." Not so! Money itself is neither good nor evil; it is morally neutral. It is the use to which it is put that is either good or evil. Thus the *"love"* of money becomes *"a root of all kinds of evil."* This love of money is called greed. And greed has a way of becoming all-consuming. I preached a sermon not long ago with the title, "How Much Is Enough?" Until we answer that question specifically and measurably, we will never withdraw ourselves from greed's grasp. To Paul, the boundary was drawn in verse 8: *"And having food and clothing, with these we shall be content."* Where do we draw the line that says, "This is all I need"? Where there is no line, the love of money becomes a dominant passion.

The second thing that needs to be clarified in this oft-misquoted text is the use of the indefinite rather than the definite article. *"The love of money is* **a** *root of all kinds of evil."* Evil confronts us on many fronts, and to regard money as the only or even the major root of evil may be misleading or naive. One of the tough challenges of Christian discipleship is confronting evil on many fronts at the same time. Some of us discovered that while we were fighting the evils of racism, the evils of the abuse of our environment, God's creation, were in need of confrontation. Then we were confronted with numerous other evils: child abuse, spouse abuse, pornography, violence, crime, war—and the danger is that we run from cause to cause, never seeing anything through to a significant change. I see the multiplicity of evil as a call for diversity in the church as the Body of Christ. No individual, not even a pastor, can possibly develop all of the knowledge and skills necessary to confront every avenue of evil in our world. I have discovered the remarkable complexities involved in the questions surrounding our military budget, the nuclear arms race, the issues of criminal justice, racial justice, and the roots of poverty and hunger. I'm learning that I do best to focus on an issue or two and then to encourage others within the church to do the same. I hope that in every congregation we will be active on many fronts at all times in our witness and work for justice and righteousness.

We have too great a tendency to judge others on the basis of whether they share our concern in a particular area. How much better that we celebrate our diversity in the Body of Christ so that some are prophets, some evangelists, some are working in every area of witness and concern (Eph. 4:11–16). It is this wide range of diversity in function that enables the church to function as a unit. A body that is just one big eye or one big foot is too ludicrous to imagine (1 Cor. 12:12–21).

It is the "love" of money that is "a" root of all kinds of evil.

A SOLEMN AND JOYOUS CHARGE

11 But you, O man of God, flee these things and pursue righteousness, godliness, faith, love, patience, gentleness.

12 Fight the good fight of faith, lay hold on eternal life, to which you were also called and have confessed the good confession in the presence of many witnesses.

13 I urge you in the sight of God who gives life to all things, and before Christ Jesus who witnessed the good confession before Pontius Pilate,

14 that you keep this commandment without spot, blameless until our Lord Jesus Christ's appearing,

15 which He will show in His own time, He who

is the blessed and only Potentate, the King of kings
and Lord of lords,
      16 who only has immortality, dwelling in
unapproachable light, whom no man has seen or can
see, to whom be honor and everlasting power. Amen.

1 Tim. 6:11–16

As we come to the end of this magnificent letter, we cannot be
certain whether Paul intended to conclude with this charge to Timothy
and the benediction in verses 15 and 16, or whether verses 11–16
were a parenthesis before continuing to address the issue of our relationship with money (17–19), and then giving a final charge to Timothy (20, 21). I prefer to regard verses 11–16 as a fitting conclusion
to the letter. But after the "Amen" of verse 16, Paul adds two postscripts before signing off.

I have a feeling that Timothy would have read this part of the
letter over and over again. It's like part of a treasured love letter to
which you return in times of special need. The *"man of God"* is con-
trasted with the false teachers and the lovers of money just confronted.

The verbs in verse 11 are dramatic: *"flee"* and *"pursue."* He is to
be in flight from the false teachings and the love of money, and he
is to be in pursuit of *"righteousness, godliness, faith, love, patience, [and]
gentleness."* Paul was fond of such lists of virtues, as with his list of
the fruit of the Holy Spirit in Galatians 5:22–23.

Flight and pursuit is a vivid way of viewing the life of Christian
discipleship. There are things that must be constantly avoided—and
not just passively. To flee implies that something is after us. Paul's
view of evil was active. He was aware of "principalities and powers"
at work in the world. While we may not choose to express our view
of sin and the devil with the same language and images of that era,
we ignore, at our peril, the active power of evil in the world. Many
of us were taught that big boys never run away. But when it comes
to active evil, wisdom calls for flight as well as fight. Yes, there are
times when we must dig in and resist. There are other times when
it is best to flee. True wisdom is choosing the right response.

Pursuit is the other side of Christian discipleship. Here is the active
and intentional pursuit of specific virtues. Righteousness has to do
with what is right—both toward God and others. Godliness is the

patterning after the nature of God as we see it revealed in Jesus Himself. Faith, love, patience, and gentleness are among those qualities always tied to Christian living.

To "flee" and "pursue," Paul adds two more verbs in verse 12: *"fight"* and *"lay hold."* Whether the word "fight" was intended as an athletic or a military metaphor, the emphasis is not upon competition or combat, but upon a disciplined and determined struggle. Faith is a continuous struggle requiring intentional effort. I find this so true in personal experience. With regularity, I lapse into the kind of thinking that questions whether God really cares or is present. Again and again, I focus my efforts and energies on financial security and success. And, believe me, it's a constant struggle to keep my faith in God first and foremost in the nitty-gritty of daily living.

The tense of the verb *"lay hold"* in Greek describes a completed reality, a single happening. This suggests that one can come to the point of holding on to the reality of eternal life as an assured possession. Again, I find this to be true. While the fight of faith is a continuing process, the assurance of life eternal by God's grace and mercy is a settled reality.

Timothy's *"good confession"* is compared with Christ's before Pilate. Most commentators interpret this confession as the basic affirmation made in one's baptism. Whether such is the case, we do well to be reminded again and again that we are a confessional community. To be a Christian is to confess Jesus as Savior and Lord. To confess is to speak out one's faith. It is to announce one's belief. I run into folks from time to time who express aversions to creeds and theological statements. One church I drive by, not far from where I live, has a sign that declares: "No creed, just Christ." But even that is a creed. For the Latin *credo* means "I believe." Whenever we say what we believe, we are making our confession. A Christian is one who confesses faith in Jesus Christ as Savior and Lord.

The commandment that Timothy is to keep is probably his confession that led to his commissioning through baptism and possibly some form of ordination. In baptism, we are commissioned as servants of Jesus Christ and thus are people under orders. Unfortunately, contemporary church membership is not widely connected with the idea of being under a command of Christ. It seems best to think of *"without spot"* and *"blameless"* in relation to Timothy rather than the commandment. We do not keep commandments spotless and blameless, but we are called to keep ourselves pure.

The section ends with a doxology and benediction unlike any other in Paul's letters. It is a magnificent ascription of praise to Jesus as *"the blessed and only Potentate, the King of kings and Lord of lords."* To Jesus is ascribed immortality, unapproachable light, and invisibility, and to Him we affirm honor and everlasting power.

It seems that Paul has concluded his letter to young Timothy—but there is more he wants to say.

Have you ever added a postscript to a letter? And even a post-postscript? Yes? Then you can readily identify with these added sentences to the letter.

P.S.: To the Rich

17 Command those who are rich in this present age that they not be haughty, nor trust in uncertain riches but in the living God, who gives us richly all things to enjoy;
18 that they do good, that they be rich in good works, ready to give, willing to share,
19 storing up for themselves a good foundation for the time to come, that they may lay hold on eternal life.

1 Tim. 6:17–19

The first postscript suggests that Paul realizes that while he had written about the dangers of loving money, he had not addressed those who were already rich as directly as he wished. While the early churches consisted mostly of people who were poor, there were some believers of wealth. They are given four specific commands: they are not to be haughty; they are to trust in God, not in their wealth; they are to do good; and they are to be rich in good works, giving and sharing.

One of the perils of being wealthy is pride. Wealth brings a sense of achievement. It also grants power and privilege. There simply is no place for pride in the Kingdom of God, and that's why Jesus said, with great compassion, "How hard it is for those who have riches to enter the kingdom of God!" (Luke 18:24). It's ironic that we make it quite easy for people with wealth to enter our churches—and even give them special attention (James 2:1–4)—but the fact is that wealth is a hindrance to God's Kingdom. Why? Because it leads to pride and a haughty mind.

It is an even greater hindrance because it diminishes the necessity for our faith in God. While the Bible never makes poverty into a virtue, there is a basic reality that people who must learn to trust God for their daily bread are indeed close to His Kingdom. To be sure, there is a fine line between having and trusting wealth. Jesus diagnosed the rich young ruler as being unable to draw that line, calling him to divest himself of his riches in order that he might be able to trust God. There's no indication that such radical treatment was prescribed for all wealthy persons, and special are those who have wealth without putting too much trust in it. And the only way they can do that is by strict disciplines of doing good, especially through giving and sharing.

Paul's principle was that of equality and fairness. We have already looked at this principle set forth in 2 Corinthians 8:13–15 in connection with 1 Timothy 6:6–10. It's significant that Paul quoted Exodus 16:18 in the Corinthian passage. "He who gathered much had nothing left over, and he who gathered little had no lack" (2 Cor. 8:15). The proper use of wealth is not saving—it is sharing. Many of us were raised on the philosophy that "a penny saved is a penny earned." We must change our thinking to "a penny *shared* is a penny earned."

I wonder. Will we ever be willing to deal with this principle honestly and realistically in the Christian church on a global scale?

It has been said that if we could reduce the world to a global village of one hundred people: seventy would be unable to read, one would have a college education, fifty would be suffering from malnutrition, eighty would live in housing unfit for human habitation, and six would control half of the money of the entire village.

If those of us among the six who are Christians are going to take Jesus seriously, how much longer can we justify controlling, spending, and hoarding half of the resources intended for all 100 of us? I'm quite convinced that we must face up to the needs of others if we are going to take our faith seriously.

It was my privilege to participate in the Congress on World Evangelization in Lausanne, Switzerland, in 1974. The five thousand participants in the Congress shaped and signed a covenant. Part of it reads: "All of us are shocked by the poverty of millions and disturbed by the injustices which cause it. More of us who live in affluent circumstances accept our duty to develop a simple lifestyle in order to contribute more generously to both relief and evangelism."

What an exciting journey awaits us! Consciously and intentionally spending less on ourselves—not in order to exalt asceticism—but to deliver more help to the poor and more evangelists to the 2.7 billion people who have not yet heard the Gospel of Jesus Christ. There are groups of Christians springing up in many places who are developing approaches to simpler, less expensive lifestyles *in order to* direct more money to helping the poor and spreading the Gospel.

You just might want to follow Paul's admonition to the affluent to give and to share—and what a beautiful way to think of giving: *"storing up for themselves a good foundation for the time to come."* It was perhaps out of this text that the saying was coined: "You can't take it with you, but you can send it ahead!" Why not?

P.P.S.: TO TIMOTHY

20 O Timothy, guard what was committed to your trust, avoiding the profane and vain babblings and contradictions of what is falsely called knowledge—
21 by professing it, some have strayed concerning the faith. Grace be with you. Amen.

1 Tim. 6:20–21

With this second postscript, Paul concludes this remarkable epistle. How he loved Timothy! And how concerned he was that Timothy remain faithful and alive in his ministry.

This admonition stands before us all as a constant warning of the danger of putting our energy into doctrinal and theological discussions at the expense of putting our faith to work and our love into practice.

Introduction to 2 Timothy

It's reasonable to believe that this is the last letter that Paul wrote. It could have been written within a few days of his martyrdom. In studying and teaching this letter, I've come to a new appreciation for it as perhaps the most intimate and moving of all Paul's letters.

While we cannot settle all of the questions surrounding the occasion of this letter, it can certainly be regarded as having been written during Paul's final imprisonment in Rome. Presumably, Paul was beheaded during the latter part of Nero's reign (A.D. 54–68) probably after the mad emperor had ordered the burning of Rome (A.D. 66) and tried to blame the Christians in order to arouse public outrage against them.

This imprisonment should not be identified with the "house arrest" with which Luke concludes Acts (28:30–31). A widely accepted view is that Paul was released after that and continued his itinerant ministry, even perhaps to Spain, before his final imprisonment in Rome.

In some of our study groups, we've found it helpful to read this letter through in one sitting at the first session, imagining that it has just come in the mail.

The Apostle Paul

What excitement must have gripped Timothy when the courier delivered this treasured scroll from Rome. Was Paul still alive? Would he be released? Would he ever return to Ephesus? At last, here was some word from the beloved Apostle.

For Paul, the end of the journey had come. In other letters, he had expressed his hope for future travels and ministry. But here is the word of finality. "The time of my departure is at hand. I have fought the good fight, I have finished the race, I have kept the faith" (4:6–7). He then asks Timothy to come to him with his books and cloak, hopefully "before winter."

This letter is Paul's final farewell. Someone called it the "dying" letter, and this is why it is of special importance. Life has to look different when you know it's about to end. What Paul is about to communicate will be his last words, not only to Timothy, but to all of us down through the centuries as well.

Timothy

To read the letter rightly, we have to get inside Timothy's sandals. For more than fifteen years, Timothy had been Paul's traveling companion throughout Asia and Greece. He had been with Paul on the second and third missionary journeys and had been sent by Paul on special assignments (1 Thess. 3:1 and 1 Cor. 4:17). He had journeyed with Paul to Jerusalem (Acts 20:1–5). He was with Paul in his first Roman imprisonment (Phil 1:1; 2:19–24; Col. 1:1). He had been left in Ephesus and appointed by Paul to be in charge of the Christian work there.

Every indication is that Timothy was much better suited to be the "number two" man. He was apparently a timid and shy person. This is implied in Paul's demand that the people in Corinth give special affirmation to him (1 Cor. 16:10–11). If Paul's gift was boldness, Timothy's was sensitivity. It is not uncommon for such sensitivity to be accompanied by digestive problems for which Paul recommended a particular tonic (1 Tim. 5:23).

It was their very differences that made them such a dynamic duo. Timothy's support and attention to detail would become indispensable to the full use of Paul's great gifts. And Paul's impetuous daring and expansive vision would become Timothy's life-blood. But now, Timothy is on his own, having to be and do so many things that he would not have chosen.

So the letter has special meaning to all of us Timothys who, regularly or periodically, are required to do things beyond our natural desires and abilities.

A Hostile World

One other factor has to grip our imaginations in order to read this letter properly. It was written at a time when the question of survival was paramount. This was not just personal survival by Paul or Timothy, but the survival of the church itself!

Our chief Apostle is in prison and about to be executed. The churches that had been established didn't have buildings, budgets, staffs, or status. For the most part, they were small gatherings of believers who met, even under cover in some places. They were not people of power or prestige, but were, generally, rather undistinguished folks (1 Cor. 1:26).

There was every reason to wonder whether this thing called the church would survive much longer. We now know that things got worse, not better. By the time John was hauled out of Ephesus to exile on the island of Patmos, it certainly appeared that Caesar, not Christ, had all the power.

So the letter comes to us from what by all human standards should have been the depths of despair. Before you study the letter, read it through as a letter that has just arrived—enjoy your morning mail!

An Outline of 2 Timothy

I. Marching Orders for a Young Disciple: 1:1–10
   A. Christ Jesus Our Lord: 1:1–2
   B. God Has No Grandchildren: 1:3–5
   C. Rekindling the Gift of God: 1:6–7
   D. The Gospel in a Nutshell: 1:8–10
II. Our Calling to the Ministry: 1:11—2:7
   A. Everyone a Minister: 1:11–14
   B. Everyone Needs an Onesiphorus: 1:15–18
   C. Strength for the Task: 2:1–2
   D. Ministry Is Difficult: 2:3–7
III. Our Work for God: 2:8–26
   A. The Power of Memory: 2:8–10
   B. Awesome Options: 2:11–13
   C. An Unashamed Worker: 2:14–19
   D. A Clean Vessel: 2:20–22
   E. A Gentle Servant: 2:23–26
IV. Coping in Troubled Times: 3:1–17
   A. The Roots of Trouble: 3:1–5
   B. The Spread of Trouble: 3:6–9
   C. Overcoming Trouble: 3:10–13
   D. The Firm Foundation for Living in Troubled Times: 3:14–17
V. Love's Last Appeal: 4:1–22
   A. The Highest Priorities: 4:1–5
   B. Hanging Up the Spikes: 4:6–8
   C. Even Apostles Have Needs: 4:9–13
   D. When Everyone Lets You Down: 4:14–18
   E. Come Before Winter: 4:19–22

CHAPTER ONE

Marching Orders for a Young Disciple

2 Timothy 1:1–10

The ancient way of starting letters with the name of the writer has distinct advantages. You didn't have to wrestle your way to the end of the scroll to discover who was writing.

CHRIST JESUS OUR LORD

1 Paul, an apostle of Jesus Christ by the will of God, according to the promise of life which is in Christ Jesus,

2 To Timothy, my beloved son:

Grace, mercy, and peace from God the Father and Christ Jesus our Lord.

2 Tim. 1:1–2

Here, the greeting is both like and unlike those in Paul's other letters. Paul's self-image centered in being an apostle. This is not to be thought of in the sense of our view of ordained clergy. To Paul this title simply meant that he was under orders from Jesus Himself. His whole purpose in life centered in obedience to Jesus Christ. His tent making work was only a way of providing the means for his true vocation. He was never off duty. And even in his last days, awaiting execution, he is still—first, last, and always— *"an apostle of Jesus Christ."*

The high sense of apostolic vocation that gripped Paul was grounded in the conviction that this was the will of God for his life. A current TV commercial offering a particular credit card as the key that can open the door to the good life, flashes a definition of success on the screen: "Success is the freedom to live your life the way you want to." The scene then shifts to a couple using their credit card in a Swiss resort! Paul knew a great deal about travel, though his accommodations were sometimes provided by the government. His definition of success was more like: "Success is to live your life the way God wants you to."

The widespread belief in our time that success and happiness are tied to self-seeking pursuits must be challenged. Our strategies for self-fulfillment simply will not work unless they are tied to the pursuit of God's will. And perhaps no one expressed that will more precisely than the prophet Micah:

> "He has shown you, O man, what is good;
>   and what does the Lord require of you
> but to do justly,
>   to love mercy,
> and to walk humbly with your God?"
>
> Micah 6:8

The unique part of Paul's greeting is the phrase *"according to the promise of life which is in Christ Jesus."* The idea that "the will of God" and "the good life" are one and the same is not always evident. The good life, in our culture, is tied to wealth, leisure, recreation, and material possessions. The will of God, throughout the Bible, is tied to love, mercy, justice, caring for the poor—all requiring giving and sacrifice. We have to choose, again and again. Jesus Christ promises us abundant life. He insisted that "it is more blessed to give than to receive" (Acts 20:35).

Don't miss the fact that in this greeting, Paul uses the name *"Christ Jesus"* three times. A writer uses repetition in order to make a strong emphasis. The emphasis on Christ Jesus is intentional. Christianity *is* Jesus Christ. It is not primarily the church, nor theology, nor ethics, nor religion—it is Jesus Christ.

In addition to this triple use of Christ Jesus, Paul also uses the term *"Lord,"* and in verse 10, "Savior." While Paul sometimes used "Jesus Christ" and sometimes used "Christ Jesus," there is no clear significance in the order. It's worth reflecting on these names and titles.

Jesus. His name is Jesus. As with most people of that time, he had only one name. Jesus was a common name, the Greek form of the Hebrew name Joshua. Many Jewish mothers named their sons Joshua, after the great military leader of Israel. The Hebrews put great significance on names, and Joshua meant "God is salvation." While there were many called Joshua and Jesus, Jesus of Nazareth was to become known as *the* Jesus.

To call Him "Jesus" is to affirm His genuine humanity. That's not always easy for us to do. The profound mystery of Jesus is at the intersection of His humanity and His deity. Christians have always affirmed both. From the New Testament on, we confess Him as human and divine. I have friends who admit to tough intellectual struggles with this mystery. Some have no difficulty accepting Him as truly human, but find it difficult to understand Him as God Incarnate. Others have come to clear faith in His Deity, but can't really see Him truly as one of us with all of the human limitations implied.

It's clear to me that in orthodox circles it's more acceptable to hedge on His humanity than on His deity. It seems to me that we do best to admit our inability to fit Jesus into any of our categories and celebrate the mystery of His uniqueness. And if we call Him Jesus, we are affirming that He really was and is one of us. When He hit His thumb with a hammer, it hurt; when He cut His finger with a saw, it bled. He experienced all the feelings we do and shared our common joys and sorrows. In holding that He was without sin (Heb. 4:15), let us not make Him something other than truly human.

Christ. As was mentioned previously in the commentary on 1 Thessalonians, the Greek word *Christos* is the equivalent of the Hebrew *Mashiach,* which converts in English to "Messiah." Thus, if we were to be technically correct, we would always refer to Jesus as *the* Christ. The hope for the Messiah begins with God's promise to David. The reign of David had been the golden age of Israel. Through Nathan, God had promised David a descendant whose throne and kingdom would be forever (2 Sam. 7:12–16). From that time, Israel lived in hope for the Anointed One of God, the Messiah, the Christ. The promise of a throne and kingdom came to be viewed in terms of political and military might. Thus, a Christ from Nazareth, a backwater town; a Christ without an army; a Christ who talked about loving enemies and going the second mile, was a caricature.

To regard Jesus as the Christ, the promised seed of David, required a radical redefinition of Messiah. How blessed were those who came to that understanding of Jesus as the Christ. In Him the Messianic age has begun and His kingdom shall never end. To live in Him is to live as a citizen of the Kingdom of God.

Savior. Here is a word that is neither a name or a title but a description of His work. He described Himself as having come "to seek and to save that which was lost" (Luke 19:10).

We can't very well call Him "Savior" without admitting that we're lost, and that's not easy for us to do. When I was in seminary, I was a summer lifeguard at one of our Southern California beaches. I was told in my training that most people would resist and resent our assistance. My initial reaction was disbelief. I assumed that anyone in trouble would gladly welcome help. Then came my first rescue! I was fought off, cursed at, kicked, and clawed. What a lesson in human pride. Too proud to admit the need to be helped, we cry, "I can do it myself!"

Lord. This is a word of authority. To call Jesus "Lord" is to give Him absolute authority in one's life. I wish I could say that I've come to that point. But I can't. My very lifestyle reveals the fact that I still regard much of my money and time as mine rather than His. There are still those pockets of resistance and disobedience that haven't really been surrendered to His mastery.

I'm sure that I'll never be able to say that He is truly the Absolute Master—the Lord—of everything in my life. But I'm finding that every time I make Him Lord in one more area of my life, I am blessed indeed. So I'm committed to the journey in which, step by step, I learn to call Him Lord. I'm convinced that I'll never arrive, but I know I'm in good company:

> Not that I claim to have achieved all this, nor to have reached perfection already. But I keep going on, trying to grasp that purpose for which Christ Jesus grasped me. My brothers, I do not consider myself to have grasped it fully even now. But I do concentrate on this: I forget all that lies behind me and with hands outstretched to whatever lies ahead I go straight for the goal—my reward the honour of my high calling by God in Christ Jesus.
>
> (*Phil. 3:12–14, Phillips*)

GOD HAS NO GRANDCHILDREN

3 I thank God, whom I serve with a pure
conscience, as my forefathers did, as without ceasing
I remember you in my prayers night and day,

4 greatly desiring to see you, being mindful of your
tears, that I may be filled with joy,
5 when I call to remembrance the unfeigned faith
that is in you, which dwelt first in your grandmother
Lois and your mother Eunice, and I am persuaded is
in you also.

2 Tim. 1:3–5

These three verses are characteristic of Paul—a very long sentence
with a number of ideas. The central thought of the sentence focuses
upon Timothy's faith. As Paul thanks God for that faith in Timothy,
his active mind literally bursts with three powerful ideas.

The clear conscience. The opening phrase of the first sentence has long
been an enigma to me. At first, it sounds like a self-righteous boast.
To say that one serves God *"with a pure conscience"* smacks of a claim
to perfection. We have just heard Paul's disclaimer to perfection in
Philippians 3:12–14. In 1 Timothy 1:15, Paul declared himself to be
the "chief" of sinners. Does he now claim to be perfect?

I think not. The phrase *"as my forefathers did,"* qualifies the whole
idea. How did Paul's ancestors serve God? Sometimes well. Sometimes
poorly. Some of those ancestors achieved prominence in the Old Testament. There was Abraham, a great man of God, who on one occasion
passed his wife off as his sister to sleep with King Abimelech in
order to save his own neck (Gen. 20:1–16). There was Moses, who
murdered an Egyptian soldier in cold blood and who fled into the
desert in fear when he knew he had been observed (Exod. 2:11–16).
And we all know a few seamy things about Paul's ancestor David
(2 Sam. 11). The Bible is an honest book and portrays its heroes as
real men and women with strengths and weaknesses who had good
days and bad days.

In what sense, then, did they serve God *"with a clear conscience"?*
Certainly not in the sense of *performance.* But the one thing they all
had in common was the *intention* to love and to serve God. To the
Danish philosopher Søren Kierkegaard, purity of heart was "to will
one thing."

I'm convinced that we need to focus more upon our intentions
than our performance. When we are possessed with a strong desire
to love and serve Christ, our performance will be profoundly influ-
enced. And when our performance falls short of our intention, we
experience anew the grace and mercy of God.

To serve God with a clear conscience does not require perfection in our performance. It is a matter of intention and desire to love and serve Christ—even when we fail. It's hard for us to grasp fully the fact that God honors our intentions whether or not we succeed in carrying them out. This is what is meant by grace.

The need for each other. The bulk of this long sentence (vv. 3–5) is Paul's disclosure of his tremendous need for Timothy's love and care. My image of Paul makes this all the more striking. Paul comes across to me as emotionally strong and tough. He could take all kinds of treatment and continue to hang in there. He seemed to be so possessed with his sense of apostolic mission that he would go it alone if necessary. We would say that Paul "really had it all together"—he was a very self-sufficient man. But, he was unashamed to admit to his need for Timothy.

I was reared in a generation in which the ideal, for the male at least, was self-sufficiency. It was an unwritten law that "big boys don't cry." In my twenties and thirties, I took a certain pride in the fact that I really didn't need anybody. Oh, I liked to have friends and to be with people, but I assured them that I wouldn't be a burden. Not to need help was the epitome of strength and success.

I'm so grateful for those who have helped me reject that error. The beginning of maturity and abundant living for me was at the point of discovering and admitting my great need for others. Everybody needs at least one other person as Paul needed Timothy. And most of us need more than one. Happy indeed are those who have others to whom they can express their deepest needs and receive love, care, and support.

My definition of success for a church is increasingly in this area. The successful church is a group of people where any and every person can come to find open, growing, caring relationships with a few others in mutual commitment to Jesus as Lord. If this isn't true in our churches, our standards of success are all mixed up.

The influence of the family. In verse 5, Paul celebrates the fact that Timothy was a third generation Christian. Both his mother and grandmother had preceded him in the faith. Apparently, however, Timothy's father did not share in the Christian faith (Acts 16:1).

While it's great to celebrate Timothy's faith as a source of joy because of the influence of Lois and Eunice, let's not forget the other side of the coin. As a pastor, I have witnessed many children reared in marvelous Christian families who have rejected their parents' faith and values. I've also seen a large number of deeply committed Christians who were reared in incredibly bad environments.

I'm all for exalting the Christian family. There's no question that the ideal family is Christian parents experiencing the joy of seeing their children grow in Christian commitment and discipleship. But let's affirm those Christian parents whose kids are in rebellion. Let's affirm the fact that some great kids come out of horrible homes.

That's why I say, "God has no grandchildren." In verse 5, Paul states at the beginning and the end that Timothy's faith is Timothy's—not his mother's or his grandmother's. My father-in-law used to say that being born in a Christian home doesn't make one a Christian any more than being born in the garage makes one an automobile.

Let us work for Christian families. Let us train Christian parents to provide climates in their families that encourage and nurture Christian faith. But let us neither take credit nor blame for our children's faith or rebellion, but give thanks for the grace of God.

My wife and I celebrate the fact that our girls share our faith in Christ and are each growing disciples in Christ. The temptation to take credit for that must be rejected. It is God's doing, not ours. The other side of the coin needs to be given equal attention. If any or all of them should have gone the opposite direction, we really need not take the blame any more than the credit.

REKINDLING THE GIFT OF GOD

6 Therefore I remind you to stir up the gift of God
which is in you through the laying on of my hands.
7 For God has not given us a spirit of fear, but
of power and of love and of a sound mind.

2 Tim. 1:6–7

Across the years, camping has been a joyous part of our family life. The nights around a campfire are a special treasure in the storehouse of our memories. Our girls have often called me a fire freak for at least two reasons. I can sit and stare at a fire all evening, absolutely mesmerized. In addition, I inevitably end up with a stick in my hand, continually poking at the coals and the wood, varying the dancing patterns of the flames.

Unfortunately, our translation of *"stir up the gift of God,"* loses the vivid metaphor of the word that Paul used, *anazōpureō*. This word is used only here in the New Testament. The main part of the word *zōpureō* refers to embers in which the flame has subsided. Putting the *ana* on the front of the word literally means "to kindle anew the flames of the fire." I love Clarence Jordan's translation, "I'm reminding you to shake the ashes off the God-given fire that's in you".

There's no reason to believe that Timothy's fire had gone out—you can't rekindle that. But every fire needs repeated stirring and rearranging to keep it burning brightly. Here is a powerful insight into a reason why so many Christians are more like smoldering ashes than dancing fires.

How do you rekindle the fire? Make some changes. Do some re-arranging. If your devotional life is dull, try some different approaches. If your joy in Christ has cooled, try getting closer to someone else to renew the flame. I find small groups that meet regularly are the most helpful in shaking off the ashes of lethargy and self-pity.

Don't be surprised or alarmed when the flames go down—just shake off some ashes and get some new kindling!

It's not really clear what the *"gift of God"* was which Timothy had received with *"the laying on of my hands."* Most commentators see this as an early form of ordination. I'm more comfortable not going too far beyond what is stated here. We really don't know what the act was nor what the particular gift was.

We mustn't miss, however, the importance of symbolic actions within the Christian community. The laying on of hands is a powerful symbol that expresses the transmission of gifts for ministry. It is often connected with prayer and healing as well. If anything, we should probably use this symbol more than we do. I often find there is a remarkable flow of love and power in prayer with the laying on of hands.

In our technological society, it might be well for us to make more use of symbolic actions to express the profound mysteries of ultimate reality beyond the scope of scientific measurement and classification. Baptism, communion, the laying on of hands, and simple things like a hug or a flower can be symbolic actions through which love, power, and healing flow.

This leads to the insight that God does not give us *"a spirit of fear, but of power and of love and of a sound mind."* Power in itself can be devastating and destructive—it needs the controls of love and common sense. Love can become mere sentimentalism or experimentation without the other qualities. And the sound mind all alone can become merely academic or speculative. Power, love, and a sound mind, given to us by God Himself, is the antidote to the spirit of fear or timidity.

THE GOSPEL IN A NUTSHELL

8 Therefore do not be ashamed of the testimony
of our Lord, nor of me His prisoner, but share with
me in the sufferings for the gospel according to the
power of God,

9 who has saved us and called us with a holy
calling, not according to our works, but according to
His own purpose and grace which was given to us
in Christ Jesus before time began,

10 but has now been revealed by the appearing of
our Savior Jesus Christ, who has abolished death and
brought life and immortality to light through the
gospel,

2 Tim. 1:8–10

These three verses form a priceless pearl in the midst of this very
personal letter. Notice the four "therefores" in 1:6, 1:8, 2:1, and 2:3.
They introduce four strong appeals from Paul to Timothy: 1:6—
Therefore . . . rekindle *"the gift of God."* 1:8— *"Therefore do not be ashamed."*
2:1—*"Therefore . . . be strong in the grace."* 2:3—*"Therefore endure hardship
as a good soldier."*

This appeal is perhaps a mild confrontation to some basic timidity
in Timothy. Telling him not to be ashamed could well imply that
Paul had seen some tendency towards this in Timothy. Timidity and
the *"testimony of our Lord"* do not blend, since God gives us the spirit
"of power and of love and of a sound mind" (1:7). I find the fact that this
may have been a problem to Timothy a source of great comfort to
me. How well I know the fear that often accompanies my efforts
to witness for Christ, whether by word or deed.

The power to overcome this timidity grows out of an understanding
and appreciation of the Gospel itself. And in this pearl of a paragraph
Paul gives us one of the most concise and comprehensive summaries
of the Gospel anywhere in his writings: God *"saved us," "called us,"*
"graced" us, *"abolished [the power of] death,"* and *"brought life and immortality."* Here is the Gospel in a nutshell.

He *"saved us."* The Gospel is salvation. But salvation language has
come on hard times for many of us. The image of being confronted
by a beady-eyed stranger with "Brother, are you saved?" is repugnant
to me. But we must be careful never to lose sight of the fact that
the Gospel is, first and foremost, about being saved.

It's not only the language of salvation that has met rejection. It's the concept itself. To accept salvation, you have to admit you're lost. I'm one of those people who hates to ask for help. I even resist asking for directions when driving in a strange town. Self-sufficiency ranks high among the virtues of our society. It's certainly as American as apple pie. From childhood, I've been programmed to "do it myself."

But salvation can only come to those who admit that they are lost. The cry for help is the initial step toward salvation. Our self-centered, self-seeking approach to life alienates us from God's love and mercy. Our need for acceptance and forgiveness by God can only come through His initiative. Jesus is God's way of initiating that love and forgiveness. He is God's act and offer of salvation.

He "called us." The idea of God's calling inevitably leads to a discussion of election and all of the perplexities associated with predestination. While these are questions that rightly concern Christian theology, I prefer to focus on a different aspect of God's calling us. The call, says Paul, is *"not according to our works."* This means that it is for everyone. But it is not a call in general over a universal loudspeaker. It is a call to each of us by name.

I find it awesome to ponder the fact that God calls me by name! The great God of the universe, the Creator and Cosmic Ground of all being, calls me Gary. That He calls each of us by name is the mark of His care for us. The Gospel is grounded in the reality of a personal relationship with the living God. It is personal because God calls us by name.

He "graced" us. I choose to make the noun into a verb because grace is an active word. The classic definition of grace is "unmerited favor." God's grace means that He relates to us in ways that we do not deserve. This grace is *"not according to our works."* It is an expression of God's eternal love and comes in and through Jesus Christ. It is grace, not the calling, which was *"before time began."* The experience of salvation through our response to God's call is all of grace.

We have difficulty admitting our lostness and need for salvation. And we find it even more difficult to live by grace. This was the central issue of Paul's letter to the Galatians, and the Galatian tendency is ever within and among us. To live by grace toward God means that we reject any notion that God loves us more when we're good or less when we're bad. The category of "the good" Christian has no place. There are only "graced" Christians.

It's even more difficult to live in grace toward each other. We sin

244

against grace in our relationships with others when we are most concerned to see that they get what we feel they deserve. We do not have an admirable track record in the way we respond to hurts and failure among ourselves in the Christian community. A pastor friend of mine, experiencing the pain of gossip and rejection in the midst of trouble in his own marriage, sadly said to me, "Christians seem to have a need to shoot their wounded."

And for ever so many, it's difficult to live by grace toward oneself. At the close of a Bible class in which we had studied this theme of grace, a young woman asked the question, "How can I forgive myself for what I've done?" Here was a caring, sensitive person struggling with the question of living by grace. She did not choose to share with me the source of her guilt, and I could assure her that I did not need to know. We explored, however, some of the possible roads she could take toward the acceptance of God's grace. In addition to her confession to God, she may need to share that confession with another person—a *very* trustworthy person. Or she may need to make some kind of restitution, if that is possible and potentially constructive. Or some symbolic action, such as the burning of a written confession, may be helpful. As I assured her that God "graced" her, I could only pray that she would come to accept and feel that grace.

He "destroyed [the power of] death." I prefer to translate *"abolished death"* as "abolished the power of death." If we accept *"death"* here as physical death, it is the power of death, not death itself, that is abolished in Christ. 1 Corinthians 15 is Paul's classic statement of our victory over the power of death.

We live under the power of death until we have confronted the reality of our own death in the light of Jesus' victory over death. As a pastor, I'm often with people who have terminal illnesses or with loved ones after there has been a sudden death. Most of the time, I'm forced to deal with some form of denial of the death. It is a well-established fact that ours is a death-denying culture. Even some of our funeral practices seem to be disguised to deny the reality that the person has really died.

To the Christian, the "sting" of death has been removed (1 Cor. 15:55). This means to me that Christ's victory over sin and death is mine. This is more than "accepting" death. It is more than thinking of death as a peaceful transition to whatever may lie beyond. It is a positive trust in Jesus Himself as conqueror of death.

There is nothing particularly beautiful about death. It is an intruder

into God's good creation—a result of human sin. It is an enemy.
And the enemy has been met and conquered by our Christ.

"He brought life and immortality to light through the gospel." I wrote this
paragraph on a day that began at 3:15 A.M. with a call from the
emergency room of a nearby hospital. I was awakened with the news
that one of our church's young men had just died. Kent was twenty-
eight years old, married a little more than a year. He was reared in
our church, and was one of those kids who was a mainstay in our
youth programs. He served a term as a deacon. He was a sensitive,
caring, deeply committed Christian. Without any symptoms or indications, he went to sleep last night and died of a massive heart attack.

As I stood with the family beside his body, I had no answers
that could suggest the reason for this tragedy. I could not see any
meaning in the death of this marvelous young man whose rich and
full life was suddenly cut off.

But in that very room of death, we felt the presence of God. We
felt that He did enter into our suffering, that He did share our tears,
that He was walking with us in the valley of the shadow of death.
I doubt that we'll ever find any reasons for Kent's dying. But we
believe that death is not the end for him or for us. For Jesus *"brought
life and immortality to light."* And that's the Good News of the Gospel!

CHAPTER TWO

Our Calling to the Ministry

2 Timothy 1:11—2:7

Unfortunately, "the ministry" is most commonly regarded as a special calling for people like me who are ordained. Not so! Everyone is called by God to the ministry of Jesus Christ in the world.

In this section, Paul writes both about his own ministry and that of Timothy. Rather than reading this merely as historical and descriptive, I choose to read this as contemporary exhortation to each of us as to our own lifestyle and ministry.

EVERYONE A MINISTER

11 to which I was appointed a preacher, an apostle, and a teacher of the Gentiles.

12 For this reason I also suffer these things; nevertheless I am not ashamed, for I know whom I have believed and am persuaded that He is able to keep what I have committed to Him until that Day.

13 Hold fast the pattern of sound words which you have heard from me, in faith and love which are in Christ Jesus.

14 That good thing which was committed to you, keep by the Holy Spirit who dwells in us.

2 Tim. 1:11–14

In a very real sense, each person's ministry is unique. Paul saw his ministry here as "a preacher, an apostle, and a teacher of the Gentiles." There were twelve apostles, but only one Paul. Each apostle had a special ministry. There have been countless preachers and teachers, but again, there was only one Paul. Each person is called to a particular ministry (or ministries) by God and is given the necessary gifts for that ministry.

The most comprehensive discussion of this subject is in 1 Corinthians 12–14: "Now there are diversities of ministries, but the same Lord. And there are diversities of activities, but it is the same God who works all in all. But the manifestation of the Spirit is given to each one for mutual profit. . . . But one and the same Spirit works all these things, distributing to each one individually as He wills" (1 Cor. 12:5–7, 11). How clear it is! Each one of us is called and gifted for ministry.

Years ago, Elton Trueblood entitled one of his books *Your Other Vocation.* He insisted that our true vocation is to be in ministry for Jesus Christ. Our *other* vocation is how we make our living.

In the passage before us, Paul refers to his own ministry in verses 11 and 12, and then gives Timothy some specific directions for his ministry. There are four basic concepts which provide some directions for each of us as we seek to fulfill our own ministries.

"I also suffer these things" (v. 12). In communicating and sharing the Gospel, Paul experienced all kinds of suffering and hardships. In 2 Corinthians 11:22–33, he cited an awesome list of horrendous things that had happened to him. It's not likely that any of us will ever suffer comparably because of our Christian witness.

But is there not a sense in which each person who follows Christ seriously endures some kind of suffering in his/her vocation? I believe so. We don't always like to face up to the fact that the Gospel is in many ways countercultural. Our society is strongly oriented to the accumulation and selfish use of wealth. You don't find much support for that from Jesus. If we take Him seriously there is required an entirely different attitude to wealth and possessions—and if you live in an affluent community, you will experience a kind of suffering if you choose to part from the community norms.

Serious and radical discipleship creates problems with the world around us, and those problems create suffering. Our suffering may be quite different in kind from Paul's, but it is nonetheless real.

"I am not ashamed" (v. 12). To depart from community values or standards because of one's commitment to Jesus as Lord always brings the fear of rejection. No one knew this more than Paul. The "Pharisee of the Pharisees" changed the entire direction of his life after being confronted by Jesus on the road to Damascus (Acts 9). Imagine the reactions with which he lived day after day. From the snickers and

sneers of those who accused him of intellectual idiocy to the disdain of those who confronted him with stinging rebuke, he lived daily with the reality of rejection.

I find the fear of rejection a powerful counterforce to freedom in sharing my deepest feelings and convictions about Jesus. In that sense, my ministry is often hindered by the fear of being ashamed.

The antidote? The experiential reality of Jesus Himself and the confidence that He will keep us in His care to the very end (v. 12b). Courage and freedom in the pursuit of our ministry is much more than practicing techniques that will not offend people. It is first and foremost a matter of our relationship with Jesus Himself.

"Hold fast the pattern of sound words" (v. 13). Now Paul turns from his sense of ministry to Timothy. The first admonition to his young friend is to constancy with regard to the teaching of the Gospel. There are standards to be maintained. Those standards are the "sound words" which we have received through the Scriptures. And the constant struggle throughout Christian history is the maintenance of those standards. Of necessity, they have to be reinterpreted in the context of historical and cultural changes. While our interpretation and understanding is in need of continuing change, the standards themselves are unchanging. And it's virtually impossible to distinguish accurately between the standards themselves and our culture-conditioned interpretation of them.

That's why Paul's admonition to hold the standards "in faith and love which are in Christ Jesus" is the key to the whole matter. The history of Christian orthodoxy has all too many evidences of holding the standards at the expense of the "faith and love which are in Christ Jesus." This faith and love is much more than a matter of feelings toward another. It is how we act and relate. To trust and love those with whom we are in doctrinal disagreement has not been one of our hallmarks.

Orthodoxy is more than merely holding the standards. It is holding them, and acting all the while in trust and love with those we regard as opponents—or even heretics. To love truly is to act for what I perceive to be the best interests of the other person. A good parent has to learn this kind of loving. There are many times when we must back off from our demands in order that we may be there to forgive and help after mistakes have been made. To hold the standards and hold the other person in love at the same time is a fine act that requires a great deal of wisdom and patience.

249

Keep "that good thing which was committed to you" (v. 14). A literal translation of this statement could read, "Keep the good deposit," or "guard the faith." Here the idea shifts to that of the Gospel as a rich treasure to be guarded. And that is our ministry, too. That's why Bible study is so important. I like to think of the Bible as a rich treasure—a veritable gold mine of history, poetry, literature, wisdom—all the Word of God to us. It is to be kept and guarded, not by putting it in a vault or under glass, but *"by the Holy Spirit who dwells in us."* That is, by ingesting it through reading and study, so that it guards us as we guard it. Evangelist Dwight L. Moody once said to a young person: "This Book will keep you from sin—or sin will keep you from this Book." While the power is not in the Book but in the Holy Spirit, the treasure is worth guarding.

EVERYONE NEEDS AN ONESIPHORUS

Onesiphorus will never be inducted into the Hall of Fame of the best known people in the Bible, but he is one of my favorites. I don't think anyone can function in Christian ministry (and, remember, that's *everyone's* calling) without having an Onesiphorus.

> 15 This you know, that all those in Asia have turned away from me, among whom are Phygellus and Hermogenes.
> 16 The Lord give mercy to the household of Onesiphorus, for he often refreshed me, and was not ashamed of my chain.
> 17 But when he arrived in Rome, he sought me out very diligently and found me.
> 18 The Lord grant to him that he may find mercy from the Lord in that Day—and you know very well how many ways he ministered to me at Ephesus.
>
> *2 Tim. 1:15–18*

Here are three people mentioned nowhere else in the New Testament. All we know about them is what is said here. While we tend to think of Paul as bigger than life, his opening words in this paragraph are genuinely human. In fact, I detect a note of self-pity: *"All those in Asia have turned away from me."* This is an obvious overstatement. He no sooner says it than he remembers Onesiphorus. Timothy certainly hadn't deserted him. And there must have been many others. Overstatement is a normal part of self-pity.

It's likely, when Paul was hauled off to his final imprisonment in Rome, that he was abandoned by many. Some would turn away from him out of fear—fear that their identification with him might lead to their arrest. The betrayal by Phygellus and Hermogenes, whoever they may have been, was especially galling to Paul. Perhaps they had been very special friends to him. If so, it's not too difficult to identify with his feelings that *"everyone"* had deserted him. It's quite normal to feel sorry for oneself under such circumstances.

But if Paul did experience self-pity, he didn't stay there very long. Instead of getting hooked on the negatives, he focuses on a positive reality. He could have written a diatribe on Phygellus and Hermogenes, but he wisely chose to concentrate on Onesiphorus. There's a great lesson here. Seldom is there a situation without something positive. But it's easy to get so bent out of shape with the negative that we can't even find the good or the hopeful. Then we wallow in self-pity.

Paul chooses to focus on Onesiphorus rather than the two deserters. And he avoids the pit of despair. Everyone needs an Onesiphorus! The friend who hangs in there with you no matter what. The friend who risks his own neck just to be with you. I've often asked folks in retreat settings, "Who can you call at 3:00 A.M. if you're really in need, without any fear of rejection?" If you don't have someone, you need someone. And that's what the Christian church is supposed to be about. It must provide the climate where such relationships can be found and nurtured. Small groups provide the most likely setting for this to happen.

Onesiphorus is also an example of our definition of every believer being called to ministry. *"You know very well how many ways he ministered to me at Ephesus"* (v. 18). Here is an "unknown" believer providing ministry to the prominent Apostle. We may well name Onesiphorus the patron saint of the ministry of the laity!

Frequently I'm asked, "What do you do if you don't have an Onesiphorus?" My answer, "Become one!" I'm convinced that "it is more blessed to give than to receive," as Jesus said (Acts 20:35). Not only is there a basic need for every person to *have* an Onesiphorus, but there is also a need to *be* one!

This is frequently overlooked in our culture. We have majored in strategies for self-fulfillment that often focus entirely upon what we achieve and receive for ourselves. I believe that we must revise these strategies to begin with an emphasis upon giving ourselves and not just upon finding ourselves. This is hardly an original idea: "For whoever desires to save his life will lose it, but whoever loses his life for My sake will save it" (Luke 9:24).

Of interest is the fact that Onesiphorus literally means "a bringer of profit." I find it helpful to ask myself continually, "To whom am I bringing profit?" And I find a basic need within me to be profitable both to people and to causes. I enjoy bringing profit to friends and loved ones. I find great reward in being profitable to people in times of their needs. I find it meaningful to bring profit to institutions, community, and Christian agencies. To discover one's need to give—to be of profit to others—is a major step in any strategy for self-fulfillment.

I see evidence all around me that the way to have trusting, loving, caring, supporting friends is to be one!

STRENGTH FOR THE TASK

1 You therefore, my son, be strong in the grace that is in Christ Jesus.
2 And the things that you have heard from me among many witnesses, commit these to faithful men who will be able to teach others also.

2 Tim. 2:1–2

The opening *"therefore"* seems to point back to the positive example of Onesiphorus. Not only was Onesiphorus profitable to Paul, but he becomes profitable to Timothy as well. The influence of a person like Onesiphorus goes out with strength to others like ripples on a pond.

While genuine friendships transmit strength to others, the ultimate source of strength is Jesus Himself. To be about ministry as the central theme of one's life requires strength. That strength is found *"in the grace that is in Christ Jesus."*

Ministry always involves transmission. It was transmitted from Jesus to Paul and from Paul to Timothy. Now Timothy is given the responsibility to transmit it to others who in turn will be faithful in continuing the process. Church history abounds with much disagreement as to the meaning of apostolic succession. The Roman Catholic tradition insists that it consists of an unbroken line of successors from the first pope, Peter. Others have elaborate schemes to guarantee the line of succession. I'm quite comfortable with those who find it much simpler. We are in the apostolic succession solely because this process of transmission has been faithfully carried on down through the centuries.

Apostolic succession is thus a matter of fidelity to apostolic teaching. In that sense, the extinction of Christianity is always but one generation away. But as long as one person teaches another who teaches another . . . the Christian community continues. We have yet to hear the stories that are now beginning to come out of China. In spite of the totalitarianism of communism, designed to stamp out all religions, we know now that there have been thousands of faithful people passing the Gospel along from generation to generation. They certainly must have needed special strength, and they obviously found it. As undesirable as Marxist communism is in every way, we must resist the assumption that communism is the end of Christianity. The only possible end to Christianity would be our failure to transmit the Gospel to faithful men and women who will transmit the Gospel to faithful men and women who will . . .

MINISTRY IS DIFFICULT

3 You therefore endure hardship as a good soldier
of Jesus Christ.
4 No one engaged in warfare entangles himself
with the affairs of this life, that he may please him
who enlisted him as a soldier.
5 And if anyone also competes in athletics, he is
not crowned unless he competes according to the rules.
6 The hard-working farmer must be first to partake
of the crops.
7 Consider what I say, and may the Lord give you
understanding in all things.

2 Tim. 2:3–7

Ministry is difficult. It always involves hardship. And that's a reality we keep resisting. In a day when we are being offered all kinds of secrets for everything ranging from easy success to effortless weight loss, I find psychiatrist M. Scott Peck's book, *The Road Less Traveled,* a delightful change from the usual self-help book. His opening sentence: "Life is difficult." Rather than approaching a strategy for self-fulfillment from the assumption that life will be smooth and manageable if we can just learn the right techniques, Peck insists that we do best by beginning with the premise that life really consists of solving problems of varying degrees of difficulty.

We have no basis, in fact or experience, for presenting the Gospel as a way of making life sweet and simple, much less as a road to uninterrupted happiness.

Ministry is difficult. Christian discipleship is difficult. Following Christ creates problems. Thus, Paul charges Timothy to *"endure hardship as a good soldier of Jesus Christ."* Our difficulties will sometimes be like those of others. Sometimes they will be quite different. At this point, Paul had his own particular set of problems, and Timothy had his. But each had to face certain difficulties because of his commitment to Christ.

As we read Paul's charge as if it were addressed to us personally, a very real question must be faced. What difficulties am I facing because of my commitment to Jesus as Lord? Pause a while on this one. Another way to put it is, in what ways would my life be easier if I weren't serious about Christian discipleship? In other words, what honest-to-God differences does Christ make in our lives?

Too often the "differences" abound in trivia: "We don't drink, and we don't chew, and we don't go with girls who do." We have become masters of majoring on minors. The great issues of the Kingdom of God, set forth by the prophets and majored upon by Jesus, are not at all prominent in our conversations and prayers.

There's little question in my mind that in the community in which I live, we have been much more concerned with making the Gospel relevant to our lifestyle than we have with making our lives relevant to the Gospel.

How do we respond to the Jesus who said: "I tell you not to resist an evil person. But whoever slaps you on your right cheek, turn the other to him also" (Matt. 5:39). "If anyone wants to sue you and take away your tunic, let him have your cloak also" (Matt. 5:40). "Give to him who asks you, and from him who wants to borrow from you do not turn away" (Matt. 5:42). "Love your enemies, bless those who curse you" (Matt. 5:44). "Do not lay up for yourselves treasures on earth . . . but lay up for yourselves treasure in heaven" (Matt. 6:19–20). "Do not worry about your life, what you will eat or what you will drink; nor about your body, what you will put on" (Matt. 6:25). "Woe to you who are rich. . . . Woe to you who are full. . . . Woe to you when all men speak well of you" (Luke 6:24–26). "Why do you call me 'Lord, Lord,' and do not do the things which I say?" (Luke 6:46).

The least effort to be obedient to Jesus in such matters as these will create difficulties and hardship. Instead, we develop elaborate rationalizations to support our disobedience. And out of this emerges "cultural Christianity," applications of Jesus which undergird and support our basic greed and lust for comfort. The accumulation of wealth, mostly for our own security, becomes a sacred creed. We spend an overwhelming proportion of our time, energy, and money mostly satisfying our own needs and desires, and praise God for His preferential treatment of us. We lead the world in the production and sale of weapons of destruction throughout the world, and call ourselves a nation under God. These are the marks of "cultural Christianity," the adaptation of the Gospel to our way of life.

If we dare to try to break out of these patterns of thinking and living because of our obedience to Jesus, we will experience great difficulties, and we will be called upon to *"endure hardness."*

Paul now uses three dramatic metaphors, portraying the qualities required in those called to endure hardness. The soldier portrays a sense of *priority*. The athlete models *discipline*. The farmer is the pattern of *perseverance*.

Christian discipleship and ministry require all three. As the soldier must leave all other pursuits, so the disciple must place his or her self at complete disposal to the Kingdom of God. "Seek first the kingdom of God and His righteousness" (Matt. 6:33).

As the athlete must keep all feelings, instincts, and reactions under control in order to compete according to the rules, so the disciple must live life under orders and within boundaries.

As the farmer must work long and hard, often under adverse conditions, so the disciple must persevere, perhaps for long times with little reward for the sake of being faithful to Jesus as Lord.

After Dr. Peck begins his book by establishing the fact that life is difficult, he then proceeds to the fact that problems in life can only be met with discipline and love. I find his approach to discipline most helpful and certainly applicable within these three metaphors in our passage.

Discipline requires *the delaying of gratification*. Neither the soldier, the athlete, or the farmer dare get hooked on the quick fix. In an instant gratification society, it's difficult to take the long view. "Fly now— pay later" is applied to much more than air travel. We lack staying power. We try this, then that, because we lack a sense of perspective. To serve Christ is to get things within the perspective of eternity. C. S. Lewis did this so well. He insisted that we must learn to relate to every human being as an immortal person. To live our lives in the context of eternity may well enable us to be less driven by our needs for instant results and quick fixes.

Peck's second dimension of discipline is *the acceptance of responsibility*. It's refreshing to hear a psychiatrist call us to accept responsibility for our feelings and actions, and stop blaming our much maligned parents. In pastor's seminars, I lead a unit on time management. I begin, not with techniques for more efficiency, but with this very question of responsibility. Unless I accept the responsibility for the use of my time, I will be out of control. Blaming others accomplishes nothing. Like the soldier, the athlete, and the farmer, we must take full responsibility for the quality of our lives.

The third component of discipline is *dedication to the truth*. And this is not as cut and dried as orthodox Christians tend to make it. Peck likens this to maps that need to be revised from time to time in order to correspond with reality. In middle life, I'm well aware that I've had to change some of the lines on my maps. I don't believe that Jesus or the Gospel has changed to fit my changing world, but I do believe that my changing world requires shifts in my understanding of Jesus. To follow the truth wherever it may lead requires a willingness to change one's understanding of the truth.

The final facet of discipline noted by Peck is *balancing*. Another word for this is flexibility. A classic illustration of this part of discipline is in Paul's phrase "speaking the truth in love" (Eph. 4:15). This requires delicate balancing. It's possible to use the truth to hurt and destroy. Truth can be a weapon of viciousness. There has been, in some circles, an emphasis upon absolute honesty. I've been in touch with enough damage in this area to issue a word of caution. Love must always temper our use of the truth. Love demands the best interests of the other person. Thus love and truth must balance each other—and this is not always easy to do.

Each one of us is called to a life of ministry. That ministry is done in the context of caring and supporting relationships. And it is always difficult. But in a life of discipline, like soldiers, athletes, and farmers, great are the joys and rewards of such a life. So it was for Paul. So it was for Timothy. And so it can be for us!

CHAPTER THREE

Our Work for God

2 Timothy 2:8–26

As we look at the remainder of the second chapter, Paul is still writing to Timothy about ministry, both his and Timothy's. And, we continue to read the letter as addressed to us and our ministry.

It's often said that we are what we eat. This passage begins by suggesting that we are what we remember.

THE POWER OF MEMORY

8 Remember that Jesus Christ of the seed of David was raised from the dead according to my gospel,

9 for which I suffer trouble as an evildoer, even to the point of chains; but the word of God is not chained.

10 Therefore I endure all things for the sake of the elect, that they also may obtain the salvation which is in Christ Jesus with eternal glory.

2 Tim. 2:8–10

Paul has clearly stated his conviction and experience that life and ministry are difficult. No soldier, athlete, or farmer accomplishes anything worthwhile without hardship. This reality was evident in Jesus' life and in Paul's.

In calling us to *"remember"* Jesus Christ, Paul again covers a vast amount of theology in two phrases: *"of the seed of David"* and *"raised from the dead."* Here is a succinct reminder of the humanity and the divinity of Jesus. He was truly human, of the seed of David. The

THE POWER OF MEMORY

genealogies in Matthew and Luke remind us of His ancestry. While we tend to think of His virgin birth as an evidence of His divinity, there's good reason to believe that it was regarded by the early Christians as a witness to His humanity. He really was born of a woman, a human parent. Both his mother and his human father were of the lineage of David. And long ago, in Israel's golden age, God had promised David that his kingdom would last forever through his descendants (2 Sam. 7:8–16). His resurrection from the dead points to the other reality of His being. His victory over death was seen as God's declaration and vindication of Jesus' life and death as the sacrificial atonement for our sins. The Resurrection was God's declaration that Jesus was indeed His very Son (Rom. 1:4). Son of man, Son of God, truly human, truly divine—this is the profound mystery of Jesus Himself.

It is this Jesus upon whom our memory is to focus in the midst of our problems and difficulties. The power of memory must never be underestimated. In the deepest sense we are what we remember. Memory is the lens through which we view our world. We relate to the present through our memories of the past. Our present attitudes are shaped by how we remember past events. The same event can have entirely different effects, depending upon how it is remembered. I think of two people, each having been terminated by the same employer. One used the memory of the termination as a challenge to deep reflection and self-evaluation. Out of that she entered a period of renewal and growth and has become a whole and healthy person. The other has used the memory of the termination as a source of resentment and bitterness. She has been terminated from two subsequent jobs and has become, I am told, a bitter and vindictive person. Past events have great power in our lives through the way we choose to remember them.

There are times when we keep our good and happy memories readily available, while trying to hide or bury our painful memories. At other times, we focus so much upon our bad memories that our good memories are lost to mind. To bring Jesus to the center of our memory is the best way I know to keep the good memories alive and available and to make the painful memories accessible for His healing love. No memory is beyond the reach of His love and forgiveness.

I was vividly reminded of the power of memory just yesterday. I had conducted a graveside service in the cemetery where my father was buried. I visited his grave after the service and had a meaningful time of just being quiet. Many happy memories of boyhood times and adult years welled up from within me, producing happy tears and prayers of gratitude.

I laughed at myself as I remembered another visit to that grave seventeen years ago, less than a year after Dad's death. As on yesterday, I had conducted a service nearby and decided to stop at his grave on the way out. As I stood there, I was filled with anger. Dad had worked hard all his life as a streetcar conductor and a bus driver. He never had money for the lifestyle that I pretty much take for granted. For him, life consisted of long, hard hours with no material rewards. He always dreamed of going to Hawaii but couldn't afford it. He would have been impressed with the luxury of many things that I call necessities.

He took early retirement at age sixty-two because the physical demands of his work had taken their toll. On his meager pension, he and Mother were beginning to enjoy a few, simple pleasures for the first time in their thirty-eight years of marriage. A year later, he died of cancer. It all seemed so unfair. Why couldn't they have had some fun years together? In rage, I cursed and kicked the headstone. I was angry at God! The corner of the headstone tore through the leather of my shoe and the skin of my toe. There I stood, filled with even deeper resentment. As I limped away, my anger then compounded with guilt, I was surprised as a sense of God's love and peace suddenly surrounded me. It was as though God and Dad were both holding me, saying, "It's o.k.! It's o.k.! I love you."

On that visit long ago, my perception of the past was so focused upon the painful memories, that anger and resentment were in control—and out of control! Yesterday's visit produced joy and gratitude. My focus was upon the pleasant memories of good times—and I even chuckled at the painful memories, now disarmed and healed. I've even forgiven God! The difference lies in bringing Jesus Himself into all of our memories.

This is evident in Paul's reference to his own suffering and imprisonment (vv. 9–10). He practiced what he preached. As he reflects upon his chains, he remembers Jesus Christ. And he celebrates the fact that no chains can bind the Word of God. Neither the chains of affluence or of poverty, the chains of oppression or of irresponsible freedom, or any other forms of threat or fear can restrict the flow and the power of the Word of God. Remember Jesus Christ!

AWESOME OPTIONS

11 This is a faithful saying:
   For if we died with Him,
   We shall also live with Him.
12 If we endure,
   We shall also reign with Him.
   If we deny Him,
   He also will deny us.
13 If we are faithless,
   He remains faithful;
   He cannot deny Himself.

2 Tim. 2:11–13

Before Paul concludes this section, he pauses, perhaps singing a stanza of a well-known song. Many scholars believe that these verses represent a portion of an early Christian hymn. It reinforces the theme of this section: ministry involves hardship.

The hymn is built around two themes applicable to Christian discipleship and ministry. The first relates to those who are true to Christ. The second to those who are false. It is best to disregard the verse divisions because the two themes divide at the middle of verse 12.

The first option is that of fidelity. To be faithful is to choose to die with Him and to endure with Him. To die with Him is to live with Him. This is central to the life in Christ. "For whoever desires to save his life will lose it, but whoever loses his life for My sake will save it" (Luke 9:24). Elsewhere, Paul said, "I have been crucified with Christ; it is no longer I who live, but Christ lives in me" (Gal. 2:20).

It really shouldn't surprise us that so many of our strategies for self-fulfillment aren't working. The renowned social researcher Daniel Yankelovich deals with this in his book *New Rules*. His central thesis is that in recent years in America, we have shifted from denial-of-self ethics to duty-to-self ethics. By this, he means that the belief that we find our lives through service and commitment to others has been replaced with the belief that we must take care of ourselves first. This has been accompanied by an intensive focus upon finding oneself by looking inward. Yankelovich insists that the "me first" outlook is at the root of the decay and disorder of our day. Though he does not profess to be a Christian, in our sense of personal commitment to Christ, he states, "The Christian injunction that to find one's self one must first love one-self, contains an essential truth any seeker of self-fulfillment needs to grasp."

Not only are we called to die with Him, but also to endure with Him. The Word *"endure"* is our old friend *hupomonē*, translated "patience" in 1 Thessalonians (1 Thess. 1:3). Recall that it is an active word, going beyond passive thoughts of survival. It is to take that which is painful and transform it into something creative and constructive. Christian discipleship, then, is to take the problems and difficulties and shape them into something beautiful for God. To endure with Him, in this sense, is to reign with Him. To reign is to be in charge. Those who live by *hupomonē* are truly in charge of their lives—their problems and their hurts.

I call this an awesome option—to live and to reign! But now the hymn presents a negative option that is awesome. It, too, has its fruits.

This option is to deny Him and to be faithless. Denial takes many forms. There is overt denial, such as in Peter's pitiful performance on that dark night in Gethsemane (Luke 22:54–62). Most of us are never likely to be faced with the martyr's option in which open confession results in imprisonment or death. But it is well for us to remember that we have thousands of brothers and sisters in other parts of the world for whom this is a daily reality. They should be much in our hearts and prayers.

In our situation, denial takes less overt forms. There is a growing awareness among us that our lifestyles may be a form of denial of Christ. A lifestyle of conspicuous consumption in the midst of a hungry world is a denial of the Jesus who calls us to feed the hungry and care for the poor. Likewise, a life that is not expressing genuine love and care for spouse, children, and friends is a denial of the Jesus who commands us to love one another. Are not the tactics and power struggles common to some church boards a flat denial of Him who calls us to be servants to one another? Before we conclude too quickly that we would never deny Him, we might well ponder the many forms denial can take.

The word translated *"faithless"* (v. 13) is used in the New Testament both to mean "not believing" and "betraying a trust." The King James Version preferred the former: "If we believe not, yet he abideth faithful." Our translation sees this, rather, as a matter of fidelity in living: *"If we are faithless."* Because we are a culture in which instant gratification is paramount, the living out of commitments has come on hard times.

The awesome consequence of denial and infidelity is His denial of us. While this may rub against the grain of our desire for an indulging God, it is based on the words of Jesus Himself: "Therefore whoever confesses Me before men, him will I also confess before My Father who is in heaven. But whoever denies Me before men, him will I also deny before My Father who is in heaven" (Matt. 10:32–33).

We would expect the hymn to repeat the parallel in its conclusion to the effect that if we are faithless, God is faithless. But notice the dramatic shift: *"If we are faithless, He remains faithful; He cannot deny Himself."* Because of this shift, the meaning is not easy to pin down.

On the one hand, it might appear that God's faithfulness, "no matter what," offsets the fear engendered by the thought of Jesus' denial of us. If pressed, this leads to a concept of unconditional love on God's part in which, ultimately, our actions have no lasting consequence. God will always tidy up our messes.

On the other hand, this statement can be read as a statement of dreadful finality. His faithfulness is to Himself. Thus, as our denial of Him results in His denial of us, so our faithlessness to Him results in His faithfulness to Himself—which is to judge us for our infidelity.

I don't think we have to get pressed to either extreme. Don't forget that this was likely a hymn, not a theological treatise. I'm satisfied that both notes need to be sounded. Denial and infidelity, in their many forms, must be taken seriously. Grace and unconditional love must never be distorted to mean that our actions do not have meaning or consequences. We must be responsible for our conduct—with God and with others. In this sense God's faithfulness must mean that He cannot contradict Himself. The God of love and mercy is also the God of justice and righteousness.

The prophet Hosea is the classic spokesman to this problem. He saw clearly the denial and faithlessness of the people of God. He boldly portrayed Israel's behavior in terms of his own unfaithful wife. God is seen both as bringing judgment upon Israel and as finally wooing and winning her back. "How can I give you up, Ephraim? How can I hand you over, Israel? . . . I will not execute the fierceness of My anger . . . for I am God, and not man" (Hos. 11:8–9).

Paul's words to the Corinthians seem to say the same thing. In 1 Corinthians 3:11–15, he portrays the Christian life as building upon the foundation which is Jesus Christ. The deeds of our lives are likened to "gold, silver, precious stones, wood, hay, straw." In our final accounting to God, our works will be tested by fire—some will endure, some will be consumed as worthless. But Paul's conclusion affirms God's ultimate mercy: "If anyone's work is burned, he will suffer loss; but he himself will be saved, yet so as through fire" (1 Cor. 3:15). I take this to be bad news and good news. For God to be faithful to Himself, our behavior must have meaning, and that means that our actions have consequences that God Himself will not abridge. But God also promises us salvation in Christ. Whether or not our works endure the test of fire, in Christ we will be saved.

The central motive for faithfulness to God is not the fear of being rejected by God. The driving force for fidelity to God is the positive desire to please the One who loves us so!

An Unashamed Worker

14 Remind them of these things, charging them before the Lord that they not strive about words to no profit, to the ruin of the hearers.

15 Be diligent to present yourself approved to God, a worker who does not need to be ashamed, rightly dividing the word of truth.

16 But shun profane and vain babblings, for they will increase to more ungodliness.

17 And their message will spread like cancer. Hymenaeus and Philetus are of this sort,

18 who have strayed concerning the truth, saying that the resurrection is already past, and they overthrow the faith of some.

19 Nevertheless the solid foundation of God stands, having this seal: "The Lord knows those who are His," and, "Let everyone who names the name of Christ depart from iniquity."

2 Tim. 2:14–19

As Paul began the second chapter with three metaphors of Christian life and ministry, he now concludes with three more. The first three: the soldier, the athlete, and the farmer. The second three: an unashamed worker, a clean vessel, and a gentle servant.

The call is to be *"a worker who does not need to be ashamed"* (v. 15).
This certainly supports the theme of the lasting value of our work
for God. Here, the key thought has to do with the way we relate
to others in our conversations about the Gospel. The obvious assumption is that Christians will normally talk about their faith. One of
the many things I have come to treasure in growing relationships
with some Christians in Kenya and Uganda is the way in which
their conversations regularly move to Jesus and the Gospel. If Jesus
is central in our lives, He will naturally be a part of our talk.

But Christian talk must not degenerate into mere doctrinal slogans
and shibboleths. In Paul's words, we are not to *"strive about words to
no profit"* (v. 14); we are to be *"rightly dividing the word of truth"* (v. 15);
and we are to *"shun profane and vain babblings"* (v. 16).

The word translated *"rightly dividing"* in verse 15, literally means
to "cut straight." In the history of the interpretation of this passage,
this has been taken to mean a number of things such as cutting a
sacrificial animal into pieces, a piece of land into sections, a cloth
into strips, or a father cutting bread for his family. I prefer the concept
of making a straight road as with John the Baptist's proclamation:
"Prepare the way of the Lord, make His paths straight" (Luke 3:4).
To "cut straight" in this sense is to be as direct as possible in getting
to the destination.

Every preacher and teacher needs to give constant and careful attention to "making straight paths." I have to confess that I have preached
and heard all too many sermons that are anything but straight paths.
I heard it said of one preacher, "He is a master of circling the field
without ever landing."

I don't quarrel with the right of theologians and biblical scholars
to develop their own vocabulary and to carry on their work in ways
that cannot be understood by the uninitiated. But I plead with my
students in the seminary classroom not to take their lecture notes
into the pulpit. The task of the local preacher or teacher, in my judgment, is to be a broker between the professional theologian and the
person in the congregation. I pity the congregation whose teachers
are not in touch with contemporary biblical and theological scholarship. Like every other field, our knowledge is expanding day by day.
I also pity the congregation whose teachers become enamored with
their ability to impress at least themselves with *"profane and vain babblings."*

There are two negative results from *"words to no profit"* and *"profane and vain babblings."* They *"ruin the hearers"* (v. 14), and *"increase to more ungodliness"* (v. 16). It is a profound responsibility to teach or preach the Word of God. On the one hand, teaching has the potential of building people up in their faith. On the other hand, it also has the potential of tearing people down. Such was the result of the ministry of Hymenaeus and Philetus. Having developed some kind of special interpretation of the Resurrection, the end result of their teaching was *"overthrow [of] the faith of some."* I doubt very much that this was their intention. It's not likely that many preachers or teachers deliberately set out to overthrow anyone's faith. But when the teaching becomes too much a matter of clever words and exotic doctrine, the end result is often tragic. The incredible tragedy of Jonestown is a stark example of this in our time.

The contrast of the two kinds of teaching is portrayed in the phrases *"rightly dividing the word of truth"* (v. 15), and *"strayed concerning the truth"* (v. 18). To *"rightly divide"* is literally "to cut straight." The verb, stray, comes from the word for a target. The Greek verb literally means "to miss the target." The goal of every Christian teacher, then, is to cut straight and to hit the mark.

The bottom line, however, is that the future and the stability of the Kingdom of God does not wax and wane on the basis of our teaching and preaching. The foundation stands secure. Most frequently, in the analogy of a building to the Kingdom of God, the foundation is Jesus Himself. It is customary on foundations or cornerstones to have inscriptions. The inscriptions for the foundation of God are set forth in verse 19. It is likely that these are all taken from the story of the rebellion against Moses led by Korah, Abiram, and On (Numbers 16). The first inscription is based on Num. 16:5, and the second on Num. 16:26.

The first inscription points to a reality grounded in God's knowledge. *"The Lord knows those who are His."* I've always felt uncomfortable with the way in which some Christians express great certainty as to who the "unsaved" are. I wish we could have a moratorium on that way of talking. It is best that we stay with the simple fact of this inscription.

The second inscription on the foundation is an open reality. If we claim to be the Lord's, naming the name of Christ, we are to *"depart from iniquity."* While we cannot know who are the Lord's— only He knows that—we can see who are His by the quality of their lives, or in Jesus' words, by the fruit that they bear (Matt. 12:33).

A Clean Vessel

No sooner does Paul refer to "departing from iniquity" than another metaphor leaps into his mind:

> 20 But in a great house there are not only vessels
> of gold and silver, but also of wood and clay, some
> for honor and some for dishonor.
> 21 Therefore if anyone cleanses himself from these,
> he will be a vessel for honor, sanctified and useful
> for the Master, prepared for every good work.
> 22 Flee also youthful lusts; but pursue
> righteousness, faith, love, peace with those who call
> on the Lord out of a pure heart.
>
> *2 Tim. 2:20–22*

We must be careful not to press this metaphor too far. The picture is of the utensils in a home of affluence. Some are used for special occasions (*"honor"*); some are used for menial tasks (*"dishonor"*). The contrast between the silver goblet used for a toast and the garbage bucket comes to mind. The context would indicate that Paul is still dealing with the contrast between true and false teachers, with Hymenaeus and Philetus still in mind.

Is Paul saying that God intentionally has both kinds of teachers in the church? I think not. For Paul quickly departs from the metaphor and makes his appeal to Timothy to be a vessel for honor, which has to do with being clean. It's no longer a matter of being *"gold and silver"* or *"wood and clay."* The focus clearly shifts to the possibility of being a clean and honorable vessel. I'm always fascinated with the mind of Paul—so quick and active. Here he puts forth the metaphor, and as quickly as it was said, he leaves it to make his point, again telling Timothy to be a true teacher.

To be a *"vessel for honor,"* Timothy must *"cleanse himself from these."* Presumably *"these"* refers to the false teachers and teaching, the vessels for *"dishonor."* Three beautiful things are said about being a vessel for honor. Such a vessel is *"sanctified," "useful for the Master,"* and *"prepared for every good work."*

What more could anyone desire? To be *"sanctified"* is to be set apart for God's service. There is no greater calling than this. To be *"useful for the Master"* is the most noble expression of a basic human need. We can be an Onesiphorus to Jesus Himself! To be *"prepared for every good work"* is the mature product of a walk with Christ. Such is the joy and reward for vessels of honor.

The way in which we can cleanse ourselves to be such vessels is described in both negative and positive terms in verse 22. To *"flee"* is a negative or defensive move. To *"pursue"* is a positive or offensive action. There are times for both responses. The classic example of appropriate flight is Joseph scrambling away from Potiphar's wife (Gen. 39:7–12). Sexual temptations do not, however, comprise the entire agenda of *"youthful lusts."* Timothy must have been thirty-six or thirty-seven years old at this point, hardly a young man just getting in touch with his sexual feelings. Youthful lusts can also be selfish ambition, undue focus upon one's self, stubbornness, arrogance, and the like. None of these are confined to youth, but they are the central issues of maturing.

Perhaps they are best seen in contrast to the four marks of Christian maturity set forth in verse 22: *"righteousness, faith, love, [and] peace with those who call on the Lord with a pure heart."*

"Righteousness" is right-ness. It is integrity, truthfulness, fairness, and justice. *"Faith"* is a constancy of trust in God rather than in our own carefully devised securities. *"Love"* is acting in the best interests of the other person. *"Peace"* is that harmony and unity with those who are brought together in a common commitment to the Lord. These are the things we are to pursue with a passion.

Often, the Christian life is portrayed in contrasting terms: to die with Christ and to live with Him (Gal. 2:20), to put off the old and put on the new (Col. 3:5–11), to flee youthful lusts and pursue righteousness. This is how one becomes a vessel of honor in God's great house.

A GENTLE SERVANT

With the following metaphor of a gentle servant, Paul now brings this magnificent section to a close:

23 But avoid foolish and ignorant disputes, knowing
that they generate strife.

24 And a servant of the Lord must not quarrel but
be gentle to all, able to teach, patient,

25 in humility correcting those who are in
opposition, if God perhaps will give them repentance
to the acknowledgment of the truth,

26 and they may come to their senses and escape
the snare of the devil, having been taken captive by
him to do his will.

2 Tim. 2:23–26

Again, Paul's mind moves from one idea to the next. With the
admonition to pursue "peace with those who call on the Lord out
of a pure heart" flashes the awareness of the harsh realities already
mentioned. *"Foolish and ignorant disputes"* abound in religious circles.
These disputes are the cause of an unwritten law forbidding the discussion of religion in barbershops. Sometimes we tend to operate
as though we have been commanded to win arguments rather than
to love people. The reason we are to avoid arguments is stated simply:
"They generate strife." Strife is never the climate for communicating
the love of God or developing human relationships.

Let's differentiate here between strife and controversy. Strife grows
out of my need to win an argument for the sake of winning. Strife
is an ego contest with the opponent. Strife is frequently marked by
an attack upon the other person. Controversy on the other hand, is
unavoidable in communicating and applying the Gospel. Jesus Himself is a source of controversy. He either is or is not God's Son, our
Savior. How do we handle His command to love our enemies without
getting into controversy as to what that means? How do we apply
the Beatitudes to everyday life without being controversial? What
do we really do with the Sermon on the Mount?

Paul gives us clear guidelines for handling conflict and controversy,
avoiding strife. It is the gentle servant who provides the kind of
leadership in the midst of controversy that transcends strife. A great
deal has been said and written in recent years about servant leadership.
Here is one of Paul's great contributions to the subject.

The servant of the Lord is not quarrelsome, *"gentle to all," "able to
teach," "patient,"* and *"correcting."*

To describe the servant of the Lord as not quarrelsome amplifies the necessity of avoiding strife. In our community we live with a large and active group of Mormons. Many of them are quite aggressive in their efforts to evangelize. Try as I do to be open to all people and to welcome discussion on any subject, my conversations with Mormons on substantive matters of faith most often become quarrels. I can tell you, it's difficult to keep the lines of conversation open once you've really sworn off quarreling. But the four remaining characteristics of a servant of the Lord do create an entirely different climate.

Gentleness is the first step. More and more, I think of gentleness as a major mark of maturity. It is a fruit of the Holy Spirit (Gal. 5:22–23). My picture of gentleness is a large linebacker-like man holding a little baby, tenderly and securely. All of the man's strength and power is focused on providing the baby with care, comfort, and security. I see gentleness as the quiet use of strength to bear up the other person. It is being sensitive to the feelings and needs of the other, acting to help and never to hurt.

To be *"able to teach"* is also a necessary skill for the servant of the Lord. The best teachers I know are gentle people who out of their gentleness and quiet strength draw out the best in people. This is the root meaning of *educate*—to "draw out" from another. Teaching is much more than pouring information into people through some imagined funnel in their heads. It is engaging persons in ways that stimulate their thinking and behavior to respond to truth.

And this requires patience. Patience is the art of allowing the other person to be human. Patience is seeing the plank in our own eye as we take on the speck in the other's eye (Matt. 7:3–5). Patience is acting toward others as we would want them to act toward us (Matt. 7:12). Patience is to deal with others in the way that Jesus deals with us.

Finally, we are to correct others who are in opposition to the Gospel, *"in humility."* To correct in humility is to recognize that our present understanding of truth is a gift of God and not our own achievement. It is also to recognize that we may not have the final word on every subject at this time, and to be open to change. As a parent, I'm well aware that there are two ways to correct. The one that I am most inclined to use is the way of verbal violence: "How often have I told you not to do that! I'm sick and tired of you!" This is clearly and demonstrably the least effective method of correction, usually making matters worse. The most effective way of correction comes through gentleness and patience, accompanied with good teaching.

Here is the portrait of the gentle servant—a most uncommon person, desperately needed at every level of life in today's world.

As we go about our ministries, our daily work for God, let us approach each task, each person, each conflict, each stretching challenge as unashamed workers, clean vessels, and gentle servants.

CHAPTER FOUR

Coping in Troubled Times

2 Timothy 3:1–17

Any thought that being an unashamed worker, a clean vessel, and a gentle servant leads to comfort and security is quickly dispelled by the about-to-be-beheaded Apostle. Christian life and ministry is lived out in the midst of trouble. As a matter of fact, it often brings trouble.

THE ROOTS OF TROUBLE

1 But know this, that in the last days perilous times will come:

2 For men will be lovers of themselves, lovers of money, boasters, proud, blasphemers, disobedient to parents, unthankful, unholy,

3 unloving, unforgiving, slanderers, without self-control, brutal, despisers of good,

4 traitors, headstrong, haughty, lovers of pleasure rather than lovers of God,

5 having a form of godliness but denying its power. And from such people turn away!

2 Tim. 3:1–5

The opening three words *"But know this,"* remind me of the way announcements were made when I was in the marine corps: "Now hear this." These were code words to get our attention, frequently to things we already knew. Paul is not saying anything here that Timothy didn't already know. Rather, he is calling for special attention as he is about to underscore and amplify things already known by Timothy. Learning and growing is not always hearing new things. It comes mostly through being reminded of things we already know.

The phrase *"the last days"* may seem at first to refer to the period just before the return of Christ. When taken in this sense, there's a tendency to assume that things have to get worse in order for Christ to come. This could lead to resignation rather than to a resistance to evil.

I prefer to interpret *"the last days"* as sometimes having a broader meaning. While *"the last days"* is used in the specific sense of the final judgment (John 6:39, 40, 44, 54; 11:24; 12:48), it is also used to describe the present (Acts 2:16–17, Heb. 1:2). In this sense *"the last days"* can mean the entire period from Jesus' first coming to His final coming. Here, *"the last days"* can best be interpreted as all of church history. In Jesus, the Kingdom of God has broken into history, the new age has begun, the last days are now until the last day when He shall come.

"Perilous times" are thus characteristic of all times and places where men and women take Jesus seriously. The word Paul uses for *"times"* can have the sense of "the state of the times." Some translaters use "seasons," emphasizing that troubles come and go with some regularity.

The word translated *"perilous"* is used only here and in Matt. 8:28 in the New Testament. It is used in classical Greek to describe wild animals or the raging sea. It can mean "hard to bear, menacing, fierce, violent, or troublesome." Thus when Paul says *"in the last days perilous times will come,"* I find it best to regard this, not as a prediction of some future time, nor as a "sign" that Jesus is about to come. Rather, this is a description of a recurring reality for all Christians in all times and places. Later in this chapter, he insists that all who follow Jesus will suffer persecution (3:12), as Jesus Himself had warned (John 15:18–20).

This raises a very troubling question for me. Why are Christians in America so comfortable? Why are we so accepted and well-received? One of two things must be true. Either we live in a Christian culture that naturally provides a climate of acceptance and support, or we have accommodated ourselves to the values established by our non-Christian culture. I don't find enough evidence to convince me that ours is a Christian culture. Our comfort and acceptance can only suggest to me that we have been tamed by the world around us and have acquiesced with the world's values much more than we realize or dare admit.

This becomes quite evident as Paul describes the roots of troubled and perilous times in verses 2–5. The reasons that Christians will be persecuted in troubled times grow out of the distorted values of people around and among them. Paul lists twenty characteristics of people who often unintentionally create a climate of trouble for those who would take Jesus seriously.

We catch the essence of the entire list in what can be called the four *philos* words at the beginning and ending of the list. *Philos* is the Greek word for love, emphasizing the love of a person for people or things. Paul's use of four Greek compound words leaps out of this long list: lovers of themselves, *philautoi* (v.2); lovers of money, *philarguroi* (v. 2); lovers of pleasure, *philēdonoi*, (v. 4); rather than lovers of God, *philotheoi* (v. 4).

In between the *philos* words are the products of human behavior that grow out of distorted values. Of the four *philos* words, three of them are used only here in the New Testament. *"Lovers of money"* occurs only one other time in the New Testament in Luke 16:14, describing the Pharisees. The basic source of trouble in the world is people—people who direct their love to themselves, to money, and to pleasure rather than to God. Trouble begins with misdirected love! And love is misdirected in three basic ways.

"Lovers of themselves." We are created to love God. Jesus summarized the meaning of love: "You shall love the Lord your God with all your heart, with all your soul, and with all your mind. . . . You shall love your neighbor as yourself" (Matt. 22:37, 39). The Shorter Catechism states the theme a little differently: "What is the chief end of man? Man's chief end is to glorify God, and to enjoy him for ever."

But our capacity to love God all too readily gets turned inward upon ourselves and outward to money and pleasure. A fine distinction must be made between healthy self-love and destructive self-love. The words of Jesus Himself direct us to a love of self as the basis of a proper love of the neighbor: "love your neighbor as [you love] yourself." This love of self, however, must always be tied to the love of neighbor. When self-love becomes an end in itself, trouble begins.

I believe that we are going to see some major changes in our approaches to counseling and psychotherapy. It's quite clear that the "me first" approach is hurting more than helping. Merely focusing upon oneself as some kind of independent entity to be "found" is not producing the kind of wholeness often promised. In recent years, as a pastor, I've seen more and more people who come to me after long, intense quests of trying to find that elusive self. Frequently, that all-encompassing quest has resulted in the dissolution of relationships and a growing isolation from satisfying, healthy friendships. Just as there is healthy love of self, so there is unhealthy self-love. The love of self that is constructive is always tied to the love of others.

"Lovers of money." Money readily becomes the object of misdirected love. In most churches, money is a touchy subject. One of the most regular complaints directed to pastors is that we're "always talking about money." This whole matter needs careful attention.

The issue, to me, is not *whether* the pastor talks about money but *why*. Jesus is recorded as having said more about wealth and possessions than any other subject. Why did He place such a strong emphasis upon this? He wasn't a fund raiser. He had no budget, buildings, or staff. As far as we can tell, He never took up an offering. There had to be another reason for His emphasis.

I'm convinced that Jesus majored upon the theme of money because of His concern for people. He understood and emphasized what the love of money does to people. Nowhere did Paul capture the essence of the issue more clearly than in his previous letter to Timothy (1 Tim. 6:9–10). There is nothing inherently good or bad about money. It is the use to which it is put that determines its quality.

This, then, leads to a crucial distinction between fund raising and stewardship. Fund raising can be done apart from stewardship. But stewardship cannot be separated from fund raising. To the pastor and church leader, the distinction is crucial. If our speaking about money is only geared toward raising funds, we may get impressive results in any given appeal, but we may not be leading our people into genuine stewardship. On the other hand, to address stewardship in our affluent culture without raising many questions about our attitudes and usage of wealth is a copout.

Again and again, Jesus emphasizes the incredible power of riches to distort and disintegrate our lives and relationships. And yet, it's difficult to live in today's world—especially our suburban world—without being preoccupied with the spending and accumulation of money.

The stories of brokenness in the midst of relative affluence are legion. If having wealth really produced what all of the ads promise, pastors and psychotherapists might become low-handicap golfers! Wealth in itself cannot produce joy and meaning in life, but preoccupation with wealth can certainly destroy it. Again, the love of money is misdirected love.

As with a healthy self-love, I believe there can be a healthy love of money. Such love ties money to God and to others, and this means giving it away. Only when we regard money as a means of serving God and others—particularly the poor and needy—can we be liberated from its destructive power. What would happen if we worked to make money in order to give it away?

"Lovers of pleasure." The third area of misdirected love is stated in verse 4: *"lovers of pleasure rather than lovers of God."* In one sense, we are very fortunate to live in a time and place where large numbers of people are able to participate in a lifestyle once (and still in many parts of the world) only known by the wealthy and powerful. Billions of dollars are spent each year in America on leisure and recreational pursuits.

I don't think we need try to eliminate this vast industry. Among other things, it does create millions of jobs for people who might otherwise be unemployed, and who, because of their employment, are able to participate in some leisure for themselves.

The issue is not whether we should *have* pleasure but whether we should focus our affection upon pleasure. It's the same as with love of self and love of money. And like them, pleasure has a way of possessing us. Even our recreational pursuits have a way of becoming sources of problems to us. I've known men and women over the years whose golf games and handicaps are more a root of irritation and anger than a wellspring of pleasure.

I know, because I was once one of them. Due to some changing demands and priorities, I had to decide whether to give my golf game the time required for me to maintain a low handicap, whether to give it up entirely, or whether to learn to enjoy it occasionally realizing that my scores would be poor. I tried the latter for awhile and experienced great frustration. I couldn't accept the poor performances. Then I realized that I had confused pleasure and work. Golf had become a demand. Not until I could genuinely accept mediocre golf as a pleasure could I enjoy it occasionally.

The issue is our attitudes toward our pleasures. If they become the focus of our energies and resources, we are on a road that we probably did not consciously choose to take. It is the road of idolatry.

Idolatry is always the result of misdirected love. The love of self, the love of money, the love of pleasure—rather than the love of God—is idolatry. Only when we subordinate these loves to God Himself do we worship God with our innermost being.

We may well have *"a form of godliness"* (v. 5), but there is no dynamic in such lives. This is precisely why there is so little life-changing power in so many of our churches. As long as we baptize our love of self, money, and pleasure, and call it the love of God, we may well go on with all the forms, but the power will be missing.

A "me first" strategy for fulfillment, a high priority on financial success and security, and a consuming preoccupation with pleasure inevitably produce the fifteen behaviors listed in verses 2 and 3. What a list! But it's all too true of the realities we all experience day by day. Commenting on each of these problem areas would be too tedious for our purposes. But we must view them as symptoms of misdirected love—the inevitable results of idolatry. Each one is a symptom that must be dealt with, but nothing short of a systemic conversion of our misdirected loves to God can bring about the healing and wholeness we need.

To those of us who generally think that Christian love is a matter of infinite toleration of most anyone and anything, Paul's closing statement of verse 5 may be shocking. While the advice must be cautiously applied, there are times when some people are to be avoided. Paul now gives specific illustrations to support his counsel.

THE SPREAD OF TROUBLE

6 For of this sort are those who creep into
households and make captives of gullible women
loaded down with sins, led away by various lusts,
7 always learning and never able to come to the
knowledge of the truth.
8 Now as Jannes and Jambres resisted Moses, so
do these also resist the truth: men of corrupt minds,
disapproved concerning the faith;
9 but they will progress no further, for their folly
will be manifest to all, as theirs also was.

2 Tim. 3:6–9

The idolatry of misdirected loves is tragic enough, but when it becomes evangelistic, trouble multiplies. And it was apparently going on in Ephesus. While some read this passage as a put-down of women as weak and gullible, it seems best to regard it in the light of what must have been a local situation. Women figured prominently in the life of the early church. Some, who perhaps were significant there, had been led away by false teachers.

Whatever their *"sins"* and *"lusts"* were, the most descriptive phrase of their folly is in verse 7: *"always learning and never able to come to the knowledge of the truth."* I don't think that Paul meant to imply that anyone can come to the place of having it all together. But there has to be some point of commitment to the truth, even without having to profess to have all the answers. I like to think of the truth as being quite static. It is my perception and understanding of the truth that is the variable.

The truth is embodied in Jesus Himself. The knowledge of the truth, then, always centers upon Him. He cannot and does not change, but our understanding of Him does. It seems to me that Paul is making an appeal here to act on the truth in Jesus as we see it, in contrast to constantly be in search of truth yet undiscovered. The false teachers then probably used the same techniques that are used now. The most common is to pretend to have all the truth. Frequently, this is tied to some particular type of religious experience. Having the experience is said to validate the claim to truth. Here is another road to idolatry, in which the religious experience becomes an object of misdirected love.

Paul's reference to Jannes and Jambres as illustrations of false teachers is of special interest because their names are nowhere to be found in the Old Testament. The most widely held view is that they were the Egyptian magicians in Pharaoh's court (Exod. 7:11). Whoever they were, Paul likens their opposition to Moses to the opposition of the false teachers in Ephesus.

These are the kind of people to be avoided. It appears that Paul is willing to conclude that it's best to direct one's energies elsewhere than in endless arguments with such folks. And that's not easy. The other day, I received a letter from a person who informed me that she had discovered "the truth" in another religion and was thus leaving our church. She asked me to spend an evening with her new teachers so that I might come to see "the truth."

My initial reaction was to take them on. Competitive challenges always ring my bell. I chose to avoid them—a more difficult thing for me to do. Instead of spending the evening that way, I took an evening at home with my family. It was an excellent trade-off!

We can avoid them because they are not going anywhere (v. 9). It's possible to take some people and things much too seriously. To spend too much time and energy contending with those I believe to be false teachers may give them more credibility than they deserve. The folly of their teaching will sooner or later become clear. In the meantime, I choose to pursue the truth that centers in Jesus Himself, knowing full well that "now I know in part, but then I shall know just as I also am known" (1 Cor. 13:12).

OVERCOMING TROUBLE

10 But you have carefully followed my doctrine, manner of life, purpose, faith, longsuffering, love, perseverance,
11 persecutions, afflictions, which happened to me in Antioch, in Iconium, in Lystra—what persecutions I endured. And out of them all the Lord delivered me.
12 Yes, and all who desire to live godly in Christ Jesus will suffer persecution.
13 But evil men and impostors will grow worse and worse, deceiving and being deceived.

2 Tim. 3:10–13

Paul closes this chapter by giving Timothy some very personal advice. Paul bases his appeal to Timothy on his own experience. Timothy is called to turn away from the false teachers and to stand alone, if need be, and take persecution for his fidelity to Jesus. In this section, Paul reminds Timothy of their intimate bonds.

Here is another of Paul's testimonies. I'm more and more convinced that the sharing of our stories is vital and essential and really constitutes the basis of the Christian community. The Gospel is the story of Jesus. Christian witness is telling one's story, the story day by day of how Jesus' story shapes and directs my story.

There is a movement in some contemporary theological circles to emphasize this story aspect of the Gospel. To those of us who major on communicating the truth in biblical and theological concepts, this can be like opening the window to a fresh breeze.

On my first trip to Africa, after two all-night flights from Los Angeles to London to Nairobi, I arrived in time to attend a service of dedication of a Christian Training Center in Nairobi by African Evangelistic Enterprise. As a member of the board of A.E.E., I had gone to Kenya for the meeting of our international council. After the dedication, we were driven to Nyeri, the site of our meeting.

About fifty miles north of Nairobi, one of our Volkswagen vans broke down—not an uncommon event, I was to learn. I found this quite exciting, for we rolled the van into a little village, hoping to find some help. Here I was, less than three hours in Africa and actually in a real, native village.

The presence in our group of the Rev. John Wilson, a Church of Uganda pastor and evangelist, gave me a sense of security. Soon, John was talking in Swahili (I assumed) to a number of people who had gathered around us. Camera-nut that I am, I was in a photographer's heaven. As I was busily snapping pictures, John said to me, "Say a word to the people." As I hesitated, the silence was deafening. Then John said, "Give your testimony!" "Testimony," I thought, "I'm a preacher. I don't give testimonies!" Not to be denied, John said, "Say a good word for Jesus!"

So I gave my testimony. I told my story, as simply as I could— the story of Jesus, and how He shapes my story. During the next two weeks in Kenya and Uganda, we had other roadside stops, and each time I was called on to give my testimony. Since then, I've chosen to give my testimony from our pulpit on Easter Sunday— not just the story of that beginning interaction with Jesus long ago, but the up-to-date sharing of His story as it shapes mine.

Paul, the great theologian, was at his best telling his story. Here he refers to nine areas of his story, ranging from his doctrine to his sufferings. Here, the testimony clearly blends belief and behavior, theology and practice. Doctrine, with Paul, was never an end in itself, but always a means to right living. He begins by linking *"doctrine,"* *"manner of life,"* and *"purpose."* Out of them issues *"faith, longsuffering, love [and] perseverance."* One is reminded here of Paul's favorite trilogy of faith, love, and hope, since we meet again our old friend *hupomonē,* here translated *"perseverance,"* and always related to hope.

Since Timothy was from Lystra, he knew what had happened to Paul there and in the neighboring Galatian towns of Antioch and Iconium. The account of the persecutions in those cities is found in Acts 13:13—14:20, culminating with Paul being stoned, dragged out of the city, and left for dead. And again Paul insists that all who *"live godly in Christ Jesus will suffer persecution"* (v. 12).

In Alan Paton's historical novel, *Ah, But Your Land Is Beautiful,* he portrays the human tragedies of apartheid, the official doctrine of the separation of the races by which South Africa is ruled. Emmanuel Nene is a black who has chosen to be a part of the Defiance Campaign of 1952 to 1958 in which countless numbers of blacks, whites, Indians, and coloreds were persecuted, imprisoned, and martyred for their stand for justice and equality for all.

There is a beautiful moment in the novel where Mr. Nene is visiting with Robert Mansfield, a white school headmaster and former South Africa cricket hero. Mansfield has resigned his headmastership because he could no longer support apartheid. Emmanuel Nene had come to see him to express his respect and support, and by the end of the visit, an obvious bond had been formed. Nene had made it clear to Mansfield that there were indeed wounds and suffering ahead for them both: "Mr. Nene rose, and looked cheerfully around him. 'I don't worry about the wounds. When I go up there, which is my intention, the Big Judge will say to me, "Where are your wounds?" and if I say I haven't any, he will say, "Was there nothing to fight for?" I couldn't face that question.'"

And Paul believed that it would always be this way, *"evil men and impostors will grow worse and worse, deceiving and being deceived"* (v. 13). Come to think of it, Jesus said the same thing: "Blessed are those who are persecuted for righteousness' sake, For theirs is the kingdom of heaven" (Matt. 5:10).

THE FIRM FOUNDATION FOR LIVING IN TROUBLED TIMES

Following his testimony, Paul now directs his personal challenge to Timothy. Paul again calls his young friend to be faithful to Jesus.

> 14 But you continue in the things which you have learned and been assured of, knowing from whom you have learned them,
> 15 and that from childhood you have known the Holy Scriptures, which are able to make you wise for salvation through faith which is in Christ Jesus.

16 All Scripture is given by inspiration of God, and
is profitable for doctrine, for reproof, for correction,
for instruction in righteousness,
    17 that the man of God may be complete,
thoroughly equipped for every good work.

2 Tim. 3:14–17

The call is not to develop something new or different, but to be faithful to the things we have received. In the midst of much needed calls for church renewal, we must ever guard against seeking renewal merely through novel innovations. I'm still not convinced that genuine renewal will always produce more members in a given church. I'm not yet convinced that great numbers of people in affluent suburbs are bumping into each other in eagerness to work for justice and righteousness and to give their money to the work of the Kingdom of God.

To live for Christ in costly commitment means that there will be wounds. There will be storms and trouble. That's why a strong foundation is essential. In the closing parable of the Sermon on the Mount, Jesus made this clear. The foundation upon which the wise person builds is the Word of God (Matt. 7:24–27).

In Christian thought, the Word of God and the Scriptures are virtually synonymous. The classic formula is that Jesus is the Word of God Incarnate, and the Scriptures are the Word of God written. Nowhere does Paul state more clearly his firm convictions about the unique role of the Scriptures in our lives.

To Paul and to Timothy, the Scriptures were the writings contained in the Old Testament, very likely the same collection of thirty-nine books in our Bible today, though our Roman Catholic brothers and sisters recognize some others. It would be fun to ask Paul or any of the other authors of New Testament books such as Matthew, Mark, Luke, or John whether he was aware that his writings would come to be bound in the same book that he called the Holy Scriptures. I'm certain that his answer would be an unqualified no. I don't think he would ever have entertained such a thought.

That's why the very existence of the New Testament as the Scriptures speaks strongly to me about God's remarkable way of using very ordinary people and things. Paul was just writing letters, the most common way of communicating across distances and separation.

God chose to use those letters as His continuing way of speaking to us. We rightly stand in the tradition of those men and women of long ago who both gathered and recognized the twenty-seven writings, now called the New Testament, as being a part of the Word of God written.

In recent years, especially among some American and British theologians, there has been a lot of heated debate about whether or not the Scriptures *can* contain any errors in such things as historical or scientific data. I emphasize *can,* because the simple fact is that the manuscripts that have come down to us *do* contain some such problems. The amazing thing to me is that they contain so few. Paul shows no interest here in our philosophical questions. He is primarily interested in what the Scriptures *do,* not in what they *are.*

As to the nature of the Scriptures, Paul states that they are all *"given by inspiration of God."* The word that Paul uses here is a compounding of *theos* ("God") and *pneustos* ("breath or spirit"). Scriptures are here said to be breathed by God. Paul does not go beyond this simple but profound statement. How God did this, we'll never know. On the one hand, the writings are certainly human. The writings of Paul, for instance, are clearly distinguishable from those of Matthew, and those of Matthew from Mark, and those of Mark from Luke. On the other hand, we affirm them as the Word of God written, for indeed we find them to be God's Word to us as we read and study them. Is there not a parallel here to the mystery of Jesus Himself? He is both human and divine. I'm satisfied that the Word of God Incarnate and the Word of God written need no verification by our logic to establish their authority. I would rather trust the Scriptures themselves than my theories about them.

The greater concern of Paul is to state what the Scriptures are able to do. They are *"able to make you wise for salvation through faith which is in Jesus Christ"* and *"profitable for doctrine, for reproof, for correction, for instruction in righteousness."* I know of no other writings for which such claims can be made and demonstrated.

The Scriptures bring us to salvation through faith in Jesus Christ. Without them, we would have little significant—and certainly no saving—knowledge of Jesus.

They are our source of doctrine. All of our teaching must be grounded in them. They are the standard by which our ideas must be measured. I love the definition of a sermon in the *Directory for the*

Service of God of my denomination: "a sermon is properly an exposition of Scripture." Book reviews and commentaries on current events are never in themselves sermons.

They are *"profitable . . . for reproof."* That's a fascinating phrase to me, for I do not readily think of reproof as something desirable. Deeper reflection reminds me that reproof is often necessary for growth. Without confrontation, life tends to go on, directed by the same prejudices and guided by the same assumptions. Lately, we've required manufacturers of certain products to provide labeling which indicates their dangers. Perhaps we should place labels on our Bibles which read, *Danger: this book may upset you!*

But the Bible also corrects us. Reproof in itself can be devastating and discouraging. I never had a coach who wasn't strong in reproof. Not all of them, however, were as able in correcting. In this sense, the Bible is a lamp to our feet and a light to our path (Ps. 119:105).

And it instructs us in *"righteousness."* Righteousness is a word of relationship—relationship with God and with others. Thus it has to do with justice as well. I am sure that we are well within the mark to claim that the Scriptures have given rise to more movements for righteousness and justice than any other writings in the world. Even Karl Marx, whose ideas of justice and righteousness became demonically distorted, was initially inspired by the writings of the Scriptures. If only he would have been fully instructed by them!

If you want to come to a growing appreciation for the Word of God in the Scriptures, spend some time focusing upon Psalm 119, all 176 verses of it! It can be used with great profit by taking one or two verses a day as a basis of reflection. Reading this Psalm for three or four months in this way can be most worthwhile.

Here, the bottom line for Paul is in verse 17: *"that the man of God may be complete, thoroughly equipped for every good work."* The Scriptures are not given to us to develop theology as an end in itself. They are given to us to produce good works in and through us. To be serious about the Scriptures, we must ask ourselves again and again, "In what ways are good works being produced through our lives because of our study of the Bible?"

In these troubled times, let us build our lives and our deeds upon the strong foundation of the Scriptures.

CHAPTER FIVE

Love's Last Appeal

2 Timothy 4:1–22

Paul now comes to the conclusion, not only of this letter to Timothy, but of his life on earth as well. These words are dictated, probably to Luke, perhaps within a few days of his beheading by the executioner on the Ostian Way. For the past thirty years he has traveled, witnessed, worked, and preached throughout the Mediterranean world. He has been loved and hated, supported and attacked, praised and cursed. Whatever else can be said of his life, it certainly wasn't dull! Anticipating the executioner's axe, he passes the baton to his young friend, Timothy, and entrusts to him the next lap of the race.

Life and ministry involve the daily working out of priorities. For each of us, there is more to do in a given day than can be done. There is much more we would like to do than can be done in a lifetime. Therefore, the establishing of clear priorities is a matter of extreme importance. In Paul's closing appeal to Timothy, five priorities are given the highest place.

THE HIGHEST PRIORITIES

1 I charge you therefore before God and the Lord Jesus Christ, who will judge the living and the dead at His appearing and His kingdom:

2 Preach the word! Be ready in season, out of season. Convince, rebuke, exhort with all longsuffering and teaching.

3 For the time will come when they will not endure sound doctrine, but according to their own desires, because they have itching ears, they will heap up for themselves teachers;

4 and they will turn their ears away from the truth,
and be turned aside to fables.

5 But you be watchful in all things, endure
afflictions, do the work of an evangelist, fulfill your
ministry.

2 Tim. 4:1–5

Paul begins his last appeal with a word of deep solemnity. *"I charge you therefore before God and the Lord Jesus Christ"* echoes the solemn opening of a courtroom trial. It would certainly get Timothy's utmost attention, as it should ours.

The authority of Paul to make this sacred charge is grounded in Jesus Christ, the King and Judge who will come again. A strong belief that history will culminate in Christ's appearing, with the judgment and the final establishment of His Kingdom, cannot fail to make a profound impression upon our lives and ministries. There can be both a sense of love and of fear in our accountability to God. While we tend to regard fear as a negative, we do well to remember the ancient words of wisdom: "The fear of the Lord is clean, enduring forever" (Ps. 19:9); "The fear of the Lord is the beginning of wisdom" (Ps. 111:10); "The fear of the Lord is to hate evil" (Prov. 8:13); "In the fear of the Lord there is strong confidence" (Prov. 14:26); "the fear of the Lord is a fountain of life" (Prov. 14:27); "and do not fear those who kill the body but cannot kill the soul. But rather fear Him who is able to destroy both soul and body in hell" (Matt. 10:28).

Five specific commands now ring out like military orders.

"Preach the word!" In the light of what has just been said (3:14–17), there is no question as to what that word is. It is the Word of God written, the Scriptures of the Old Testament, and to us the New as well. We are first, last, and always to be proclaimers of the Word of God. Here is the picture from the ancient world of the town crier, "Hear ye, hear ye . . . !" Among all the things that demand our time and energy, nothing is to have higher priority than preaching the Word, be it from the pulpit or in a conversation in the company cafeteria.

"Be ready in season and out of season." The verb here translated *"be ready"* is also translated as "be urgent" and "be instant." The verb itself literally means "to stand by, to be available." But the context demands a stronger reading connoting urgency and forcefulness.

However, such urgency must be controlled with common sense. Urgency is no excuse for insensitivity. There is a time for speaking and a time for silence, to paraphrase the wisdom of Ecclesiastes. "To everything there is a season" (Eccles. 3:1). We are to be urgent in all seasons, whether we preach or not.

"Convince." This word is also translated "reprove." It is related to the word translated "reproof" in 3:16, describing what Scripture does. The emphasis may be upon the idea of reasoning in order to convince the unbeliever of the truth of the Gospel.

"Rebuke." This can hardly be regarded as the most sought-after task of Christian ministry. And yet I wonder if the gift of rebuking should not be added to our list of spiritual gifts. How fortunate for David that Nathan had this gift. Nathan must have had both the courage and the gift to rebuke David through the parable of the unjust rich man, with his "You are the man" (2 Sam. 12:7). Thus, David came to himself and confessed, "I have sinned against the Lord." To Nathan was given the high privilege of declaring God's forgiveness: "The Lord also has put away your sin; you shall not die" (2 Sam. 12:13). The other side of the coin of the gift of rebuking is the joy of declaring forgiveness to the one who repents.

"Exhort." This is the Greek word *parakaleō* which is used to mean "to encourage" or "to bring comfort." It is the word used of the Holy Spirit elsewhere in the New Testament. Some suggest that *"convince"* addresses the intellect, *"rebuke"* confronts the emotions, and *"exhort"* appeals to the will. While this application cannot be used rigidly, exhortation is clearly intended to mean encouragement and inspiration. Rebuke without encouragement can be deadly.

All of these priorities are to be carried out in a climate of *"longsuffering and teaching."* Paul's word for patience is *makrothumia*. This is the word generally used of God's patience with us. To be patient with others as God is patient with us is the environment of all Christian ministry. This is the essence of teaching. To educate means to draw out. True teaching patiently draws out the very best in another.

Our task is all the more difficult because of the proclivity of people for the strange malady of *"itching ears."* Nothing is more humorously descriptive of the world in which we are called to live and minister. The phrase *"itching ears"* literally means "having the hearing tickled." Ticklers of the ears abound in every generation, and as long as people love to have their hearing tickled, such teachers will have followers.

I have to confess my discouragement as a pastor at the remarkable success of so many ear-ticklers in our time. Television and radio have provided them with the ideal media. Ear-tickling thrives in a climate of fantasy in which real relationships are imagined with people whom we neither know nor touch. The ear-tickler designs the message to communicate what the audience wants to hear. I thank God for those few in mass media ministries who refuse to be mere ear-ticklers; notable among them is Billy Graham.

The temptation for ear-tickling is just as real to the preacher in the local congregation. The major difference, however, is that the pastor and people live together, ideally, in the same community and become seen and known on a personal basis in places like markets and drug stores. Ear-tickling is less likely to succeed in real relationships. Sometimes people join our congregation, telling me that they are changing churches because my preaching is more to their liking. When I hear this, I'm almost certain that they'll move again before too long, at least if I'm faithful to the whole Word of God.

The appeal of Paul to Timothy, and to us, his successors, is finalized in verse 5. There are four things that every potential ear-tickler must do: (1) *"be watchful in all things,"* (2) *"endure afflictions,"* (3) *"do the work of an evangelist,"* and (4) *"fulfill your ministry."*

The literal translation of *"watchful"* is "to be sober." Getting a following, becoming well liked, being admired can be downright intoxicating. We need to have all of our faculties at full command lest we sell our souls for the pottage of being adored by folks with itching ears.

To *"endure afflictions"* is again mentioned by Paul as the lot of the faithful servant of the Lord. It may well be that because many people *"will not endure sound doctrine"* (v. 3), we will have to *"endure afflictions."* The persistent question remains: If we are not being met with some affliction, why not?

To *"do the work of an evangelist"* may or may not be a reference to a specialized form of ministry. It certainly is such a reference in the only other place where the word occurs in the New Testament (Acts 21:8; Eph. 4:11). As we have seen, however, this can also be applied in the broader sense of sharing the Good News as everyone's vocation.

To *"fulfill your ministry"* is to complete the task already begun. Life and ministry is a journey based upon our marching orders from God. To follow the orders is to fulfill the ministry.

Through Paul's final appeal, the priorities for all of us who follow in Timothy's tracks are established. He doesn't promise us comfort or an easy way. But whatever else may be said of this life of ministry, it certainly won't be dull!

HANGING UP THE SPIKES

6 For I am already being poured out as a drink offering, and the time of my departure is at hand.

7 I have fought the good fight, I have finished the race, I have kept the faith.

8 Finally, there is laid up for me the crown of righteousness, which the Lord, the righteous Judge, will give me on that Day; and not to me only, but also to all who have loved His appearing.

2 Tim. 4:6–8

One of the most poignant moments in the history of baseball was the final farewell of Lou Gehrig in Yankee Stadium. Suffering from an incurable disease, the great and revered first baseman stood at the plate and tearfully said farewell to the fans who had cheered him on for many years. Sooner or later, the time comes when each of us must "hang up the spikes." That time had come for Paul. What a farewell speech!

This 52-word speech (in Paul's language) has to rank as one of the great valedictory addresses of all times. I would place it at the top of all such great statements, including Lincoln's Gettysburg address. In these few words, Paul captures the essence of his whole life.

He begins with two vivid metaphors expressing his view of his forthcoming martyrdom. First, he sees himself as *"a drink offering"* about to be poured out. The word he uses is a technical term used of a cup of wine in a Roman sacrifice poured out to the gods. There's reason to believe that every Roman meal ended with this symbolic act. Though he was about to be executed, he chose to regard this as an offering to God. This was the natural conclusion of his belief that the whole of life is to be regarded as "a living sacrifice, holy, acceptable to God, which is your reasonable service" (Rom. 12:1).

The second metaphor of his death is *"the time of my departure."* This is another of those Greek words capable of various meanings. Two are most often cited. The word is used of the loosening of the ropes when taking a tent down. It is also used of the release of the lines when a ship leaves the dock. Paul sees himself as a soldier, gathering his tent for the next stop, and as a sailor launching out on a new journey. Let's herald this as the Christian view of death.

I'll never forget my last visit with my father before he died. He knew and I knew that his cancer would soon take its toll. One of the last things he said to me was, "Gary, don't cry for me. I'm about to leave on the most exciting trip of my whole life." Dad had been a bus driver, as I have mentioned, and this was his trip beyond all trips. In Christ, we view life as a journey and death as the time of our departure. In eleven words, Paul has expressed most magnificently his view of death.

In the remaining forty-one words he states his view of life. I choose to read verses 7 and 8 as one analogy, taken from the Greek and Roman games. It is the picture of a runner who competed honorably in the race. In the phrase *"I have fought the good fight"* the final word comes from a word which means any contest in the games. It need not be confined to a boxing match. The word is *agōn*, presumably the source of our word agony. It pictures an athlete coming off the field, having given his very all. As he prepares to hang up his spikes, he can honestly say that he has given the race his total effort. A well-known athlete friend once said to me, "I would rather lose, having done my best, than win without being pressed."

Having given his best, Paul now sees himself as crossing the finish line. The focus is not on winning as much as it is on finishing. There are many joggers in our community, and a few of them have become marathon runners. To be sure, every marathon race has a winner, but far more important to the dedicated marathon runner is completing the race. A delightful woman in our church recently traveled to New York City to compete in the marathon there. She had no illusions of winning over the fifteen thousand other runners, but you couldn't help being warmed by her joy in finishing! Christian life and ministry is not a competition to run better than others. It's a commitment to run all the way to the finish.

In the context of this metaphor, when Paul says he has *"kept the faith,"* he is saying that he has competed according to the rules. Apparently, the Greek athletes took a solemn oath before the games that they would compete honorably and honestly. Here is Paul, at the end of the race, affirming that his vows had been kept. The keeping of vows has come on hard times. Long-range commitment is often replaced by short-range gratification. A woman was reportedly asked on her fiftieth wedding anniversary, "In all of these years, did you ever consider divorce?" "No, never. Murder often, but never divorce!"

Finally, there is the reward. The crown in the Greek games was a laurel wreath awarded to the victor. In the case of our Christian race, the crown goes not only to Paul, but also *'to all who have loved His appearing."* Any thought that only "superChristians" get special awards is abolished. It means a lot to me to know that my dad will receive the same crown as Paul. He never did anything great for God, by our standards, but to him there shall be the garland of victory on that Day.

Such is Paul's view of death and life—and all in fifty-two words! What a way to hang up the spikes!

EVEN APOSTLES HAVE NEEDS

9 Be diligent to come to me quickly;
10 for Demas has forsaken me, having loved this present world, and has departed for Thessalonica— Crescens for Galatia, Titus for Dalmatia.
11 Only Luke is with me. Get Mark and bring him with you, for he is useful to me for ministry.
12 And Tychicus I have sent to Ephesus.
13 Bring the cloak that I left with Carpus at Troas when you come—and the books, especially the parchments.

2 Tim. 4:9–13

It would seem that anything after Paul's magnificent valedictory address would be anticlimactic. For a long time, I more or less ignored these closing verses of the letter. I tended to regard them as being of limited local and historical interest. But I've since come to a joyous appreciation of these closing words of Paul's last letter.

They are very human words. In this section, we are very much in touch with Paul as a normal human being with some simple, but very real needs. Three of them are expressed: (1) the need for the presence of friends, (2) the need for physical comfort, and (3) the need for intellectual stimulus.

There are times when the need for the physical presence of a friend transcends all other needs. Such is this time for Paul. Though he has soared on the wings of eloquence in his final speech, he now descends to the reality of his longing to have Timothy with him, and soon! The need is heightened by the painful desertion of Demas, and the departures of Crescens, Titus, and Tychicus on "church business."

We know little about Demas. In Colossians 4:14 and Philemon 24, his name is linked with Luke, and he seems to have been regarded as one of Paul's fellow workers. The cause for his defection, *"having loved this present world,"* gives us no real indication of his reasons. The tragedy is that here is one who at one time was running well but now has dropped out of the race. Fidelity in Christian life and ministry must be constantly renewed. Yesterday's trophies do not win today's races. And I've never known any parents who named their children after Demas. How sad.

Crescens does not appear elsewhere in the New Testament. His journey to Galatia was apparently accepted by Paul, as was that of Titus for Dalmatia. Presumably, Titus had completed his mission in Crete. Tychicus was a special person to Paul, having been a messenger for him with his letters to the churches in Ephesus and Colossae and to Titus (Eph. 6:21–22, Col. 4:7–8, Titus 3:12). He was on his way to Ephesus at Paul's request, perhaps to release Timothy to come to Rome.

Having come down to Luke as the only remaining companion, Paul now asks Timothy to come and to bring Mark with him. This warm reference to Mark must be given special attention.

Mark first appears in relationship with Paul as a member of the team for the first missionary journey (Acts 12:25). For some reason, Mark had abandoned the team in Perga, returning home to Jerusalem (Acts 13:13). To Paul, Mark was a deserter, as became clear when Barnabas wanted to take Mark with them on the second missionary journey. Paul was so adamant in his refusal to give Mark another chance, that he separated from his close friend Barnabas. With that, Paul and Silas went one way, and Barnabas and Mark another (Acts 15:36–41).

We'll never know the middle of the story, but by the time Paul wrote Colossians, healing has occurred, and Mark is with Paul in his first Roman imprisonment. And now, at the end, Paul wants *"useful"* Mark with him. Mark thus stands as the patron saint of all who recover from previous failures. Today's defeats can be forgiven and overcome. Ask Mark and Paul!

But the unsung hero is clearly cousin Barnabas. He was willing to take a chance on Mark. He believed so strongly that Mark could make it, given another opportunity, that he risked a lot for his young cousin. We can't separate Mark's recovery from Barnabas' risk and trust. Thank God for the cousin Barneys who will stand by us in our failures. There are two questions here. Who has been a Barnabas to me? The second is more demanding. Who needs me as a Barnabas?

Paul also dealt honestly with his physical needs. The dungeon was cold, and Paul needed his cloak. How comforting to know that this great spiritual giant didn't find any virtue in needless shivering! The cloak was a large blanketlike garment with a hole for one's head in the center. We're not likely to discover who Carpus was or why Paul left his cloak at Troas. As one who has left a couple of topcoats on airplanes, I like to think that Paul had the capacity for that sort of thing, too!

The need for intellectual stimulus was also expressed in his request for the books and parchments. Happy is the person who early in life discovers books as friends. While Paul wants his close friends with him, he is also aware that other friends can be present through books. Some survivors of concentration camps found that one of the worst parts of the experience was having nothing worthwhile to read.

The need to learn never ends for the Christian. Here was Paul, about to die, asking for his books. My father-in-law, a veteran pastor and preacher, recently died at age eighty-six. In my study at home, I kept a special section of newly published books that I felt would interest him. The first thing he did on every visit was to greet me with "What's new, kid?" and then head for the shelf. How refreshing it was to bask in the glow of his hunger for learning right up to his final disabling sickness.

Our gratitude is to Paul for being human enough to deal with these simple but very real needs.

Paul also shows us his human side in expressing some legitimate anger at one who had harmed him. At the same time, Paul looks beyond human spite to divine faithfulness.

WHEN EVERYONE LETS YOU DOWN

14 Alexander the coppersmith did me much harm. May the Lord repay him according to his works—

15 of whom you also beware, for he has greatly
resisted our words.

16 At my first defense no one stood with me, but
all forsook me. May it not be charged against them.

17 But the Lord stood with me and strengthened
me, so that the message might be preached fully
through me, and that all the Gentiles might hear. And
I was delivered out of the mouth of the lion.

18 And the Lord will deliver me from every evil
work and preserve me for His heavenly kingdom. To
Him be glory forever and ever. Amen!

2 Tim. 4:14–18

We know nothing about Alexander the coppersmith other than
what is said here. In some way, he resisted Paul's teaching and apparently brought intentional harm to him. Some think that he may have
been an informer who gave clues leading to Paul's arrest. Whatever,
Alexander was an object of Paul's anger. Paul was also angry at the
fact that no one stood with him at his first defense in the courtroom
in Rome. That's incredible! Paul had written his great letter to the
Roman Christians. Where were those friends in Rome when he most
needed them? To be sure, some may have been out of town and
others may have had their reasons, but was there not one single
Christian in Rome to testify on Paul's behalf?

Was Paul angry? If Alexander and the silence of his friends didn't
make him angry, what would? The deeper question relates to what
Paul did with his anger. He did two different things.

In the case of Alexander, he consigned him to God's judgment.
"May the Lord repay him according to his works." This was the same Paul
who wrote to the Christians in Rome: "Repay no one evil for evil.
. . . Beloved, never avenge yourselves, but leave it to the wrath of
God; for it is written, 'Vengeance is mine, I will repay, says the
Lord.' No, 'if your enemy is hungry, feed him; if he is thirsty, give
him drink; for by so doing you will heap burning coals upon his
head.' Do not be overcome by evil, but overcome evil with good"
(Rom. 12:17–21, RSV).

I see no contradiction here between Paul's writing and his anger
expressed toward Alexander. I'm convinced that Paul would have
fed a hungry Alexander, but he rightly places him in God's hands
for justice. He was not out to get even with Alexander.

But his anger with his silent Christian friends is resolved quite

differently: *"May it not be charged against them."* Here is Paul quoting
Psalm 22, even as Jesus had used it in Gethsemane. Within the family,
the desire is for healing and forgiveness, not for judgment and vengeance.

The ultimate resolution of his anger is in his conviction that the
Lord had stood with him, even in the absence of all others and with
the opposition of some. His reference to delivery from *"the mouth of
the lion"* seems less likely to refer to Nero who is about to have him
beheaded than to Satan from whom Paul's delivery is certain. The
anger is resolved, not denied, and Paul breaks forth in praise to God.

Paul here frees us from the fallacy of regarding all anger as sinful.
Being angry is not necessarily wrong. The morality of anger lies in
how we handle it. The denial of anger can only lead to more serious
problems. The resolution of anger can come by bringing it to God—
either for His judgment or for His forgiveness. When others let us
down, anger is a normal response. To place its disposition in the
hands of God is the beginning of release and freedom from destructive
and crippling anger.

COME BEFORE WINTER

19 Greet Prisca and Aquila, and the household of
Onesiphorus.
20 Erastus stayed in Corinth, but Trophimus I have
left in Miletus sick.
21 Do your utmost to come before winter. Eubulus
greets you, as well as Pudens, Linus, Claudia, and all
the brethren.
22 The Lord Jesus Christ be with your spirit. Grace
be with you. Amen.

2 Tim. 4:19–22

With these final greetings and a benediction, the Apostle speaks
to us for the last time. Prisca and Aquila, now in Ephesus, receive
special greetings from Paul. They had risked their lives for Paul (Rom.
16:3), and always hosted a church in their home (Acts 18:2–3; 1 Cor.
16:19). Onesiphorus we have already met. Erastus we meet in Acts
19:22 on a special mission with Timothy. Erastus had lived in Corinth
when Paul wrote to the Romans, and he was the city treasurer (Rom.

16:23). Trophimus had been with Paul on his return journey from Greece to Asia (Acts 20:4) and had been involved in the controversy in Paul's arrest in Jerusalem (Acts 21:29).

Eubulus, Pudens, Linus, Claudia, and *"all the brethren"* join in the final greeting. I'm haunted by the question of where they had been at the first defense hearing. If they had let him down, it no longer mattered to Paul.

Is there not a word for us all in this poignant appeal, *"Come before winter"?* There may not be another spring. Act now. Do the kind deed today; there may be no tomorrow.

"The Lord Jesus Christ be with your spirit. Grace be with you. Amen."

Thirty years of remarkable ministry is about to end with the thud of the executioner's axe. But the word and work of the Lord will go on as long as people like Timothy and us heed Paul's last letter.

Introduction to Titus

A survey of a number of commentaries on the pastoral Epistles confirms that Titus often gets lost in the shadows of 1 and 2 Timothy. Titus has not received a great deal of attention, and I am sure it is not the focus of many sermons.

Perhaps because I enjoy rooting for the underdog, I decided to read Titus with a new openness and expectancy, with prayer and imagination. And, believe me, this little letter has come alive for me for the first time ever!

Paul's Special Ambassador

The first thing that tugged at me was a need to get to know Titus himself. We know very little about him, as compared to Timothy, for references to him are scarce. His name never occurs in Acts and appears in only three of Paul's other letters, 2 Corinthians, Galatians, and 2 Timothy.

But the little information we have indicates that Titus was one of Paul's closest and most trusted friends. The very greeting in Titus 1:4, "my true son in our common faith," witnesses to a special relationship. And the fact that Titus was on a special assignment for Paul in a very tough place like Crete speaks powerfully about Paul's regard for Titus as a competent leader and pastor.

Chronologically, we meet Titus first in Galatians 2:1–5. The occasion was a crucial moment, not only in Paul's life, but also in early Christian history. Tension had been mounting as to whether the Jerusalem church was going to accept Paul and his approach to baptizing

Gentiles without insisting that they first become Jews by being circumcised and subscribing to Jewish laws and rituals. The decision
on this issue would determine the shape of the Christian church
for all time. When Paul went to Jerusalem to fight for his approach
to the Gospel of salvation by grace through faith alone, he took
Titus with him as his prime exhibit of a Gentile convert worthy of
full acceptance in the church, apart from the ritual of circumcision.

Paul's choice of Titus on this momentous occasion was vindicated!
With what joy he wrote: "Yet not even Titus who was with me,
being a Greek, was compelled to be circumcised." (Gal. 2:3). The
outcome of the confrontation was an agreement that Paul and Titus
"should go to the Gentiles and they to the Jews" (Gal. 2:9, NIV).
The others "desired only that we should remember the poor, the
very thing which I also was eager to do" (Gal. 2:10). What an impression Titus must have made upon James, Peter, and John that
day—and because of it, the history of the Christian church has been
different! And to us Gentiles, centuries later, what a difference!

We can assume from various references in 2 Corinthians that Titus
became Paul's most trusted troubleshooter. The actual number of
assignments and trips is not certain, but the picture of Titus is not
unlike that of our secretary of state being sent again and again on
shuttle missions of diplomacy. No church gave Paul more cause for
concern and anger than Corinth. They were a wild bunch, for Corinth
was a wild place. Before writing 2 Corinthians, Paul sent Titus to
Corinth to collect an offering for the needy in Jerusalem (2 Cor. 8:1–
6, 16–24). On another occasion, he sent Titus again to straighten
out some messy situations and to confront some of Paul's opponents
there. The mission was a success and brought great joy to Paul (2
Cor. 7:6–7, 13–16).

And now, Paul writes to Titus, who is on special assignment to
Crete, to bring some order and direction to the churches there. When
Paul wanted someone to do a tough job, he called on Titus. We
might say that Titus was one of Paul's most trusted and capable
ambassadors, if not his secretary of state.

Truth Is in Order to Goodness

The second thing that has gripped me in a new way in this brief
letter is its simple but profound approach to church life and governance. My denomination (Presbyterian) places a great emphasis upon

doing everything "decently and in order" (1 Cor. 14:40). Because I teach a course on Presbyterian polity at Fuller Theological Seminary, I have special appreciation for the assignment given Titus to "set in order the things that are lacking, and appoint elders in every city as I commanded you" (Titus 1:5).

But what impresses me more deeply with this letter is its central emphasis upon the relationship of practice to polity, behavior to belief, conduct to creed. One of the fundamental principles of church order in the Presbyterian constitution is "that truth is in order to goodness; and the great touchstone of truth, its tendency to promote holiness, according to our Savior's rule 'By their fruits ye shall know them.' . . . We are persuaded that there is an inseparable connection between faith and practice, truth and duty. Otherwise, it would be of no consequence either to discover truth or to embrace it" (*Book of Church Order* of the Presbyterian Church, USA, "Form of Government," 1.0304).

If this letter to Titus can be said to have a central text, it has to be: "This is a faithful saying, and these things I want you to affirm constantly, that those who have believed in God should be careful to maintain good works" (3:8).

The inseparable relationship of doctrine and good works is the basis of the entire letter. And how important this is for the church in every generation! We have a tendency to emphasize one at the expense of the other. When either truth or doctrine becomes an end in itself, we produce a legalistic orthodoxy, often lacking in genuine love and care in action. However, when goodness is emphasized at the expense of truth ("it doesn't matter what you believe as long as you are sincere and loving"), we produce platitudes without power, often lacking in long-term commitment.

In Titus, Paul calls us to sound doctrine that expresses itself continually in good works. I pray that this commentary will be as helpful to you in the reading as it has been to me in this writing—to discover this powerful gem, too often lost in the shadows of the other letters of Paul.

An Outline of Titus

I. The Christian and Truth: 1:1—2:1
   A. The Doctrinal Basis of Truth: 1:1–4
   B. The True Leader: 1:5–9
   C. Confronting False Teachers: 1:10—2:1
II. The Christian and Goodness: 2:2–14
   A. Goodness in Maturing: 2:2–3
   B. Goodness in Marriage and Family: 2:4–5
   C. Goodness in Christian Leaders: 2:6–8
   D. Goodness in Christian Slaves: 2:9–10
   E. The Doctrinal Basis for Goodness: 2:11–14
III. The Christian and Good Works: 2:15—3:15
   A. Good Works and Good Citizens: 2:15—3:2
   B. The Doctrinal Basis for Good Works: 3:3–7
   C. The Usefulness of Good Works: 3:8–11
   D. Good Works in Action: 3:12–15

CHAPTER ONE

The Christian and Truth

Titus 1:1—2:1

The opening greeting is much longer in proportion to the total length of this letter than that in any of Paul's other letters. This is good reason in itself to take it seriously. It consists of the standard three parts of a greeting: the writer, the reader, and the greeting.

THE DOCTRINAL BASIS OF TRUTH

1 Paul, a servant of God and an apostle of Jesus Christ, according to the faith of God's elect and the acknowledgment of the truth which is according to godliness,
2 in hope of eternal life which God, who cannot lie, promised before time began,
3 but has in due time manifested His word through preaching, which was committed to me according to the commandment of God our Savior;

4 To Titus, my true son in our common faith:

Grace, mercy, and peace from God the Father and the Lord Jesus Christ our Savior.

Titus 1:1–4

Paul does not begin this letter with any reference to his personal circumstances, nor does he state the purpose of his writing. Later in the epistle, it appears that he is on a journey which has included a brief stay on the large island of Crete before its continuation to Greece and Macedonia.

Since there is no place in Luke's narrative in Acts for such a journey, it seems best to assume that Paul was released from the imprisonment with which Acts closes, enabling him to travel for awhile before being imprisoned again in Rome prior to his execution. If this was the case, this letter to Titus was probably written between the first and second letters to Timothy.

While the purpose of the letter is to instruct Titus and the Christians in Crete in some practical matters in need of correction, Paul begins by establishing his authority to give such instructions on the basis of his own commitment to the truth revealed in Jesus Christ.

This is much more than a personal letter to Titus. It is an official communication to Titus as the one in charge of the congregation in Crete. Paul first bases his authority to write such a letter upon his being *"a servant of God"* and *"an apostle of Jesus Christ."*

In Romans, Galatians, and Philippians, Paul calls himself "a servant of Jesus Christ." Only here does he use the term "servant of God." I take this change in language to be significant, not in a theological sense, but in a very practical way. Paul must have changed his customary phrase here in order to communicate more meaningfully with the people in Crete. Even the language *"God our Savior"* in verse 3 is different from his more common usage. While this is not a major point, I celebrate this indication of Paul's sensitivity and flexibility as a communicator. I have a friend who begins every letter he writes with the phrase "Greetings in the blessed name of our precious Lord and Savior Jesus Christ." I have received indications from some people that they are turned off by that particular greeting, to the point that they read the rest of the letter with negative feelings.

All communicators need to be sensitive to the possible feelings elicited by each word they use. In one circle a particular word or cliché may evoke a positive response. In another, it may have the opposite effect. It is our task as communicators to be sensitive and flexible to the feelings of our readers and hearers. I regard Paul as a good model.

Even as Paul presents his credentials, he makes a profound doctrinal statement of his understanding of truth: his authority is grounded in *"the faith of God's elect"* (v. 1). The preposition translated *"according to"* in this phrase means that Paul's apostleship, and thus his authority, is fully consistent with the faith which God's elect have received. *"The faith"* is the standard of measurement by which the Cretans were to measure and evaluate their life. To Paul, there was always an objective and fixed data base in Jesus Himself by which all doctrine was to be measured. In a time when we often rush to the latest scheme to make the Gospel "relevant" to the modern world, we might well ask ourselves what *"the faith of God's elect"* really is.

The second part of this doctrinal statement is neglected at great peril. Truth is *"according to godliness."* Doctrine becomes deadly when it is divorced from godly living. Truth must produce goodness, or it is not truth. The history of orthodoxy witnesses to this again and again.

Godliness must not be defined in terms of any particular set of pet pietisms. Godliness consists of expressions in everyday living of the character of God. If God is love, godliness consists of loving in word and deed. If God is mercy, godliness consists of being merciful. If God is patient and kind, godliness is expressed through patience and kindness. While our expressions and behaviors will never achieve godly perfection, we are called upon to reflect the nature of God Himself through our devotion and obedience to Christ.

And this is never portrayed as some superhuman task of appearing to be something other than what we are. It is rather an expression, however imperfectly, of what we really are by virtue of God's creating and redeeming love. Godliness is not an achievement of a special few. It is the natural flow of a life in a relationship with Jesus Christ.

Thus, truth is always inseparably linked with godliness. The tradition in which I have been spiritually nurtured has made two consistent errors. The first has been the promotion of doctrine as a virtual end in itself; the second has been the defining of godliness too narrowly.

Salvation has been proclaimed to be basically a matter of "believing" the right things about God, Christ, the Bible, and whatever other doctrinal matters deemed to be essential. This has led to perpetual civil war among Christians. It even allows doctrinal distinctions to become the justification for hostile and destructive words and actions. If truth is always tied to godliness, and godliness has to do with love, mercy, forgiveness, justice, and the like—then doctrine can never be the basis for justifying their opposites.

At the same time, godliness has been truncated by some definitions. If the measure of godliness is limited primarily to one's sexual morality and speech, vast areas of life are ignored. I've known too many folks who heap unkind and unloving abuse upon their spouses and children, but regard themselves as godly because they don't "smoke, drink, or chew."

For us to remember that "truth is according to godliness" is the beginning of wisdom, both in doctrine and in practice.

The third part of Paul's doctrinal statement in this greeting is the *"hope of eternal life"* (v. 2). Of this, Paul says three things: (1) it was promised by God before time began; (2) it is now manifested through preaching; (3) Paul's preaching of this was commanded by God.

Eternal life is a hope because it is not yet a completed reality in our experience. In one sense we have eternal life in Christ now. But in another sense, it is yet to come. To be in Christ is to have eternal life. "He who has the Son has life" (1 John 5:12). We don't have to wait until we die to receive eternal life. In this sense, eternal life refers to quality more than duration. But eternal life is also an affirmation that death is not the end of our lives. We will not experience the reality of that aspect of eternal life until we die, and in that sense we live in the *hope* of eternal life. And this hope is not a mere wish-dream because of Jesus' victory over death in His resurrection.

It is upon these doctrinal foundations that Paul lays his claim to truth and authority. He can call the church in Crete to particular standards of behavior and relationships because truth is nailed down in Jesus Himself.

He writes to Titus as his *"true son in our common faith."* Happy indeed are those who are blessed with children in the faith. A friend shared with me the other day a source of great joy to her. Years ago, she had served as a leader in a youth group in the church. A letter had come from one of the young people who had been in the program and is now a mature adult with children of his own. He wrote to thank her for being such a strong influence in his life in those formative years, expressing his love for her as a "parent" in Christ. To be involved in the birth and nurturing of sons and daughters in the faith is one of the greatest and most rewarding privileges in all of life.

Paul could convey *"grace, mercy, and peace"* to Titus with warmth. These three qualities are integral to Christian truth. While textual evidence does not warrant the inclusion of the word *"mercy"* in verse 4, its usage elsewhere presumably encouraged our translators to add it here. The greeting of grace and peace brings two remarkable thoughts together. Grace, of course, is the undeserved and unearned favor of God at work in our lives through Jesus. It results in a sense of harmony and well-being, the *shalom* of God.

THE TRUE LEADER

5 For this reason I left you in Crete, that you should set in order the things that are lacking, and appoint elders in every city as I commanded you—

6 if a man is blameless, the husband of one wife, having faithful children not accused of dissipation or insubordination.

7 For a bishop must be blameless, as a steward of God, not self-willed, not quick-tempered, not given to wine, not violent, not greedy for money,

8 but hospitable, a lover of what is good, sober-minded, just, holy, self-controlled,

9 holding fast the faithful word as he has been taught, that he may be able, by sound doctrine, both to exhort and to convict those who contradict.

Titus 1:5–9

No organization can rise higher than the quality of its leadership. The church in Crete must have been suffering from a lack of quality leadership, because Paul had placed Titus there to lead them toward a life that would be a faithful expression of the doctrinal standards.

The very structure of this letter defines pastoral theology for all time. Not only do we have the inseparable relationship of truth and goodness, but we also have a clear statement of the primacy of leadership development. The pastor who neglects this will ultimately fail in the pastorate. I learned this the hard way.

In the first congregation I served as senior pastor, I decided that I wanted to move much faster than the elders were willing to move. I proceeded to develop programs and emphases without allowing them to share in their development and leadership. While there was "success" and "growth," the fact was that many of those programs did not continue after I left that congregation. It pretty much went back to its old ways of doing things.

When I came to the congregation I have now served for more than nineteen years, I determined from the start that I would place my highest priority on leadership development and that new programs and emphases would grow out of the leadership of the Session, our official church board. As I look back, it took much longer than I anticipated to develop a new breed and style of leaders. Significant and lasting changes didn't really develop until after five or six years. But when I look back at the last ten years, I wouldn't tackle it any other way.

And this isn't a matter of a particular form of church government. Whether the form of government is congregational and autonomous, or episcopal with more centralized authority, the quality of the leadership determines the quality of the life of the congregation. And leadership is always a shared responsibility of pastor and people. Whether it's a vestry, session, or board, the principle is the same. Whether the authority is vested in the clergy or the laity, the principle still holds. The essential role of the pastor (Titus) is to develop leadership (elders).

Leadership development begins by having agreed-upon and articulated standards. We may or may not choose to require the exact qualifications as set forth here and in 1 Timothy 3, though we cannot miss the mark by far in taking these two similar lists seriously. But of crucial importance is having high standards.

I'm appalled at the casual and careless processes of leadership selection in many churches. Often the pastor is either given carte blanche authority to choose the officers or learns to be a clever manipulator of the nominating committee. Both can be avoided by developing clear standards and procedures for the selection and training of officers.

The selection or nominating committee does well to begin its work by reviewing and clarifying the standards. The goal is to find the people who measure up to the standards rather than to shape the standards to fit the people. Again and again, pastors tell me that if the standards are high in terms of commitment and performance, they can't find enough people to fill the offices. When that is the case, the pastor has one of two choices. One can either accept the status quo and limp along hoping for another call, or one can accept the challenge to place a high priority on developing the kind of leaders needed.

And how is this done? By intentional identification, cultivation, and training of individuals with the potential and the commitment required of true leaders in the church. The pastor who doesn't make time for this kind of activity is doomed to mediocrity. Ignoring this area of pastoral leadership is as disastrous to a church as is neglecting research and development to a business. Many American businesses are paying in the 1980s the high price of their neglect of research and development in the '60s and '70s. All too many churches are suffering from decades of pastoral ignore-ance of intentional, individual leadership development.

Care must be taken that such efforts do not degenerate into picking the pastor's pets. That only produces a sick church. When leaders are selected because they can be trusted to support the pastor's programs, the basic ingredients for a half-baked church are present. I can't state the appeal strongly enough: Pastors and lay leaders, place a high priority in identifying and training those folks who will measure up to high standards of commitment and leadership!

We have already written in this volume concerning the specific qualities for elders set forth in 1 Timothy 3 and encourage you to review that section in conjunction with this passage. In comparing the two, don't miss the strong emphasis upon *"sound doctrine"* in verse 9. The exemplary life of the elder is a product of sound doctrine. We simply cannot emphasize either practice or doctrine at the expense of the other.

The assignment given to Titus was not only to develop strong leaders, but also to *"set in order the things that are lacking"* (v. 5). While leadership development is crucial, so is the confrontation with false teachers. The "for" in verse 10 gives us the reason it is so important for the elders to hold sound doctrine.

Confronting False Teachers

10 For there are many insubordinate, both idle talkers and deceivers, especially those of the circumcision,

11 whose mouths must be stopped, who subvert whole households, teaching things which they ought not, for the sake of dishonest gain.

12 One of them, a prophet of their own, said, "Cretans are always liars, evil beasts, lazy gluttons."

13 This testimony is true. Therefore rebuke them sharply, that they may be sound in the faith,

14 not giving heed to Jewish fables and commandments of men who turn from the truth.

15 To the pure all things are pure, but to those who are defiled and unbelieving nothing is pure; but even their mind and conscience are defiled.

16 They profess that they know God, but in works
they deny Him, being abominable, disobedient, and
disqualified for every good work.

1 But as for you, speak the things which are proper
for sound doctrine:

Titus 1:10—2:1

I find it best to approach this kind of passage by recognizing that
we best grasp its impact by recognizing that the same problems are
present in and among our churches today, even though they may
not exist in the exact forms they had taken in Crete.

We need not focus on trying to determine exactly who these rebel-
lious and unruly people were. That they were Jewish converts insisting
on the preservation of circumcision is clearly stated. I'm not aware
of any such individuals in our churches today, but their descendants
are legion. How many teachers do you know who are insisting that
in order to be a Christian you have to practice or avoid doing certain
things? How many teachers have you heard who insist that their
particular doctrinal fine point is "essential" to the Gospel?

Are you aware of teachers and leaders whose very teaching is upsetting and ruining whole households? And are you aware of some
who purvey their teaching for the sake of "filthy lucre," as the King
James Version translates it? Paul has already pointed out to Timothy
that "the love of money is a root of all kinds of evil" (1 Tim. 6:10),
and the temptation is real when our teaching becomes a source of
financial gain. Radio and television ministries are especially dangerous
because of the vast potential they carry for generating huge sums
of money.

You don't have to look very far to discover that even though the
false teachers may not wear the same clothing or teach the same
things as those rascals in Crete, they are ever present in the church
of every age and place. The words that Paul uses in verse 10 to
describe them have timeless and universal application.

They are *"insubordinate,"* which is to say they are unruly and undisciplined. A mark of false teachers in every age is their unwillingness
to be under discipline. They are fiercely unaccountable. With all of
its problems, I appreciate denominational life because of its demands
for accountability. Though the processes may be cumbersome, we
are less likely to become misleading and false teachers when we submit to some forms and structures of discipline.

The false teachers were also described as *"idle talkers."* One of the tragedies of our time is our failure to match the quality of our technology with the content of our communication. We are moving from an industrial to an informational society. We have developed the capabilities of instant and unlimited communication on a global scale. But we don't have much of value to communicate. If we in the church are *"idle talkers"* and not doers of love, peace, mercy, and justice, we merely take our places alongside the false teachers of Crete.

They were *"deceivers."* Smooth and glib talk by undisciplined speakers can become charmingly deceptive—and financially productive. Such teaching leads people away from the truth rather than to it. Any teaching that adds to or detracts from a basic love for and commitment to Jesus Himself is ultimately deceptive.

The hard thing in all of this is the action Paul requires of Titus. He is told that their *"mouths must be stopped."* The Greek word used here implies a process of reasoning. Stopping their mouths is not to be a silencing by force or violence but by teaching and reason. This kind of silencing may lead to rebuke and admonition, but its goal is always to produce soundness and wholeness in the faith. And it's so easy to lose sight of this goal when confronting false teachers. If we're not careful, we become more interested in winning the argument than in winning the person. Silencing the false teachers does not mean destroying them. Rebuking them does not mean demolishing them, even though they may be *"abominable, disobedient, and disqualified for every good work"* (v. 16).

There are two maxims in this paragraph worthy of special attention. The first is by a Cretan prophet, *"Cretans are always liars, evil beasts, lazy gluttons."* This may shock us as a racist epithet, and it is. I doubt that Paul would use this kind of statement were he writing in a day like ours when our sensitivities have rightly been heightened to the dangers of such kinds of ethnic generalities. But in Paul's defense, two things can be said. First, he lived in a day when sensitivities such as ours were undeveloped. It's not likely that anyone would have raised an eyebrow at this kind of statement. The second thing to be said is that Paul was quoting one of their own prophets, Epimenides of the sixth century before Christ. It would have been one thing for Paul the Jew to have said this of Cretans—probably a sure way to start a riot. It was apparently acceptable for him to quote one of their own. And the Cretans had developed their own reputation for these characteristics. Sometimes people have a way of living up— or down—to their cultural images. The Greeks developed a word, *kretizō,* "to Crete-ize," which meant "to lie" and "to cheat." As the

Corinthians had developed their image as lovers of parties and orgies, so the Cretans had developed their own specialty. Because of this Cretan reputation, Paul was all the more concerned about dealing directly and openly with the false teachers.

The second maxim of note is in verse 15: *"To the pure, all things are pure, but to those who are defiled and unbelieving nothing is pure."* This is, in fact, a double maxim, concluding with: *"They profess that they know God, but in works they deny Him."* In these phrases, Paul is confronting the false teachers both with the test of character and with the test of conduct.

The Cretan false teachers apparently placed a high priority upon the proper observance of outward ritual at the expense of inner integrity, as with the Pharisees of Jesus' day. Regulations about food and drink and various behaviors have always had a strong appeal to religionists. Jesus was specific in his rejection of such approaches: "There is nothing that enters a man from outside which can defile him; but the things which come out of him, those are the things that defile a man" (Mark 7:15). Paul is clearly not saying that impurity exists only in the mind or that sin is only in the eye of the beholder. He is, however, striking the same blow that Jesus struck: it is our inner attitudes and motivations that determine the quality of our actions. It is indeed the pure in heart who are blessed, for they do see God. Søren Kierkegaard defined purity of heart as "willing one thing." When we will the one thing of knowing and loving God, all things have a way of becoming pure and beautiful. The test of character takes us beyond mere performance based upon external rules.

The test of conduct measures our knowledge of God by our actions, not by our claims. Words of love without deeds of love do not a loving relationship make. Talk of mercy without kindness and forgiveness only denies the presence of God. Pontifications about justice without the actions to match quickly become a travesty. It is our actions, not our claims, that witness to our knowledge of God.

The most effective antidote to a false teacher is a true teacher. I prefer to tie Titus 2:1 to the preceding paragraph and to begin chapter 2 with verse 2. The charge to Titus to silence and rebuke the false teachers comes to its perfect conclusion in the admonition to *"speak the things which are proper for sound doctrine."* Here is a clear appeal to that beautiful blend of character and conduct, belief and behavior, words and deeds, which is always the mark of a true teacher.

CHAPTER TWO

The Christian and Goodness

(*Titus 2:2–14*)

It seems to me that this section of Titus is a beautiful summary of everything contained in the pastoral Epistles. All of the emphasis upon sound doctrine and the proper ordering of life in the church has little, if any, significance unless it produces changed lives that demonstrate a high quality of life and love. And that quality of life will have varying characteristics at different stages along life's journey.

William Barclay entitles this section of Titus "The Christian Character in Action." Here are guidelines for the Christian life for older men and women, for younger men and women, for slaves, and for good citizens. And in the midst of the passage is one of the truly beautiful and succinct summaries of Christian doctrine anywhere to be found in Paul's writings.

This chapter is, to me, one of the gems of the entire New Testament.

GOODNESS IN MATURING

2 that the older men be sober, reverent, temperate,
sound in faith, in love, in patience;
3 the older women likewise, that they be reverent
in behavior, not slanderers, not given to much wine,
teachers of good things—

Titus 2:2–3

Paul begins with instructions to Titus for his teaching of older men and of older women. It is clear that the older people in the church are to be leaders and examples to the younger. The assumption is that they have lived long enough to sift and sort out the differences between that which is truly abiding in value and that which is of little or no value.

Far from being a threatening or frightening process, aging can be a rich and rewarding experience. We can either fear it and fight it, or we can flow with it and enjoy it. Here, Paul sets before us the rich potential of the aging process for men and for women.

Four goals are set forth for men. And the word *"likewise"* in verse 3 implies that these same goals are just as valid for women. The first goal is that of sobriety. The Greek word is *nēphálios,* a word whose primary meaning is "sobriety in contrast to drunkenness from overindulgence in wine." But the word is also used in the wider sense of clear-headedness in general. Here is the picture of a person who has achieved perspective in life—one who is not under the influence of outside forces, whether alcohol, money, anger, lust, or greed. Whatever else the experiences of aging should do for us, they should enable us to develop a perspective in which our values are brought into line with God's intentions for us. In the course of my pastoral work, I meet a lot of people in every stage of life. I'm saddened by folks in their forties and fifties who are still madly pursuing the same ephemeral goals they were chasing in their twenties and thirties. In a couples' conference not long ago, I was sharing some of the changes in my own values, especially with regard to wealth and possessions. In an open discussion period, some of the couples in their twenties confronted me with the statement: "This is all well and good for you in your fifties—you've had your fun. If you want to settle down and simplify your lifestyle after all these years of acquisition, travel, and all the rest, that's fine. But we're going to do our thing for a while at least—just like you did!"

My knee-jerk reaction was to give the "fatherly advice" response: "Yes, my child, I understand. But, after learning my lessons, I hate to see you make the same mistakes I've made. Take my advice, and start in your twenties from where I am, approaching sixty." But you and I know that this approach doesn't work any better in the twentieth century than it did in the first. The hardest thing for us older folks to accept is that the younger generation is going to learn these things pretty much the way we did—by trial and error. That's why I say that I'm more concerned with those my age who are still chasing the same goals that they started pursuing thirty years ago. When maturing is part of aging, our perspectives and values grow into sobriety, a clear-headed way of viewing everything around us.

The second goal of maturing in our older years is reverence. The Greek word is *semnos,* describing serious and mature behavior. This need not point to dullness or drabness. I know a man in his eighties who embodies this quality. He's fun to be around. He radiates a reverence for life, for people, for nature—for everyone and everything around him. There's always a sparkle in his eyes and voice that indicates his continuing enjoyment of life.

The third goal is to be *"temperate."* Here the word is *sōphronas* which can be translated "prudent" or "sensible." It portrays a person whose actions have a high degree of correspondence with his best judgment. I've often thought that it was Paul the younger man who described his struggle: "For the good that I will to do, I do not do; but the evil I will not to do, that I practice" (Rom. 7:19). Maturing is narrowing the gap between our best judgment and our actual behavior. Part of the challenge in this area of growth is involving both our mind and feelings in the process of shaping our judgments. When good judgment is primarily a matter of rational precision, it becomes cold and impersonal. When it is primarily shaped by feelings, it has a way of becoming irresponsible.

The fourth goal is descriptive of the product of the first three: *"sound in faith, in love, and in patience."* Here is the trilogy we first met in Paul's earliest letter: "your work of faith, labor of love and patience of hope" (1 Thess. 1:3). Faith has a way of growing with the years, not necessarily in the intellectual sense, but in the sense of simply trusting God more. If anything, I have more intellectual questions and struggles the more I study and learn, but I find myself trusting in God more and more, even as I trust my ability to understand less and less. Growth in love is growth in our ability to act in the best interests of others. And this ties us back to our old friend *hupomonē,* the patience and endurance that enables us not merely to survive, but to transform hardships into things of beauty for God.

Yet another goal of maturing is set forth, specifically to the older women, *"that they be reverent in behavior."* There is widespread agreement among the commentaries that the language here describes a sacred priest carrying out her duties. Thus, the picture is one of a person who sees her entire life as worship to God. The words of Paul to the Romans comes to mind: "I beseech you . . . that you present your bodies a living sacrifice, holy, acceptable to God, which is your reasonable service" (Rom. 12:1). The word translated "service" is the word used of priestly ministry in the temple. Maturing in Christ is to grow in the awareness that all of life is sacred and that everything we do has a direct relationship to God. Happy is the person who sees desks and kitchen sinks as altars rather than artifacts.

I group the last three goals of maturing, for they relate closely to each other: *"not slanderers, not given to much wine, teachers of good things—".* Slandering is the spreading of stories, true or false, that bring hurt or pain to others. And what a deadly combination there is in one who indulges in that kind of talk and who is inclined to drink too much wine! One of the effects of alcohol is to impair our control over our judgment and discernment.

Healthy and constructive speech (being *"teachers of good things"*) requires alertness and discipline. Sobriety is essential to such behavior. Such speech is described by Paul as "speaking the truth in love" (Eph. 4:15). We must never use honesty as a license for destroying others. Love requires that some things be stated and that others be left unsaid. The maturing person is able to make the distinction.

In these two verses, less than half of a Pauline sentence, we are given profound guidelines for maturing. And it's clear that maturing can be the best part of the aging process. We cannot mature without aging. The tragedy is aging without maturing. Blessed are those who do both together.

Verses 4 and 5 are the continuation of the sentence beginning with verse 1. From his counsel to the older men and women, Paul now focuses upon younger women and men. One of the goals of maturing is to be able to teach those who are younger. This is clear in the opening words of verse 4. It is the older women who are to be *"teachers of good things"* to the younger women.

GOODNESS IN MARRIAGE AND FAMILY

> 4 that they admonish the young women to love
> their husbands, to love their children,
> 5 to be discreet, chaste, homemakers, good,
> obedient to their own husbands, that the word of God
> may not be blasphemed.
>
> *Titus 2:4–5*

It would be natural for antifeminists to pounce on these verses with a "now I've gotcha" cry of triumph. For those who believe that a woman's place is in the home and that God created women to be subservient to men, the first reading of these verses seems to lend a word of support.

There is a sense in which the traditional roles of wife and mother are affirmed. The young women are *"to love their husbands"* and to be *"obedient to their own husbands."* They are *"to love their children," "to be discreet,"* to be *"chaste,"* to be *"homemakers,"* and to be *"good."*

What better description of a good wife and mother? There doesn't seem to be a provision for the young woman pursuing a career in the world of business, or for the young mother dropping her child off at the day care center on the way to work. Doesn't this passage make the sole role of the woman as wife and mother quite clear?

At one time, my answer was emphatically affirmative. But I no longer feel this to be true, for a number of reasons. I don't think the principles of the importance of being a good wife and mother ever change. But the application, of necessity, must change from time to time and from place to place. In Crete, at the time of this writing, young women had no option to marriage and motherhood. As far as we can tell, the only employment for a young woman outside of the home was as a prostitute on the streets or in a pagan temple. Moving west from Crete, through Athens to Rome, we would meet a few women in business, such as Lydia from Thyatira. But she was probably an older woman, with grown children, for "she and her household" were baptized together (Acts 16:15). Young women really had no options other than marriage and motherhood.

It is in the light of that cultural reality that we must try to understand what was happening in the early churches, such as the one in Crete. As women and men came to Christ, they came to the realization that in their baptism into Christ "there is neither male nor female, for you are all one in Christ Jesus" (Gal. 3:28). For people who had been raised in a culture in which women were regarded as inferior and treated as chattel, the Christian view introduced an entirely different way of thinking. That this new way of thinking would change the outward forms of the community has been validated by history. But we must understand the tension created by the Gospel in this and other areas of human relationships.

The danger for the early Christians was the danger of every new movement: single-issue overemphasis.

If, for example, the church had come across primarily as an antislavery movement, the central meaning of the Gospel in the life, death, and resurrection of Jesus could have been obscured. It seems to me, in issues like this, that Paul was saying, "Don't make the break with culture so fast that you blur the focus upon Christ Himself." That this could be abused as a rationalization for continued oppression and injustice goes without saying, but some tension is inescapable.

I believe that Christ ultimately breaks the power of all oppressive and inhuman forces and systems. In this sense, Christianity is always a liberation movement. The power of Christ broke the power of slavery, though the early church studiously avoided being known as a single-issue antislavery movement. The power of Christ also breaks the power of the oppression of women, but the church is not primarily a woman's liberation movement. Christianity is Jesus Himself, and no issue must be allowed to upstage Him.

Clearly, the problem for the early Christians was how to relate their new experiences of freedom in Christ to the oppressive structures of the world around them. That is not the problem in our day for women in the Western world. If anything, the situation is the reverse. In the first century, the church was the liberator of women, while the world was relegating women to a role of subservience to men. In our day, in the West, the culture has been in the vanguard of women's rights, and the church, for the most part, has been the standard-bearer for keeping women in subservient roles.

In that time, the radical affirmation of the church to the world was that women were created, with men, in the image of God and that women were the recipients, with men, of salvation and of the gifts of the Holy Spirit.

In our time, a different affirmation is needed. The culture around us has moved a long way in its commitment to the equality of women. In some circles it even implies the superiority of women. The recognition of women through ordination is well established in many of our churches. But have we been faithful to the emphasis of the Bible upon the dignity and importance of marriage and motherhood for younger women? Is it not time for us to affirm with equal vigor young women as wives and mothers? I think so.

I've had this conversation with some of my women students in seminary. I'm deeply concerned about those who express a disdain for marriage and motherhood. One said to me: "If I wanted to take the easy way, I'd just settle down, get married, and raise some kids." I'm glad she's not representative of most of the women in ministry that I know. I don't believe any woman is going to have significant ministry, inside or outside of the church, who does not exalt, to the same extent that the Bible does, marriage and motherhood.

In our day, not every woman can or should be married. Contemporary women are fortunate indeed to have more options than Paul or Titus could have imagined. But without a large proportion of younger women seriously committed to marriage and motherhood as a high priority, the future of our culture, as well as of the church, would be in jeopardy.

The principle of *"obedience to their own husbands"* in verse 5 must always be viewed in the context of mutual submission to each other, growing out of their mutual submission to Christ as developed by Paul in Ephesians 5:21–33.

The admonition to the younger women ends on the note of Paul's concern *"that the word of God may not be blasphemed."* A strident, single-issue approach to the Gospel is always in danger of bringing discredit to the Gospel itself.

The younger men are also reminded of their responsibility to be a credit to the Word of God. The specific admonition to them is straight to the point: "be sober-minded." The same Greek word is used in verse 2 to the older men, translated "temperate." Here, we're back to the struggle to narrow the gap between our best insights and our behavior. This is a lifelong process in human growth, and the sooner young men identify and deal with it, the more quickly they will achieve true maturity.

Not only is Titus to teach the older and younger men and women, but, as is the emphasis of this entire letter, he is to be a living example of what he teaches.

GOODNESS IN CHRISTIAN LEADERS

6 Likewise exhort the young men to be sober-minded,

7 in all things showing yourself to be a pattern of good works; in doctrine showing integrity, reverence, incorruptibility,

8 sound speech that cannot be condemned, that he who is of the opposition may be ashamed, having nothing evil to say of you.

Titus 2:6–8

The three basic strands of the life of the Christian leader are *"good works," "doctrine,"* and *"sound speech."*

In good works, the Christian leader is to be a pattern. The Greek word for pattern is *tupos,* from which we get our word "type." It conveys a picture of the impression made by a stamp or a die. Whether or not we like it, people, to some degree, will emulate their Christian leaders. The quality of our lives will be stamped upon others. We have little control over that. What we can control, however, is the kind of mark we make.

In doctrine, Titus is called to *"integrity, reverence, [and] incorruptibility."* The word for integrity means untainted, especially with reference to motives, and in contrast to the false teachers. The temptation to use our Christian position of leadership to draw attention to ourselves, to lord it over people, and to feather our own nests is ever-present. And it's never easy to be absolutely certain of our motives. Eternal vigilance is the task assigned to each of us. We do well to recognize that there is always some impurity even in our best intentions— and trust in God's mercy and grace.

The word *"reverence"* brings us back to its use in verse 2, where we saw its meaning, not as dullness or drabness, but as a sparkling, mature enjoyment of all of life. This word reminds me of the Shorter Catechism's "What is the chief end of man?" "Man's chief end is to glorify God and to enjoy Him forever." The word in our text translated "incorruptibility" has very little support by the evidence of manuscripts and is dropped by virtually all modern translations.

In *"sound speech,"* the goal is to teach in such a way that we do not invite or allow rejection because of our carelessness or shabbiness. As a professor of preaching at the seminary, I listen to a lot of sermons by our fledgling preachers. I try to listen to these through the ears of a nominal Christian or an antagonistic unbeliever. By pointing out flaws in logic, carelessness in structure, or lack of clarity in thought, I hope they can be helped toward *"sound speech that cannot be condemned."*

The goal that our opponents will have *"nothing evil to say"* of us cannot be intended to mean that we will not be attacked or maligned. The thought is obviously that such confrontation will not be the result of our own shoddiness of speech.

Christian leaders are always on trial, whether or not we concede the fact. We can only give constant, prayerful attention to our own conduct, doctrine, and speech. I find the challenge of such leadership quite exhilarating!

As is often the case when Paul is writing about practical matters of Christian goodness, he has a word for those early Christians still caught in the ambiguities of living in a culture that practiced slavery as a key part of its economic structure. In this case, he addresses only the slaves.

GOODNESS IN CHRISTIAN SLAVES

9 Exhort servants to be obedient to their own masters, to be well-pleasing in all things, not answering back,
10 not pilfering, but showing all good fidelity, that they may adorn the doctrine of God our Savior in all things.

Titus 2:9–10

One of the most difficult things for me as a Christian leader is living with ambiguity. There are a significant number of absolutes in Christian thought and life—enough to tempt me to believe that everything can be put into the categories of yes or no, true or false. Haven't we all done this with our spouses or our children or a close friend? "Now just give me a straight answer—yes or no!" The tough questions in life are those that can't be answered in unambiguous categories.

Slavery had to be one of those tough questions for the early Christians. Whether viewed from the standpoint of a slave or a slave owner who had come to Christ, the complexities were enormous. Take the case of the slave owner becoming a Christian. His relationship with Christ must have demolished any notions that one human being could be the owner of another, since God alone is the Father of everyone. But what are the viable options? One would be the immediate release of all the slaves. But this could be disastrous, not only for the owner, but also for the slaves who would have nowhere to go. Another option would be to move from slavery to partnership or employment. But it's not likely that this could be done in a matter of weeks or months—or even years. The only practical option for most was that of trying to be a caring, loving master—at best a temporary and partial solution; at worst an invitation to disaster, especially with the possibility of unscrupulous slaves who might abuse this new system.

Or take the case of the slave who became a Christian. If his or her master was not a Christian, it's certain that the same kind of mistreatment would continue. How could that person handle such abuse once he or she had tasted a new sense of self-worth in Christ? But now that he/she was aware of the fact that his/her patience and integrity might be the witness that could point his/her master to Christ, open rebellion might not be as attractive. Or if the master was also a Christian, the Christian slave might expect preferential treatment as a brother or sister in Christ, when such treatment could create a disruption of the entire operation.

There just weren't any easy answers, and those dear folks, Christian slaves and Christian masters, had to live with a lot of ambiguity. In this passage, there is no indication whether the masters were Christians. The teaching is directed to slaves who were Christians, presumably under both Christian and non-Christian masters. The instructions were plain and simple, needing no special comment.

The principle was that in such goodness as a slave, the *"doctrine of God our Savior"* would be adorned *"in all things."* This is a fascinating idea, applicable to all areas of human relationships. There is a sense in which our behavior can make the Gospel attractive. It is not the prerogative of the master to demand submission of the slave on the grounds that it is the slave's responsibility to adorn the Gospel.

But it is the prerogative of the slave to choose to submit—even to injustices—if by so doing the Gospel can be attractively adorned. This principle of voluntary submission is frequently more powerful in changing social structures than the way of violence. Many of us have been reminded of this in the movie *Gandhi.*

Paul closes this remarkable section on Christian goodness with the second of these brief theological summaries in this letter. The first we saw in 1:1–4, which we labeled the doctrinal basis of truth. The third we shall come to in 3:3–7 which we shall call the doctrinal basis of good works. Here, in one of Paul's characteristic long sentences is the doctrinal basis of goodness in maturing, in marriage and family, in Christian leaders, and in Christian slaves, whom he has been addressing.

THE DOCTRINAL BASIS FOR GOODNESS

11 For the grace of God that brings salvation has appeared to all men,

12 teaching us that, denying ungodliness and
worldly lusts, we should live soberly, righteously, and
godly in the present age,
13 looking for the blessed hope and glorious
appearing of our great God and Savior Jesus Christ,
14 who gave Himself for us, that He might redeem
us from every lawless deed and purify for Himself
His own special people, zealous for good works.

Titus 2:11–14

What a remarkably concise summary of our faith! If we had taken Paul more seriously along the way, some of our historic creeds and confessions would be much simpler and shorter.

The doctrinal basis of goodness is grounded in the incarnation. The key word in verse 11 is *"appeared."* This is like the language of John: "That which was from the beginning, which we have heard, which we have seen with our eyes, which we have looked upon, and our hands have handled, concerning the Word of life—" (1 John 1:1).

While our faith both lends itself to and requires doctrinal formulation, we must never lose sight of the fact that Christianity is Jesus Himself. It is a person, not a set of ideas. God didn't drop a scroll of theology out of heaven; He came Himself! His coming is His grace that brings us salvation. In these two words— *"grace"* and *"salvation"*— we have a summary of the meaning of God's incarnation in Jesus.

Out of the profound mystery of the incarnation has come the teaching of what we need to know about the meaning of life. In a day when so many messages are being beamed at us, purporting to tell us how to find the good life, this one may appear to be deceptively simple. It is stated negatively and positively: negatively— *"denying ungodliness and worldly lusts;"* positively—living *"soberly, righteously, and godly in the present age."*

To deny ungodliness (a double negative) is simply to affirm godliness. To affirm godliness is to recognize God in all of life. Ungodliness is to live as if there were no God. This raises that interesting question to those of us who readily and regularly profess faith in God. In what specific ways are our lives being lived differently than they would be if we did not believe in God? Or, as it has been stated, "If you were on trial for believing in God, what evidence would you give?"

To deny worldly lusts is an extension of the same thought. Worldly lusts are all desires centered in and growing out of the social, political, and economic systems of this world. These systems are always portrayed over against the Kingdom of God—the world as it would be if it were really ruled by God—or the world as it was really intended to be in God's design.

To live this life *"soberly, righteously, and godly"* conjures up—too readily, I'm afraid—a picture of life dressed in basic black. This is the third time Paul has used the word in this chapter, and it has the same meaning as in verses 2 and 6. Our translation renders "temperate" in verse 2, "sober-minded" in verse 6, and *"soberly"* here. My preference would be to translate it as "prudent" or "sensible" in all these verses. Recall that we defined this as a life that has a growing correspondence between what is believed and what is practiced.

The emphasis of *"righteously"* is rightness—doing what is right. The biblical idea of righteousness is a happy one. There's a beautiful thought in Hebrews, in which the life of discipline in order to produce goodness is portrayed as yielding "the peaceable fruit of righteousness" (Heb. 12:11). Righteousness is a rewarding way to live. There's always a good feeling when you know you've done what's right by the motivation of God's love and grace.

The cycle is completed with the word *"godly."* All of life finds its deepest meaning when lived in the conscious—and unconscious— awareness of God's loving care and presence.

The third great theme of this doctrinal statement is *"hope."* We move from the incarnation, through the style of our lives, to the hope that keeps us going. The doctrine of Christ's return is vital to our staying power in the tough issues of Christian obedience and discipleship. It is unfortunate when we make a test of orthodoxy out of some particular version of this hope. I've often thought that it must be the strategy of Wormwood himself (a "junior tempter" in charge of a young male "patient" in C. S. Lewis' *The Screwtape Letters*) to get Christians fighting over whether the return of Christ is before, during, or after the Millennium or the Great Tribulation. Whatever your view of the manner of His coming, let the hope of His return be your sustaining joy and strength.

The fourth and final theme of Paul's doctrinal summary is *redemption.* He gave Himself to *"redeem"* us—literally purchase us at the cost of His own life—from *"every lawless deed."* The picture here, to me, is one in which sin has us within its grasp and power. Christ literally buys us out of its power to be His own people, cleansed and eager for good works.

The theme of good works now becomes the focus for the rest of the letter.

I hope you agree with me that this chapter in Titus is a beautiful summary of everything in the pastoral Epistles. How it whets our appetite for active goodness in all of the stages and relationships of our lives—goodness grounded in grace and redemption that is in Jesus Himself—our great God and Savior!

CHAPTER THREE

The Christian and Good Works

Titus 2:15—3:15

With this last chapter of Titus, we come to the third and final theme of this great pastoral letter. We move through the letter from truth to goodness to good works. Three times in this chapter we hear the tune of "good works" (vv. 1, 8, 14). The doing of good works is related primarily to the unbelieving folks around them. The doctrinal basis of such good works is clearly stated in verses 3–7.

I prefer to begin this chapter with chapter 2, verse 15 because it clearly connects the previous doctrinal section with the admonition to the Christians in Crete to be good citizens. The organic unity between the three major doctrinal sections of 1:1–4, 2:11–14, and 3:3–7 and the practical appeals of the entire letter stand as a permanent model of the necessary relationship of doctrine and behavior.

GOOD WORKS AND GOOD CITIZENS

15 Speak these things, exhort, and rebuke with all authority. Let no one despise you.
1 Remind them to be subject to rulers and authorities, to obey, to be ready for every good work,
2 to speak evil of no one, to be peaceable, gentle, showing all humility to all men.

Titus 2:15—3:2

Before Paul gives Titus further directions on the need to instruct the Cretans as to the importance of their practice of good works in the community, he pauses to give Titus one more word of personal encouragement. Titus is reminded that he has been given the authority by Paul to exact strong leadership in the church at Crete. A clearer reading of *"Let no one despise you"* would probably be "Don't let them wear you down!" There's no way that we can ultimately control who likes or dislikes us, without losing our integrity. But we can choose how such responses will affect us.

Good citizenship is not an elective for the Christians in Crete— or anywhere else. The same theme is found in Romans 13:1–7 and 1 Peter 2:13–17. It seems safe to assume that these admonitions to good citizenship were based upon the fact that at the time of writing, the Roman government was an encourager of good works (Rom. 13:3, 1 Pet. 2:14). This is the normal, God-given role of government. This admonition was of special importance to the Christians in Crete, for Cretans were notoriously turbulent and unruly when it came to politics. The obvious strategy was for Christians to set an example in good citizenship, thus not implicating the young church in political agitation.

The danger in these New Testament passages is in their misuse by applying them directly as universal principles for all times and places. The history of the German martyrs in the confessing Church under Hitler is but one of numerous examples in our time of situations in which these admonitions from another setting and time simply cannot be applied across the board. I've talked first hand with Christians in Uganda who survived the terrorist regime of Idi Amin. You'll never convince them or me that a dedicated Christian could honor the emperor. For a man like Bishop Festo Kivengere, the obvious act of obedience to God meant the denunciation of Amin by leaving the country by night and going into exile.

Even in our own United States, good citizenship is not without tension-producing decisions. Does being subject to the authorities mean that we must not question their decisions? Does *"speak[ing] evil of no one"* mean that we do not raise our voices in protest to actions and decisions felt to be unjust or unfair? Not at all. When the demands of the state contradict the demands of the Kingdom of God, the Christian has no choice but to take the costly stand and to speak out—whether it means ostracism, punishment, exile, or even death.

Even protest can be expressed within the basic limits of our passage. One does not have to attack and vilify persons to express protest. One can be peaceable and gentle in taking a stand for what is believed to be right, *"showing all humility to all men."*

The key to the entire matter is in the phrase *"to be ready for every good work.''* In our case, let us be grateful for the many aspects of our government which we as Christians can genuinely support without reservation. How fortunate we are to live in a land with a long history of providing quality public education, of developing health services to the poor, and of providing some measure of relief to the needy. We're far from perfect, but we have a strong history in such areas.

At the same time, let us be grateful that we live in a political system where we have a wide range of freedom to express our disagreement with those whom we have elected to govern us. And let us be sensitive and alert to every attempt to curtail and limit that freedom. The tragic story of the way in which all American citizens of Japanese ancestry were stripped of their freedom in 1941 to 1942 in the name of national security must stand unforgotten as a solemn warning of the ease with which liberty can be lost.

And all the while, let us be quick to join with any and all, Christians and non-Christians alike, whenever there is an opportunity to do good works. When there's a need for the relief of human suffering in Namibia or Uganda or Coalinga—let us be the first *''to be ready for every good work.''*

THE DOCTRINAL BASIS FOR GOOD WORKS

Again, Paul's penchant for theological precision bursts forth for the third time in this letter. In another characteristically long sentence, Paul sets forth the essence of the Gospel.

> 3 For we ourselves were also once foolish,
> disobedient, deceived, serving various lusts and
> pleasures, living in malice and envy, hateful and hating
> one another.
> 4 But when the kindness and the love of God our
> Savior toward man appeared,
> 5 not by works of righteousness which we have
> done, but according to His mercy He saved us, by
> the washing of regeneration and renewing of the Holy
> Spirit,
> 6 whom He poured out on us abundantly through
> Jesus Christ our Savior,

> 7 that having been justified by His grace we should
> become heirs according to the hope of eternal life.
>
> *Titus 3:3-7*

It's a great theologian who paints himself into the picture. Before Paul articulates the doctrinal basis for the good works required of believers, he begins with his personal testimony. Perhaps, as he considered how difficult it would be for some of the Cretan Christians to undergo a virtual character transplant from their tendency toward political agitation to becoming persons majoring in good works, he felt a surge of love and hope for them—for he, too, had undergone a similar surgery of the soul many years ago. It is often in remembering our past that the grace of God becomes even more precious. In 1 Corinthians 6:9-11 and in Ephesians 4:17-24, Paul had used similar lists of sins to describe the former behavior of some of the converts in those churches. But here, he adopts a list of sins as his very own. And what a line of credits! *"We ourselves were also once foolish, disobedient, deceived, serving various lusts and pleasures, living in malice and envy, hateful, and hating one another."*

We mustn't forget that Paul was a good man by all reasonable human standards. His list of good things prior to his conversion to Christ was set forth in Philippians 3:4-6. How can he point to himself as blameless concerning the righteousness which is in the law (Phil. 3:6) in one breath and then admit to this list of sins in the next?

The apparent dissonance dissolves once we get a handle on the pervasiveness of indwelling sin. We tend to measure sin and unrighteousness primarily in terms of outward acts. But the Bible penetrates more deeply into the inner recesses of our very being.

Look again at Paul's list of sins in our passage. Recall that as Paul lists them as his own, this is Paul the Pharisee, Paul the religious perfectionist, Paul the striver-for-goodness, who now admits to these elements of his former behavior.

Do you get the point? Sin is not necessarily a matter of destructive or unacceptable outward behavior. It is also a matter of inner attitude and maturation. How clearly Jesus spoke to the "good" people of His day: "For from within, out of the heart of men proceed evil thoughts. . . . All these evil things come from within and defile a man" (Mark 7:21-23). And at greater length in the Sermon on the Mount, Jesus dealt with this fundamental aspect of sin (Matt. 5-7).

As long as we major on the outward aspects of sin, we'll never understand the real nature of sin. There is nothing in Paul's list here that is always expressed or measured in gross outward behavior. One can serve *"various lusts and pleasures"* in very respectable ways. While we tend to think of such a phrase in sexual terms, Paul's words *epithumia* and *hēdonē* describe desires and pleasures not necessarily to be regarded as evil in themselves, but as the thorns—"the cares of this world, the deceitfulness of riches, and the desires for other things" that "choke the word" and render it unfruitful (Mark 4:19).

The same holds for *"being hateful"* and for *"hating one another."* Hate is not always expressed in violent behavior or words. We talk a great deal these days about child and spousal abuse. We are quick to declare physical abuse as criminal. We also recognize to a lesser degree the unacceptable nature of verbal abuse. However, we readily overlook and ignore the expression of hate through withdrawal or of the withholding of love. This may well be the most common and devastating form of hate, all the more pernicious because it can even be done under the guise of righteousness. The descendants of Saul—those who express their hate, even in religious activity, to "the glory of God"—are legion.

We will never fully appreciate the grace and mercy of God until we stand alongside Paul as the "chief" of sinners (1 Tim. 1:15).

It is this awareness of our own sinfulness, as good as we may be, that makes the opening "But" of verse 4 so dramatic. Precisely at the point where God has every right to express His judgment of us, He chooses instead to meet us with kindness and love. Again, Paul's focus is upon the incarnation, the appearing of God our Savior in Jesus Himself.

Paul's passionate commitment to justification by God's grace alone stands at the center of this summary of the Gospel. Salvation simply cannot be achieved by our good works. It is all God's doing from start to finish. The phrase *"through the washing of regeneration and renewing of the Holy Spirit"* suggests to me the past and present tenses of God's kindness and love. The washing of regeneration portrays an act of cleansing in the past. Baptism is the obvious symbol of that act of God in which we are cleansed from our sins. The renewing of the Holy Spirit becomes a process by which we receive and experience the continuing cleansing of our sins by God.

The past and present tenses of our salvation lead us into the future as the heirs of Jesus Himself in our hope of eternal life. Our faith places great hope in the future. It is our future that calls us to take the present seriously. It is our future that renews our strength in the midst of today's hurts, failures, and frustrations.

Here, then is the doctrinal basis of good works. We are to do good works because God is good. Our good works are always tainted with the pervasive reality of sin. Our good works are not done in order to earn God's favor or salvation. They are the products of God's kindness and love at work within us through the Holy Spirit.

A great deal of life is learning the differences between what is useful and what is useless. And that's not easy. The price tags are all mixed up. Useless things are promoted and are often quite costly, while useful things go ignored and undervalued. The Gospel is greatly concerned with helping us sort things out so that we can base our lives on what is genuinely worthwhile and enduring.

THE USEFULNESS OF GOOD WORKS

8 This is a faithful saying, and these things I want you to affirm constantly, that those who have believed in God should be careful to maintain good works. These things are good and profitable to men.

9 But avoid foolish disputes, genealogies, contentions, and strivings about the law; for they are unprofitable and useless.

10 Reject a divisive man after the first and second admonition,

11 knowing that such a person is warped and sinning, being self-condemned.

Titus 3:8–11

The *"faithful saying"* is the summary statement of the Gospel in verses 3–7. We are to keep the Gospel in focus at all times and not allow other things to become primary.

Our faith in God must issue forth good works on a regular basis. This requires a high degree of intentionality. We must be careful when we say that good works are a product of God's kindness and love at work within us. For good works don't just happen as though we were passive bystanders watching God work through us. There's always that tension of the extent to which God is the source of our good works and to which we are responsible for them.

This tension is beautifully stated by Paul in his letter to the Philippians: "Work out your own salvation with fear and trembling; for it is God who works in you both to will and to do for His good pleasure"

(Phil. 2:12–13). This is the *both . . . and* of Christian conduct. It is *both* the work of God *and* our own responsibility. One without the other is not viable. Merely to be passive, expecting God to override our lethargy or fear, is unrealistic. But merely to see ourselves as unaided contestants in the struggles for justice and righteousness is a sure road to frustration. It is *"good and profitable"* for us to *"be careful to maintain good works."*

This is hard work. It requires diligent labor. Somewhere along the way, I was taught that the life of Christian discipleship was easy. It was portrayed as a mere matter of trusting God and resting in Him. I've long since come to appreciate the inner peace and rest that comes from trusting in God. But I've also come to enjoy the challenges and disciplines of trying to be a faithful follower of Jesus in His constant care for the hungry and the poor and in His insistence on justice and righteousness. He never said it would be easy, and if we dare to take Him seriously, we will experience that growing joy of taking up crosses. Such a life is based upon doing useful things—good works that are *"good and profitable to men."*

Among the useless things are religious debates and divisive people. How sad that so much time in Christian circles is spent on doctrinal nitpicking and divisive competition. *"Disputes, genealogies, contentions, and strivings about the law"* are simply *"unprofitable and useless."* People who are divisive—those who are engaged in getting followers for their particular brand of religion or their particular doctrinal distinctions—are to be rejected after two admonitions.

Would that we could hasten the day when we would invest our financial and emotional resources in the production of good works rather than good arguments or good programs. The advent of mass media, which could be such a blessing in the communication of the Gospel, has, so far, developed mostly into a competition for the ratings. And the best ratings seem to come to those who concentrate on drawing a following for themselves. The basic problem may be inherent in the medium itself. It is essentially a spectator sport. The recipient is a "viewer." The responsibility of the viewer is to support the program. The only measure of accountability is in the cards and letters. It is difficult to assess the effect of the media on the production of good works in the lives of viewers. That requires life in community together—and that's why "the assembling of ourselves together" (Heb. 10:25) is essential in the development of good works. Would that we could sort out our priorities around doing good works!

GOOD WORKS IN ACTION

And now Paul dictates his closing words to Titus. Typically, he directs them to specific individuals. But he cannot bring this letter to conclusion without one final appeal for good works.

> 12 When I send Artemas to you, or Tychicus, be diligent to come to me to Nicopolis, for I have decided to spend the winter there.
> 13 Send Zenas the lawyer and Apollos on their journey with diligence, that they may lack nothing.
> 14 And let our people also learn to maintain good works, to meet urgent needs, that they may not be unfruitful.
> 15 All who are with me greet you. Greet those who love us in the faith. Grace be with you all. Amen.
>
> *Titus 3:12–15*

Either Artemas or Tychicus was to replace Titus in Crete shortly after the receipt of the letter. While Artemas remains unknown to us, Tychicus was another of those special people in Paul's network. On another occasion, Tychicus will be sent by Paul to relieve Timothy in Ephesus (2 Tim. 4:12). Paul is eager to receive a visit from Titus while spending the winter in Nicopolis.

We don't know Zenas the lawyer apart from this reference, but Apollos is well known through various references in Acts and 1 Corinthians. It sounds as if both of them may have been in Crete. Paul is eager to see them.

The maintenance of good works and the meeting of urgent needs remains at the top of Paul's agenda for the Christians in Crete. And must not this be foremost in our agenda? What would happen if all of our budgets and programs were evaluated on the basis of the extent to which they produce good works in the world around us and meet urgent needs of people everywhere? I find myself with a growing hunger to be a part of a fellowship that would dare to order its life around such an agenda. Impossible? I think not.

This is my dream.

Bibliography

Barclay, William. *New Testament Epistles of Paul.* Philadelphia: Westminster Press, 1975.

Bartsch, Hans W. *New Testament: 1 Timothy, Titus.* Hamburg: Herbert Reich, 1965.

Blaiklock, E. M. *The Pastoral Epistles.* Grand Rapids: Zondervan, 1972.

Bruce, F. F. *Paul and His Converts.* Nashville: Abingdon, 1962.

————. *1 and 2 Thessalonians.* Word Biblical Commentary. Waco, TX: Word Books, 1982.

Calvin, Jean. *The Epistles of Paul the Apostle to the Romans and to the Thessalonians.* Grand Rapids: Eerdmans, 1961.

Ellicott, C. J. *St. Paul's Epistles to the Thessalonians.* Grand Rapids: Zondervan, 1957.

Erdman, Charles. *Thessalonians.* Commentaries on the New Testament Books. Philadelphia: Westminster Press, 1966.

————. *Pastoral Epistles of Paul: Timothy 1 and 2, Titus.* Commentaries on the New Testament Books. Philadelphia: Westminster Press, 1966.

Findlay, G. G. *The Epistles of Paul the Apostle to the Thessalonians.* Cambridge: Cambridge University Press, 1904.

Getz, Gene A. *A Profile for a Christian Life Style: Titus.* Grand Rapids: Zondervan, 1978.

Guthrie, Donald. *Pastoral Epistles.* Tyndale Bible Commentary. Grand Rapids: Eerdmans, 1957.

Hanson, Anthony, ed. *The Pastoral Letters.* Cambridge: Cambridge University Press, 1966.

Hubbard, David A. *Thessalonians: Life That's Radically Christian.* Waco, TX: Word Books, 1977.

Jeremias, Joachim. *Die Briefe an Thimotheus und Titus.* Göttingen: Vanderhoeck & Ruprecht, 1975.

Johnson, Philip C. *The Epistles of Titus and Philemon.* Grand Rapids: Baker Book House, 1966.

Lee, Sang Kun. *Lee's Commentary on the Epistles 1 and 2 Thessalonians, 1 and 2 Timothy and Titus.* Seoul, Korea: Korean Presbyterian Publishers, 1983.

Loane, Marcus. *Godliness and Contentment: Studies in the Three Pastoral Epistles.* Grand Rapids: Baker Book House, 1982.

Lock, Walter. *A Critical and Exegetical Commentary on the Pastoral Epistles (1 and 2 Timothy and Titus).* Edinburgh: T. & T. Clark, 1924.

Morris, Leon. *The First and Second Epistles to the Thessalonians.* The New International Commentary of the New Testament. Grand Rapids: Eerdmans, 1959.

Moule, H. C. G. *Studies in 2 Timothy.* Kregel Popular Commentary Series. Grand Rapids: Kregel, 1977.

Ogilvie, Lloyd John. *Life as It Was Meant to Be.* Ventura, CA: Regal Books, 1980.

Reuss, Joseph. *Der erste Brief an Thimotheus.* Dusseldorf, Patmos, 1963.

Rolston, Holmes. *First Thessalonians–Philemon.* Richmond: John Knox Press, 1963.

Stott, John R. *Guard the Gospel.* Downers Grove, IL: InterVarsity Press, 1973.